THE MIDLAND
& GREAT NORTHERN
JOINT RAILWAY

A. J. WROTTESLEY

DAVID & CHARLES
NEWTON ABBOT LONDON

ISBN 0 7153 8173 3

First published 1970
Second edition 1981

Library of Congress Catalog Card Number 80-85502

© A. J. F. Wrottesley 1970, 1981

All rights reserved. No part of this publication may be reproduced, stored in a retrieval system, or transmitted, in any form or by any means, electronic, mechanical, photocopying, recording or otherwise, without the prior permission of David & Charles (Publishers) Limited

Printed in Great Britain
by Redwood Burn Ltd Trowbridge & Esher
for David & Charles (Publishers) Limited
Brunel House Newton Abbot Devon

Published in the United States of America
by David & Charles Inc
North Pomfret Vermont 05053 USA

Contents

LIST OF ILLUSTRATIONS 9

1 THE BEGINNINGS 11
   Norfolk in the early nineteenth century – early schemes – the Mania – GN & EC in conflict

2 THE PREDECESSORS IN THE WEST 15
   The Norwich & Spalding Railway – the Peterboro' Wisbech & Sutton Bridge Railway – the Lynn & Sutton Bridge Railway – the Spalding & Bourne Railway – the GE Northern Extension Scheme – the L & SB opens – the first Bourne-Saxby scheme, the Midland & Eastern Railway – the S & B completed – the PW & SB opens – the Bourne & Lynn Joint – fares – goods traffic – GE expansion – proposed GN/GE amalgamation – new directors – the Sleaford—Bourne line – the GN–GE Joint – floods – the Sutton Bridge dock scheme – passenger services – literary associations

3 THE PREDECESSORS IN THE EAST 32
   Schemes in east Norfolk – the Great Yarmouth & Stalham Light Railway – the Yarmouth & North Norfolk Light Railway – the Lynn & Fakenham Railway – opening to Massingham – amalgamation plans fail – opening to Stalham – the Yarmouth Union Railway – ambitious plans – more openings – Melton—North Walsham line sanctioned – Yarmouth Union completed – towards Norwich – Melton works established – more plans for Lynn and Blakeney – amalgamation authorised – Norwich reached

4 THE EASTERN & MIDLANDS RAILWAY 51
Trouble on the board – Melton—North Walsham completed – a lavish service – extension schemes – litigation with the Midland – changes on the board – opening to Holt – 'separate undertakings' – the Lynn loop – opening to Cromer – Blakeney scheme abandoned – more litigation with the Midland – Kings Cross to Cromer – more extension schemes – alliance with the Midland – Saxby-Bourne line authorised – GN and Midland joint owners of western section – financial crisis on the E & M – in chancery – a good service under difficulties – economies – how to obtain rolling stock? – improvements on the joint line – a joint offer – the M & GN is constituted

5 THE COMMITTEE FROM 1893 TO 1914 77
Allocation of responsibilities – the locomotives – Bourne to Saxby – train services – coast erosion – staff changes – track and signalling improved – more extensions – the Norfolk & Suffolk Joint – popularity of 'Poppyland' – long non-stop runs – more Blakeney schemes – developments at Sutton Bridge and elsewhere – opening to Mundesley – the Norfolk & Suffolk Joint approved – coast line proposed again – Cromer express service changes – station changes – light railway schemes – accidents – a change of managers – more doubling – Midland expresses improved – opening to Lowestoft: Breydon viaduct – fish traffic – no M & GN at Peterboro' GE – N & S progress – a West Riding express – lack of Sunday services – the N & S completed: GE at Sheringham – fruit traffic – a pooling agreement – potato traffic – Norwich goods traffic: coal, cattle and bricks – the best years – ballast – an amalgamation scheme that failed – the through expresses, 1907-14 – strikes and floods – the Whitaker tablet exchanger – signals at level crossings – town holiday and excursion trains – fastest and longest runs – the staff – winter services – Sunday services – tickets

6 THE COMMITTEE FROM 1914 TO 1936 120
Wartime changes – passenger services reduced – naval bombardments and air raids – war work at Melton – use of concrete – M & GN staff in the forces –

Mr Marriott becomes manager – post-war problems –
restoration of passenger services – Mundesley route
improvements – fruit and fish traffic – signalling
developments – the M & GN at the grouping – passenger service developments – Mr Marriott retires –
decline of 'Poppyland' traffic – the General Strike –
town holiday and excursion trains – more Mundesley developments – the Kings Cross—Cromer expresses – more excursions – holiday camp services
and halts – Sunday trains – more Saturdays only
services – goods traffic; depression; road competition
– some short-distance goods services – more signalling developments – accidents – the staff; station
gardens – a record run – the latest new halt – the
final mileage

7 THE LNER REGIME 141

The committee – changes – fish traffic – the passenger services – the Hindolvestone accident – military
traffic – war again – air raids – wartime passenger
services – Sunday trains again – restoration of
express services

8 THE EASTERN REGION'S ADMINISTRATION 152

Nationalisation – change of station names – the
passenger services – closures and economies –
Breydon viaduct closed – concentration at Cromer
Beach – Spalding – diesel trains – goods traffic : road
competition – floods again

9 CLOSURE 159

Special investigation – the TUCC inquiry – objections –
the decision – services in the last two years – 28
February 1959 – surviving freight services – compensating services – more closures – more economies –
goods services withdrawn

10 THE ROLLING STOCK 171

Early days. Midland engines – GN engines – GY & S
engines – L & F engines – 4–4–0 tanks – 0–6–0 tanks –
Beyer 4–4–os – liveries – E & M engines – headcodes –
carriage stock – E & M engines withdrawn – assistance
by GN and Midland engines – the Johnson 4–4–os take

over – the Johnson 0–6–0s – the Ivatt 0–6–0s – classes of engines – rebuilding of Beyer 4–4–0s – new tank classes – travels of 4–4–0 tanks – Johnson 4–4–0s with large boilers – the committee's carriage stock – goods vehicles – 0–6–0s reboilered – long-lived small tanks – changes in the livery – last years of the Beyer 4–4–0s and 4–4–0 tanks – operation of the Leicesters – the LNE regime – withdrawal of M & GN engines – LNE engines – more powerful types in use – the last M & GNs – carriage stock changes – visits by named engines – the BR era – the N & S joint – the engine sheds – the last years – epilogue

APPENDIXES	193
AUTHOR'S NOTE	203
ACKNOWLEDGEMENTS	204
BIBLIOGRAPHY	206
INDEX	209

Appendixes

1	Dates of Openings	193
2	Mileage Tables	194
3	Single line sections in 1914	198
4	The Board of Directors of the M & GN Joint Committee, 1889-1936	199
5	Dimensions of locomotives	200

List of Illustrations

PLATES

Long Sutton 1862 (courtesy R. S. McNaught)	17
Martham 1890 (Dr Tice Budden courtesy Col Bucknall)	17
Melton Constable with E & M Beyer Peacock 4-4-0 (Dr Tice Budden courtesy Col Bucknall)	18
Cromer 1906 (Dr Tice Budden courtesy Col Bucknall)	18
Freight train including fish vans at Great Yarmouth (T. G. Hepburn)	35
Local train leaving Cromer Beach (T. G. Hepburn)	35
'C' class 4-4-0 in 1913 (H. Gordon Tidey courtesy Col Bucknall)	36
Johnson 4-4-0 No 40 (H. L. Salmon courtesy Col Bucknall)	36
Cromer—Kings Cross express at Wisbech North (T. G. Hepburn)	53
Cromer—Manchester express near Nottingham Midland (T. G. Hepburn)	53
M & GN six-wheeled coach (H. C. Casserley)	54
Sutton Bridge 1937 (H. C. Casserley)	54
Water tank (T. G. Hepburn)	54
Little Bytham junction (T. G. Hepburn)	71
Potter Heigham Bridge halt (R. M. Casserley)	71
Yarmouth—Leicester express (T. G. Hepburn)	72
Local train at Norwich City (H. C. Casserley)	72
Hillington for Sandringham (H. C. Casserley)	89
Sutton Bridge station (H. C. Casserley)	89
Lenwade (R. M. Casserley)	90
Hindolvestone (R. M. Casserley)	90
Yarmouth—Leicester express (T. G. Hepburn)	107
H. G. Ivatt 2-6-0 at Aylsham North (D. H. Ballantyne)	107
LMS 0-6-0 crossing the Ouse at West Lynn (D. H. Ballantyne)	108
Leicester train leaving Saxby (P. H. Groom)	108

E & M 0–6–0T at Melton (*author's collection*)   125
E & M 2–4–0 at Norwich (*author's collection*)   126
Beyer Peacock 4–4–0 No 43 at Cromer Beach
  (*Col Bucknall*)   126
Johnson 4–4–0 No 78 (*Dr Tice Budden courtesy
  Col Bucknall*)   143
4–4–0 tank No 9 at Mundesley (*Dr Tice Budden courtesy
  Col Bucknall*)   143
Johnson 0–6–0 No 65 at Melton (*Lens of Sutton courtesy
  B. L. Ridgeway*)   144
0–6–0T No 93 at South Lynn (*T. G. Hepburn*)   144
H. A. Ivatt 0–6–0 No 92 at Spalding (*H. C. Casserley*)   144

IN THE TEXT

Company seal	76
Signals	81, 82, 83
Tablet exchange equipment	111, 112, 113, 114, 115
Tickets	119
Inflammable liquids notice	183

MAPS

Peterboro'	20
King's Lynn	21
General map	26 & 27
Great Yarmouth	33
Yarmouth Beach	38
Melton Constable	42
Cromer	59
Spalding	79

CHAPTER ONE

The Beginnings

NORFOLK IN THE EARLY NINETEENTH CENTURY

In the early nineteenth century the majority of the inhabitants of the county of Norfolk were engaged in agriculture. Methods of working and, in consequence, production had improved considerably, thanks to Coke and Townshend in the previous century. Norwich was a great town but not so important as it had been when it was the third city in the kingdom. Yarmouth was an important port; its famous North Sea fisheries were developing, and it was becoming a holiday resort. Other ancient ports, Lynn, Wells and Blakeney, were somewhat decayed. There were several market towns. Cromer was a village, and Sheringham as a seaside place scarcely existed.

In medieval times the county had been well known for its woollen manufactures as a cottage industry. Many large and beautiful churches still survive, bearing witness to the one time prosperity of the industry and to the larger rural population of those days. Worstead, which still has a station on the Eastern Region, and was for many years served by a station called Honing for Worstead on the Midland & Great Northern Joint, gave its name to a form of cloth. But the industry had declined in consequence of the Black Death plague in the fourteenth century, and almost disappeared in the eighteenth century as a result of the Industrial Revolution.

But now in the west and in adjoining south Lincolnshire more land was under cultivation owing to progress in draining the fens, and the country needed better transport, outward for agricultural produce, livestock, including poultry (especially the famous turkeys) and fish from Yarmouth and smaller places, and inwards for manufactured goods and coal. Good roads were few and often narrow, though there was some seaborne traffic and inland water transport, as several Broadland rivers were wide enough for large wherries and others had been canalised under Navigation Acts.

EARLY SCHEMES

The opening of the Stockton & Darlington Railway in 1825 and of the Liverpool & Manchester in 1830 caused proposals for railways all over the country, including Norfolk. In 1826 there was a scheme for a horse-worked line into Suffolk and soon afterwards a Norwich—London line was suggested. In the early 1830s there were several schemes for a London—York line with a Norwich branch. One of these, the Northern & Eastern, was authorised only from London to Cambridge in 1836 and by 1842 had got no further than Bishop's Stortford. Norfolk investors mainly supported the Eastern Counties, which obtained its Act for a line from London to Yarmouth via Colchester, Ipswich and Norwich in July 1836.

THE MANIA

By 1843 the EC had only succeeded in building its line from London to Colchester and had announced it could not raise the money to go further. In consequence Norfolk people promoted the first railway built there, the Yarmouth & Norwich (via Reedham) opened on 30 April 1844. The Railway Mania was by this time in full swing. By the end of 1849 nearly all the principal towns the Midland & Great Northern Joint was later to serve, Peterboro', Spalding, Wisbech, Lynn, Fakenham, Norwich, Yarmouth and Lowestoft, were connected by rail with each other, the Midlands and London. But the north of Norfolk, where so much of its rails would be laid, had no railways for many years. There were several schemes in Norfolk and south Lincolnshire for lines along or close to later M & GN routes. On 29 November 1845 a Bill was deposited for a line direct from Lynn to Fakenham, to start about 1½ miles out of Lynn from the line to Dereham authorised in the previous July, with hopes of going beyond Fakenham towards Norwich later. As far as Massingham the line would have taken a more southerly course and thereafter a more northerly course than the line built in the years 1879-80, later part of the M & GN main line (see Chapter 3). But the Bill did not even reach the committee stage. In 1846 the North of Norfolk applied for powers for a line from Norwich to Aylsham, North Walsham, Cromer and Holt. This was supported by the Norfolk, an amalgamation of the Norwich & Brandon and the Yarmouth & Norwich. The proposed Norwich terminus would have been in the city near Tombland. But the committee considered there would not be enough traffic to justify construction, and there was also opposition from the cathedral authorities; so the Bill was withdrawn. In the same year a company called the Boston, Stamford & Birmingham had its proposals cut down by an Act which authorised a line from Helpston (north of Peterboro' on the authorised Midland line to Leicester) via Thorney to Wisbech. Competing Bills for a Spalding—Holbeach—Sutton Bridge—Lynn line by this concern, by another company, the Grand Union, and a parallel Spalding—Wisbech route by the Lynn & Ely (with Eastern Counties support) failed. Next year the EC, which despite many applications failed to obtain sanction for a line to Lincoln, secured powers to extend its authorised Wisbech branch to Spalding via Sutton Bridge in the face of opposition from the Great Northern (authorised in 1846) which had revived the Spalding—Lynn scheme and wished to serve Lynn harbour. The BS & B proposed a Wisbech—Sutton Bridge line (on a more easterly course) and to build docks there in alliance with the GN. Parliament said it could only build a Wisbech—Sutton line if the EC did not, but granted powers for a direct Peterboro'—Thorney line and a Wisbech harbour branch. The GN was granted running powers from Spalding to Wisbech and authority to build a short line from Sutton Bridge to Sutterton (not built) but not to Lynn.

Much of this enthusiasm for competing lines in south Lincolnshire was due to the plans of George Hudson, the 'Railway King', to connect the Midland and the EC, of both of which he was chairman, and to prevent the development of the GN, which he opposed. Part of the district was still unprofitable fenland and the valuable traffic in fruit, vegetables and flowers only developed later.

The GN absorbed the BS & B. The EC branch to Wisbech (from its Ely—Peterboro' line at March) was opened on 3 May

1847 but none of its powers for new lines were ever exercised. The GN and EC soon decided it was unreasonable to have two parallel Peterboro'—Wisbech lines, so, in exchange for abandoning the BS & B's powers, the GN in 1849 received running powers from Peterboro' to the original EC station in the southwest of Wisbech, later the goods station.

The East Anglian, an amalgamation of the Lynn & Ely and Lynn & Dereham, opened another line to Wisbech from the east on 1 February 1848, with a station in the south-east of the town where Wisbech East was later. The only extension the EC made at Wisbech at this stage, despite its powers to go on to Sutton Bridge and Spalding, was a connecting line from its station to the EA station, though a harbour branch was added later.

The Norfolk, which in 1846 had been authorised to extend to Fakenham (opened on 20 March 1849) and to Wells and Blakeney (not built), revived a Norwich—North Walsham—Aylsham scheme in 1847 without success.

GN AND EC IN CONFLICT

The GN, which opened its 'loop line' through Spalding on 17 October 1848 and its main line from London (Maiden Lane) through to Peterborough GN on 7 August 1850, again attempted to serve Lynn. In July 1851, despite criticism from shareholders, it agreed to work the EA and attempted to run trains from Peterboro' to Lynn via Wisbech. But the EC contended that the GN's running powers did not include the line between the Wisbech stations. When the first GN train reached Wisbech EC, the GN officials found the points for the connecting line shut against them and had to get the passengers to the EA station by horse-bus. When the GN applied to the court for relief, the EC further contended that the Wisbech connection had only been put in to give the EA access to an isolated section of its line at St Ives. But the judge found against the GN on different grounds, that its agreement with the EA was really a lease, invalid without parliamentary sanction. In the autumn of 1851 the GN and EC concluded an agreement on many matters in dispute between them, one of the terms being the transfer of working the EA to the EC, which was effected on 1 January 1852.

CHAPTER TWO

The Predecessors in the West

THE NORWICH & SPALDING RAILWAY

Many local people besides the GN were disappointed at the failure of all the promoters to provide a line from Spalding to Lynn with the advantage of serving the harbour and chances of going further into Norfolk later, either over the EA or by a separate line. So a new company, the Norwich & Spalding, was promoted by local residents with some assistance from contractors and financial people, and obtained an Act on 4 August 1853. Despite its title it was only authorised to revive the Railway Mania scheme for a line from the GN at Spalding eastwards through Holbeach to Sutton Bridge, near the mouth of the Nene, and from there to Wisbech. There were hopes of going on to Lynn and Norwich later. But for the present, despite grand words in the Act about the importance of the line as a through route, the only easterly outlet was to be a junction with the EA just west of its Wisbech station, where the dispute had occurred between the GN and the EC two years before. The Wisbech section was regarded as so important that the N & S was not allowed to open any other part of its line unless it could show it was proceeding with the construction of that section. Traffic facilities were contemplated via the EA and EC all the way to the Norfolk, and to the Eastern Union (Colchester to Ipswich, Bury and Norwich). Mr J. C. Cobbold, of the famous Ipswich family, MP for that town and chairman of the EU, was on the N & S board. Mr Wilkinson, a contractor, was chairman, and other directors included Sutton Bridge and Holbeach residents.

As the line was through flat country, there should have been no serious constructional difficulties. But the company found it hard to raise the money, partly because of the Crimean War. The little railway only succeeded in reaching Holbeach, 7½ miles from Spalding, for goods traffic on 9 August and passengers on 15 November 1858. The single line started from a junction with the GN just south of Spalding station, curved round to the east, crossed the Welland and was then level throughout, with stations at Weston, Moulton and Whaplode. Under an agreement of 2 September 1858 the GN undertook to work the line for three years and provided four trains each way taking 25 minutes generally, but one, first and second class only, took 20 minutes. There was an additional train on Tuesday, market day. Weston and Whaplode were stops 'by request only'. There were no Sunday trains.

The other powers had expired; so on 13 August 1859 a further Act was obtained, regranting the Holbeach—Sutton Bridge powers but not those to Wisbech. This section however was still regarded as so important that the Act added that no dividend could be declared unless the company proceeded with its promotion. It was stated that further powers were being sought and that the EC would not oppose; but they were refused in 1860.

On 1 March 1862 the GN agreed to work the line for ten years from 1 November 1861 for 50 per cent of the gross receipts and to put the sleepers of the existing line in proper order. The line was completed from Holbeach to Sutton Bridge, 8 miles, on 1 July 1862. It was single and level, with stations at Fleet, Gedney and Long Sutton. The station at Sutton Bridge was to the south of the later passenger station and on the site of the later goods station west of the Nene. The same number of trains was operated taking from 45 minutes to 1 hour from Spalding to Sutton Bridge, but the fast train, first and second class only, took 35 minutes. Fleet and Gedney were stops 'only when required'.

THE PETERBORO' WISBECH & SUTTON BRIDGE RAILWAY

Powers to build the line to Wisbech were again refused in 1862-3; but on 28 July of the latter year another company, the Peterboro', Wisbech & Sutton Bridge, capital £180,000, was authorised to build a line between those places almost

Page 17 *Nineteenth-century station scenes:* (above) *Long Sutton in 1862 showing early* GN *coaches and* GN *2-2-2;* (below) *Martham in 1890 showing 2-4-0 No 3 and original* E & M *signals*

Page 18 *Parting of ways:* (above) *Melton Constable, Cromer line to the right.* E & M *Beyer Peacock 4–4–0 with train of ex-Midland six-wheeled coaches approaching from Lynn;* (below) *Cromer 1906. Bay platform was used for Norfolk and Suffolk route trains*

THE PREDECESSORS IN THE WEST 19

along the route sanctioned to the Boston, Stamford & Birmingham in 1846-7, and so provide the Wisbech—Sutton link. The line would pass rather to the north of the centre of Wisbech but powers were to be sought for a connecting line there with the Great Eastern (as the Eastern Counties had just become). The N & S was to have running powers from Sutton Bridge to Wisbech. The Act contained powers to make agreements with the GN and the Midland. It might have been expected that the GN would secure some control over a line which could carry out some of its 1847 and 1851 plans; but the Midland had already stepped in and agreed to work the line for 50 per cent of the gross receipts, and this agreement was scheduled to the Act. It was to cause a great deal of trouble later. The spelling in the Act was Wisbeach, a form which was used officially until 1877.

THE LYNN & SUTTON BRIDGE RAILWAY

Meanwhile two more small companies were formed to extend the N & S eastwards and westwards. The first of these was the Lynn & Sutton Bridge, authorised on 6 August 1861, £100,000 capital and £37,000 on loan. The EA, still nominally an independent company, was given powers to subscribe, and appoint directors if it did. There were powers to sell the line to the GN, subject to specific parliamentary authority. The GN promoted a Bill to acquire both the N & S and the L & SB in the 1862 session, to the great annoyance of the EC, as it was just then carrying out the amalgamations which produced the Great Eastern. It alleged that the GN was acting in breach of the 1851 agreement; but the GN did not proceed with the Bill.

THE SPALDING & BOURNE RAILWAY

The other line, the Spalding & Bourne, which had much the same directorate as the L & B (though quite different from the N & S) was authorised on 29 July 1862, capital £100,000, loans £32,500. At Bourne the line was to make an end-on junction with another small line worked by the GN, the Bourne & Essendine, and the Act provided that arrangements could be made with this concern and the GN. At this stage the spelling in the

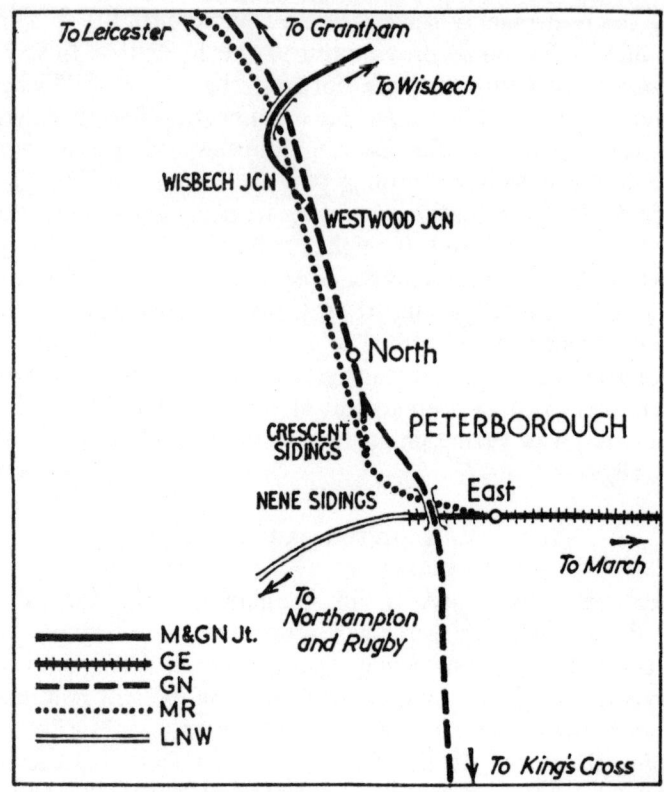

Acts was Bourn and the form Bourne was not officially adopted until 1894.

THE GE NORTHERN EXTENSION SCHEME

The Great Eastern was incorporated on 7 August 1862. To quote Grinling, 'The combined energies of the previous small companies would be directed to a revival of schemes for an advance to the north'. In 1863 the GE sought powers for a line from March to Spalding (with running powers over the GN from there to Doncaster) crossing the Peterboro'—Sutton Bridge route near Murrow. The GN countered this by proposing a March—Spalding line itself and traffic exchange facilities at March. The GN won in the Commons, where the committee approved its Bill and rejected the GE's. But in the Lords the GE secured running powers to Spalding. Next year, 1864, the GE came forward with a scheme for a line all the way from Long Stanton near St Ives, crossing the Peterboro'—Sutton near Thorney, and on via Spalding and Lincoln to join the Lancashire & Yorkshire at Askern north of Doncaster; but after a fierce parliamentary struggle it was rejected. The importance of all this is that the GE made several more attempts to secure its own line to the north and the GN naturally retaliated by supporting small lines in south Lincolnshire and Norfolk (later parts of the M & GN) by which it could send traffic if the GE plans succeeded.

In the same year, 1864, the PW & SB obtained powers to make the connecting line with the GE at Wisbech, which was never constructed, and a short line into the harbour there, which was.

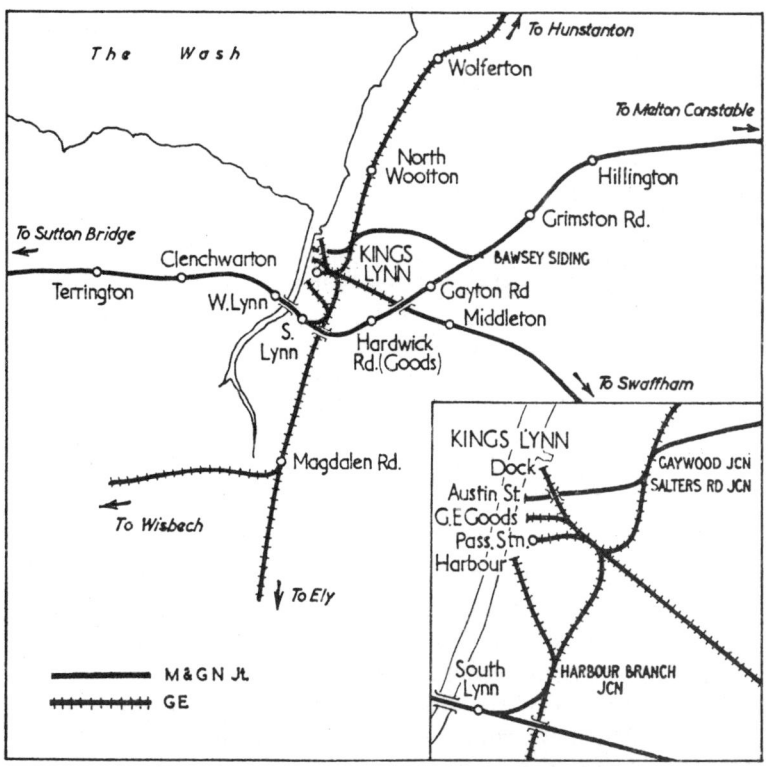

THE L & SB OPENS

By its 1861 Act the L & SB was placed under a heavy obligation to build a new rail and road bridge over the Nene at Cross Keys, Sutton, to replace the existing swing road bridge (opened in 1850), which the company was to purchase for £22,500. But in 1864 it was allowed instead to adapt and widen the road bridge for the railway. The line was opened throughout for goods traffic in November 1864 from a junction on the Lynn—Ely line (formerly EA and by this time GE) just south of the junction of the Lynn harbour line, $1\frac{1}{2}$ miles south of King's Lynn station. It crossed the Ouse by a bridge of five lattice girder spans, three central of 117 ft and two end of 70 ft, built by Messrs Waring & Eckersley, the contractors. There was a goods station at South Lynn east of the bridge, which was used with the short section from the junction with the GE as early as 2 November 1863, and a passenger station, West Lynn, west of the bridge. Then the line ran west, on the level, with stations at Clenchwarton, Terrington and Walpole, over the bridge at Cross Keys, north of the N & S passenger station, to a new station and a junction with the N & S just to the west, $9\frac{1}{2}$ miles in all from the junction at Lynn to the junction at Sutton Bridge. Passenger trains provided by the GN began on 1 March 1866. At first both passenger stations at Sutton Bridge were in use.

In July 1865 the PW & SB obtained powers to provide a branch from Eye to Crowland Abbey but this was never built.

THE FIRST BOURNE—SAXBY SCHEME
THE MIDLAND & EASTERN RAILWAY

The L & SB and the S & B proposed in 1866 to amalgamate, lease the N & S and build an extension westwards from Bourne to join the Midland at Saxby, the route which, nearly thirty years later, was to become the main Midland access to the M & GN. Naturally the Midland supported this and the GN opposed. The new concern was to be called the Midland & Eastern. During the proceedings before the Commons commit-

THE PREDECESSORS IN THE WEST 23

tee the GN's counsel said that if the Saxby extension was given up the GN would grant the Midland running powers from Bourne to Essendine and on to Stamford, over yet another small line it was working, the Stamford & Essendine (sometimes called Lord Exeter's railway), to a new junction which could be made with the Midland there; it would withdraw opposition on those terms. The promoters and the Midland agreed on 1 July, and the Bill constituting the Midland & Eastern passed on 23 July. It was further agreed that the GN and Midland would work the line jointly, guaranteeing £15,000 yearly rental.

THE S & B COMPLETED

The S & B was opened a few days later on 1 August. The line left the GN at a point called South Junction, as it was rather further south of Spalding station than the junction of the Sutton Bridge line, and curved round to run west on the level along the edge of the fens. There were hardly any villages. Small stations were built called North Drove, Counter Drain and Twenty. 'Drove' in this district meant a road across a fen with a 'lode', a ditch or stream, on either side. 'Counter' and 'Twenty' referred to drainage ditches of those names near the stations, the latter being the twentieth of a series. The end-on junction at Bourne was made with a short section of the Essendine line which extended 11 chains east of the passenger station. The latter was of unusual appearance, as it included an old sixteenth-century house associated with the Gunpowder Plot. The line was $9\frac{1}{2}$ miles long and single. The GN provided trains which connected its main line at Essendine and its loop line at Spalding with Lynn, which it had wanted to do fifteen years before. Fortunately, a L & SB Act of 1865 had provided that whoever was working that line had running powers into Lynn.

THE PW & SB OPENS

The PW & SB was opened for goods on 1 June and for passengers on 1 August 1866. The line left the Midland Peterboro'—Leicester line on the west side, just north of where there was a junction, Westwood, between the GN and Midland lines. The actual junction point was later known as Wisbech Junction. The line ran parallel with the Midland for a short distance on a rising gradient and then crossed both the Midland and the GN lines by a bridge. It then ran north-east with stations at Eye Green, Thorney, Wryde, Murrow and Wisbech St Mary to the station rather in the north of Wisbech town. Then it turned north through Horse Shoe Lane Junction where the harbour line went off, and Ferry and Tydd stations to a point on the N & S line then called Midland Junction, just west of the spot where the L & SB joined, west of the new Sutton Bridge passenger station. The line was 27 miles long, single and nearly level. The Midland provided passenger trains from and to the GE station at Peterboro', serving also the GN station. Eye Green was called simply Eye until 1 October 1875.

Joint operation of the M & E, and the new junction between the Stamford & Essendine and Midland lines at Stamford, were sanctioned in August 1867. The N & S was duly leased by the M & E but remained nominally independent. In the same year it had to obtain an Act of its own, for it could not declare a dividend because it had not built the Wisbech—Sutton section. The Act recited the troubles described above, and stated that the chairman of the committee had said that the N & S had, *bona fide*, tried to make the line, and that it had now been built by the PW & SB. So the unfortunate clause preventing payment of dividends was repealed.

THE BOURNE & LYNN JOINT

The management and operation of the M & E, which could be called the first 'M & GN', were distinctly unusual. Even at that time there was a small committee of GN and Midland directors, but it rarely met—in December 1866, February 1867 and not again until 1880. At the first meeting it appointed Mr R. Dykes, a Midland man, manager of the joint arrangements and he looked after the line with joint meetings of officers of the GN and Midland. The joint line was not called the M & GN or even the Midland & Eastern (which of course, as a company continued to exist), but the Bourne & Lynn Joint. It had its own staff and its own uniform. For many years the number of trains run daily on each section of the

Bourne & Lynn and between Peterboro' and Sutton Bridge remained much the same, about four or five each way, with extras on Saturdays and market days. The 1867 Act used the precedent of the Cheshire Lines (in which, too, the GN and Midland were both interested) which had been constituted the year before, 1866, whereby each company was empowered to run its own trains on the joint line. The terms of this clause caused some trouble later. But in practice only the Lynn—Sutton Bridge section was really worked jointly with regular passenger and goods trains of both companies. As there were only the four or five passenger trains each way, some trains had both GN and Midland coaches, and at times passengers had to change at Sutton Bridge. From January 1867 all passenger trains used the new station there and the old N & S station became the goods station. The Bourne—Spalding—Sutton Bridge section was worked almost entirely by the GN, whose trains sometimes ran through between Stamford or Essendine, reversing at Spalding, and Sutton Bridge or Lynn, but at other times only made local trips. There were some complaints of delay at first as some of the trains were mixed passenger and goods, so a separate Essendine—Lynn goods train was put on. The only workings by Midland engines were a weekly cattle train from Lynn to Bourne, which was then taken on to the Midland at Stamford by a GN engine, a daily goods from Lynn to Spalding and back, and an occasional passenger excursion from Lynn to Matlock and Buxton. There were no passenger trains on Sundays between Bourne and Lynn or between Peterboro' and Sutton Bridge.

As there was the guarantee the M & E and N & S shareholders received modest dividends, and the PW & SB holders generally did too, although the deferred ordinary holders in that concern had to wait until 1877.

As from 1 July 1877 the M & E formally absorbed the Norwich & Spalding. Under the Act the committee of GN and Midland directors which had nominally been administering the Bourne & Lynn Joint was given statutory recognition.

FARES

In those days there were first, second, third and government fares (often 'gov' in the timetables). The latter meant third-class travel at a penny a mile, which had to be provided on every line under the Act of 1844 by at least one train each way daily on weekdays. Third-class fares on the other trains might be at a penny a mile or might be more. If the third-class fare was a penny a mile by all trains that carried such passengers, the trains were often shown in the timetables as '1, 2, gov' instead of '1, 2, 3'. Some of the GN trains on the line were still first and second only but the number carrying third was increasing. The Midland trains were first, second and 'gov' in all cases (even before the Midland provided third class on all its trains in 1872), until it abolished the second class on 1 January 1875.

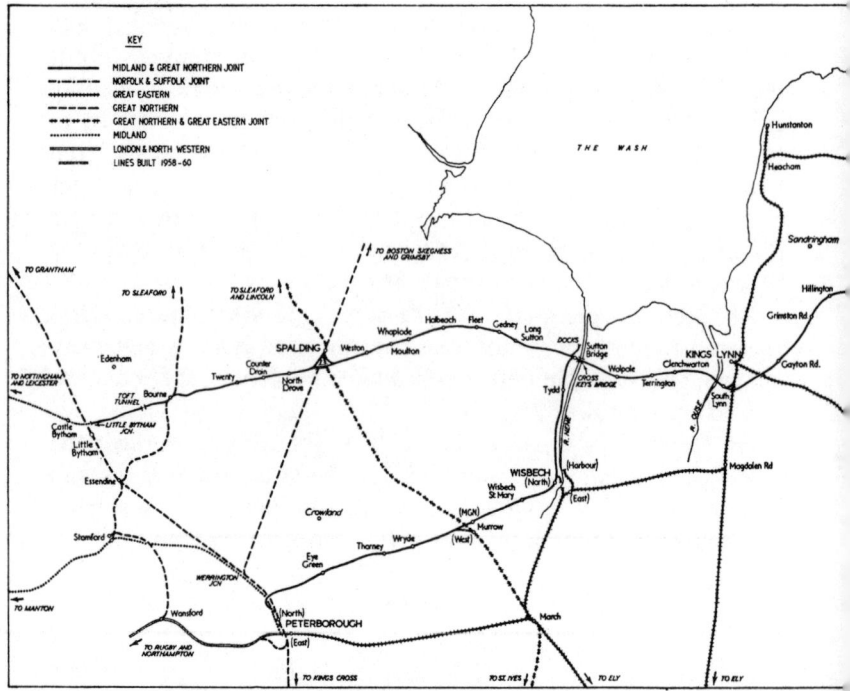

THE PREDECESSORS IN THE WEST

GOODS TRAFFIC

Goods traffic, mainly agricultural produce and cattle out of the area, and coal and general goods inwards, developed slowly. The only eastern outlet was at Lynn, as the junction with the GE at Wisbech was never built. But there was Lynn docks traffic from 1870, thanks to the King's Lynn Dock & Railway; and Wisbech harbour dealt with timber, corn and cattle cake.

GE EXPANSION

Meanwhile the GE was working lines which served north-

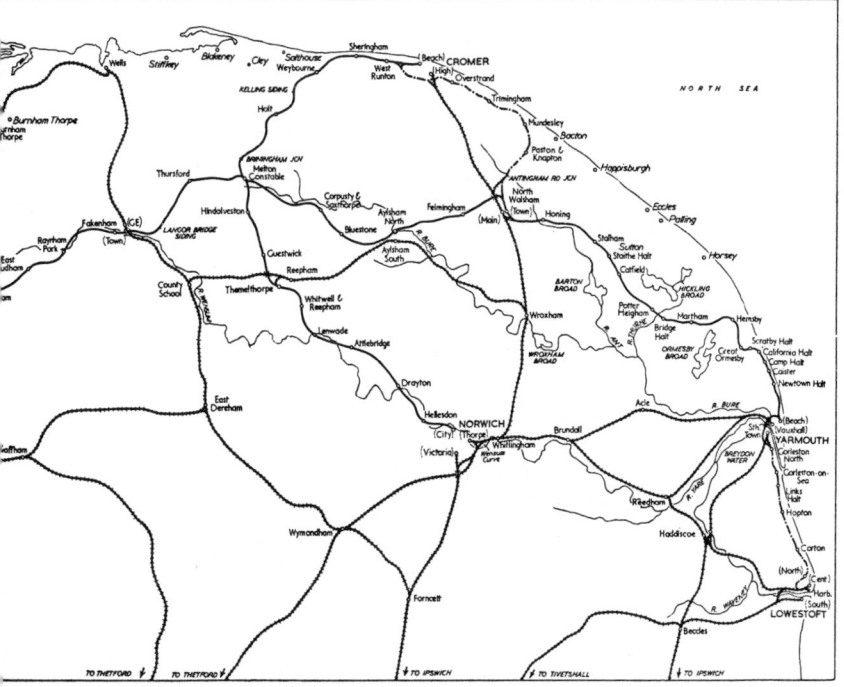

west Norfolk. These were the Fakenham—Wells, first authorised in the Mania, revived by the EC with local financial support, and opened on 1 December 1857, the Lynn—Hunstanton, opened 3 October 1862, and the West Norfolk, from Heacham on the Lynn—Hunstanton through Burnham Market to Wells and the harbour there, opened 17 August 1866. But the northeast of the county still had no railways.

PROPOSED GN–GE AMALGAMATION

The GE suffered severely in the 1866 financial crisis and was reluctant to operate still more lines of doubtful profit in quiet districts. What it really wanted was its own route to the north. The GN opened the Spalding—March line, crossing the PW & SB on the level near Murrow, with a separate station at that village, on 1 April 1867. At first it looked as if the GN and GE would make an agreement for traffic facilities between the North and East Anglia by this route but the companies could not agree on the terms. For ten years there were more GE schemes for a northern extension, alternating with negotiations with the GN for amalgamation, which nearly succeeded more than once. The relevance of these possibilities is that if the GN and GE had become one at this period, the Lynn & Fakenham, and the Yarmouth & North Norfolk (see Chapter 3), even if they had ever been built in full, would, with the M & E, have probably come into the hands of the GN–GE combine, and the Midland & Great Northern Joint would never have existed.

NEW DIRECTORS

Mr Eckersley, the contractor, was by now chairman of the N & S and on the M & E board, and his partner, Mr Waring, was soon a director of both. During the 1870s the board of the PW & SB became much the same as that of the M & E and N & S, including Mr Waring and other members of his family. Mr R. A. Read, who was to play an important role later on, became a director of the N & S in 1875 and of the M & E in 1877.

THE SLEAFORD—BOURNE LINE

On 2 January 1872 the GN opened a line from Sleaford, which joined the Spalding—Bourne line 3 chains east of the end-on junction at Bourne between GN and M & E metals, so that the Sleaford trains used this short section of the joint line. Some increase of traffic on the joint line resulted.

THE GN–GE JOINT

In April 1878, in consequence of expressions of a parliamentary committee considering yet another GE Bill for a northern extension and a competing GN scheme, the GN and GE reached agreement to establish a GN–GE joint route by existing and new lines from Huntingdon to Doncaster via March, Spalding and Lincoln. The GN had decided it was better to have a joint line and so prevent the construction of a separate GE northern extension, rather than continue disputes with the GE and opposition to its Bills. But because the GE would be able to compete with them when its joint line was finished, the GN and Midland became more interested in the Bourne & Lynn and more disposed to patronise small lines in north Norfolk, which eventually became the Eastern & Midlands and later the M & GN.

FLOODS

In the autumn of 1880, following very wet weather, there were serious floods in Lincolnshire. The Spalding—Bourne line was flooded for 2 miles to a depth of 4 or 5 ft and had to be closed from 9 October until 1 February 1881.

THE SUTTON BRIDGE DOCK SCHEME

In the early 1870s Messrs English, shipowners and merchants of Wisbech, formed a company with the object of reviving the 1846 scheme for docks near the Nene estuary at Sutton Bridge and avoiding the need for so many ships to come up the river to Wisbech through the swing bridge. It was considered that the new docks would be suitable for the export of coal from the East Midlands. The GN subscribed £20,000 of the capital and Acts were obtained in 1875-6.

When the Sutton Bridge Dock company found difficulty in raising the money the GN helped by lending a further £35,000 on mortgage. A GN director was on the dock company's board. Another Act was passed on 29 June 1880 and the works proceeded rapidly. A short branch was made to the docks and river, leaving the M & E a short distance west of the 'Midland Junction' with the Peterboro' line. Including the GN contribution nearly £150,000 had been spent, 13 acres of water were enclosed, and large warehouses and up-to-date hydraulic machinery were provided. On Saturday 14 May 1881 Messrs English's own ship *Garland* was the first to arrive, with 1,150 tons of pitch pine from Norway which she proceeded to unload; she was to take a return cargo of Derbyshire coal brought by the GN to the dock.

The next day it was found that the lock at the entrance was not watertight. When the tide came in there was too much water in the docks; when it fell there was not enough. It was discovered that the ground near the corner of the lock had sunk, leaving the wall unsupported, and also that the earth had fallen on the north side. Water came through the silt under the lock gate. The engineers tried to stop the effect of the falls by putting in quantities of sand and clay but when, some days later, the concrete facing of the west side of the dock fell, they could not suggest a speedy remedy. The *Garland* succeeded in getting away with the coal, and three or four other ships which had docked were also able to leave; but no other operations were possible. More eminent engineering advice was sought but the docks were not used again. The GN had spent £55,000 on docks which were unusable, and was deprived of valuable traffic, general goods inwards and coal outwards, over the M & E. Coal traffic into the district of course continued and remained important.

PASSENGER SERVICES

In 1875 the passenger service between Sutton Bridge and Lynn was slightly increased and in the summer of 1883 it was doubled, by running nearly all the GN and Midland trains through separately. On 1 July, as described in Chapter 3, the M & E, and PW & SB, became part of the Eastern & Midlands but the operation of the train services by the GN and Midland remained much the same for ten years.

LITERARY ASSOCIATIONS

The district served by these lines had been brought to the notice of the reading public by Charles Kingsley's famous historical novel, *Hereward the Wake*, about the English hero of Norman Conquest days, which was published in 1866. The setting is largely Bourne, Spalding, Peterboro' and the fen country generally.

CHAPTER THREE

The Predecessors in the East

SCHEMES IN EAST NORFOLK

The GE succeeded in being the first to serve north-east Norfolk but only by a small margin. Its subsidiary, the East Norfolk, authorised in 1862 and 1864 but delayed by financial troubles, was opened from Whitlingham, east of Norwich on the Yarmouth line, through Wroxham to North Walsham on 20 October 1874 but did not reach Cromer until 26 March 1877. By that time two lines which were both to become part of the M & GN had been sanctioned and were under construction, approaching the district from opposite directions. They were the Lynn & Fakenham and the Great Yarmouth & Stalham Light. Meanwhile another GE subsidiary, the Wensum Valley, was authorised in 1864 to build a line by that route from Norwich to Dereham but did nothing towards construction. A separate scheme, the Central Norfolk Light, from Norwich to Blakeney via Aylsham and Holt, although put forward in 1875 by Lord Hastings and Messrs Wilkinson & Jarvis (later a director and contractors respectively of the Lynn & Fakenham), did not even deposit a Bill.

The promoters of the Lynn & Fakenham were Mr W. Walker, a Lincolnshire man who was head of a firm in Lynn and had bought the manor house at Little Massingham, and the Rev I. L. Brereton, the rector there, who had established the school for Norfolk which later gave its name to County School station; this was the junction of the GE Dereham—Fakenham line with the line from Wroxham through Aylsham, an extension of the East Norfolk (see page 41). Meetings were held at the rectory and the support of Lord Townshend and Sir W. Browne-Folkes was obtained.

THE PREDECESSORS IN THE EAST

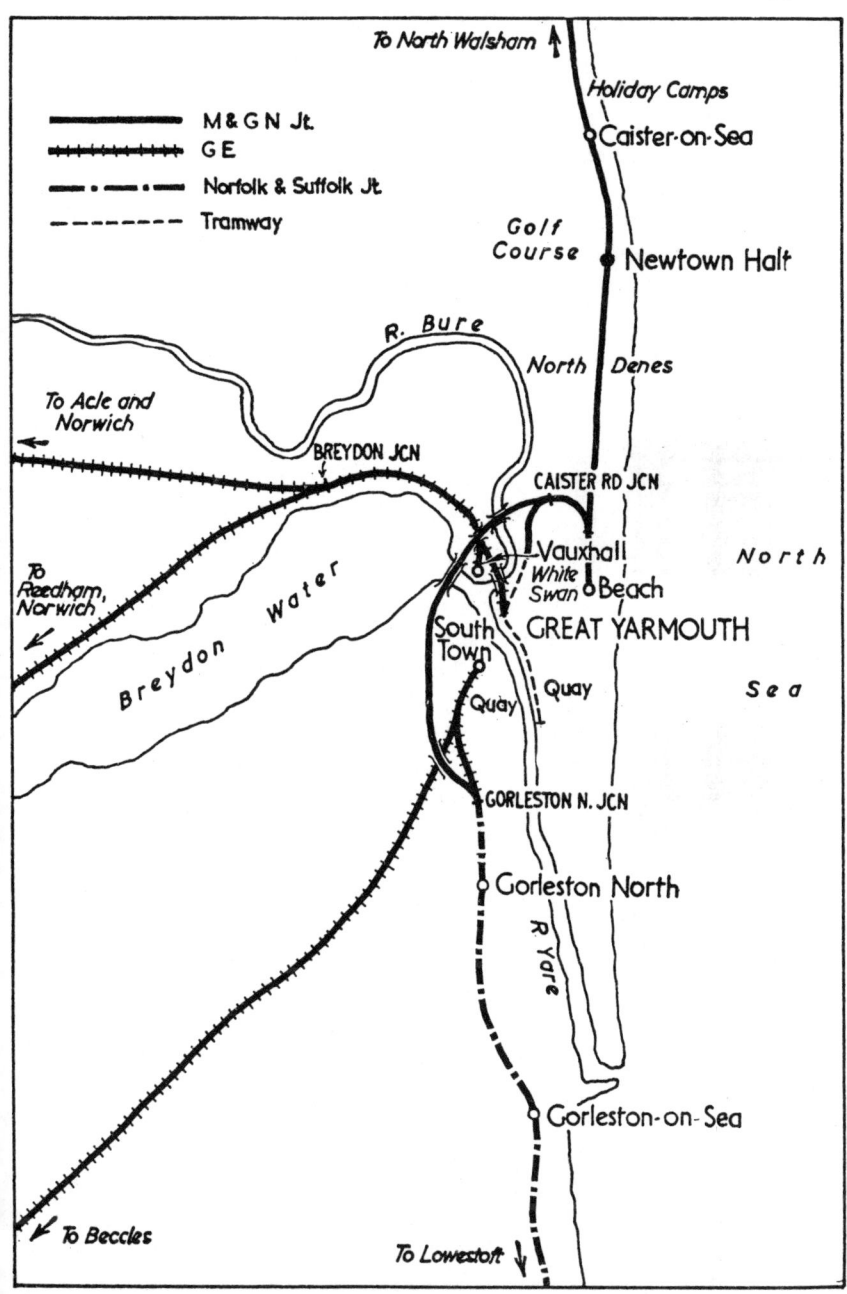

A railway between Lynn and Fakenham had first been proposed as early as 1845 (see Chapter 1); but the new scheme had good chances of success, as it also served to fulfil the hopes of the Norwich & Spalding and its successors for a separate railway eastwards from Lynn towards Norwich. When the L & F Bill came before the parliamentary committee in March and May 1876 it encountered vigorous opposition from the GE and the Hunstanton & West Norfolk, (an amalgamation in 1874 of the Lynn & Hunstanton and the West Norfolk which was worked by the GE). But the L & F obtained its Act on 13 July 1876.

THE GREAT YARMOUTH & STALHAM LIGHT RAILWAY

The Great Yarmouth & Stalham's Bill, which met with less opposition, passed on 26 July 1876 and part of its line was opened before any of the L & F. It was authorised as a 'light railway' under the Regulation of Railways Act, 1868; in practice this meant that it was of light construction and that the speed of the trains was limited under regulations issued by the Board of Trade, but it had to be sanctioned by Act of Parliament. The cheaper procedure of a public inquiry by commissioners followed by a Board of Trade order permitting construction was not introduced in England until the Light Railways Act, 1896. The provisions of the 1868 Act relating to the authorisation of light railways were in fact little used; the GY & S was one of the few occasions.

The original capital was £98,000 in 9,800 £10 shares, with borrowing powers of £32,600. The first directors were Sir Edward Lacon, Bart, MP, chairman, James Bunn, Charles Aldred, Edward Youell, and John Clowes, all well known in the district. Sir Edward was a director of Lacon's brewery and chairman of Lacon & Youell, Bankers, with Mr Youell as his partner; so this concern became the company's bankers. Mr Clowes was a Yarmouth solicitor.

The contract for the $17\frac{3}{4}$ miles from Yarmouth to Stalham was given to Messrs Wilkinson & Jarvis and work began on 15 January 1877. The Yarmouth terminus, which became known as Beach station, described as at Skinners Mill, Nelson Road, was in the north of the town less than 200 yards from

Page 35 (above) *Freight train, including fish vans, at Great Yarmouth. Loco Johnson 4-4-0 renumbered as* LNE *01 (formerly 1) but still with* M & GN *tender 1937;* (below) *local train leaving Cromer Beach. Note the somersault signals ·*

Page 36 *Interesting expresses 1910-1930:* (above) *near Cromer 1913 'C' class 4–4–0 with large boiler, ex-*GN *six-wheeled coaches,* GN *high roof bogie coach, Midland coaches for Leicester in rear;* (below) *ex-*GN *coaches headed by Johnson 4–4–0 No 40, approaching Peterboro'*

the north beach and near some of the principal hotels. But it was about half a mile from the nearest GE metals at Vauxhall, so the line was at first isolated. The country was easy, nearly flat, but to save expense the line was laid practically on ground level, which meant frequent changes of gradient and short stretches of 1 in 100. Work proceeded with vigour and the first section, 5 miles 31 chains to Ormesby, was opened on 7 August. From Beach the line ran across the North Denes close to the shore, turned slightly inland to the first station, Caister, and then ran right by the sea for about 1½ miles before turning inland north-west to a temporary terminus in the parish of Ormesby St Margaret. The station was not called Great Ormesby until 24 January 1884. Mr Charles Nicolson was in general charge as manager, secretary and engineer. All rolling stock had to be brought through the streets from Vauxhall to the GY & S station, (Beach from 5 April 1883).

The next section from Ormesby to Hemsby turned north about a mile from the shore for 1 mile 57 chains and was opened on 16 May 1878, passing just north of Ormesby broad, the largest of a series of beautiful broads which connect with each other, but have not for many years been accessible from the other broads and rivers. It then proceeded north-west, away from the sea, to Martham, 2¾ miles. But as, so far, authority for a level crossing north of Hemsby was lacking, and litigation with the local authorities followed, this section had to be opened from a temporary station beyond the crossing on 15 July. From October, there was another 'temporary' south of the crossing. Six trains daily and four on Sundays were provided each way between Beach and Martham, serving all stations and allowed 35 minutes for the journey. The fares were first, third and 'gov', with no second class. At first there were only three small 0-6-0 tank engines but in September the first 4-4-0 tank *North Walsham* arrived.

The little line proved so popular for passenger and local goods traffic that it was possible to declare a dividend of 4 per cent at a half-yearly meeting in the autumn of 1878, when completion to Stalham was expected by January 1879. Powers for Hemsby crossing were obtained in July 1879, the lines were connected, and the 'temporaries' abolished.

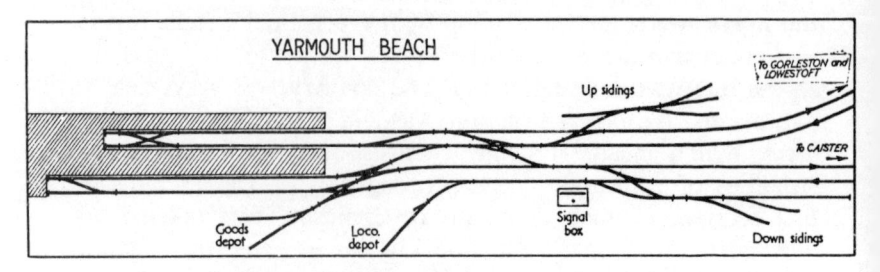

THE YARMOUTH & NORTH NORFOLK LIGHT RAILWAY

On 27 May 1878 the company obtained another Act, authorising an extension for 7 miles from Stalham to North Walsham and a change of name to the Yarmouth & North Norfolk Light. Powers were given to raise £60,000 new capital and further loans of up to £20,000.

The next sections, 2¾ miles westwards to Potter Heigham and a further 2¾ miles to Catfield, proved more difficult because of Potter Heigham Bridge. This structure, about half a mile east of the station, was described in the Act of 1876 as over the river Bure. In fact it was over the river Thurne, a tributary of the Bure. The Act provided that the bridge had to be 9 ft 6 in above 'high water' and have a span of at least 40 ft over the river. The bridge had three 79-ft spans and its main girders were of the through truss type, divided into five equal bays. The line reached Catfield on 17 January 1880.

Despite the words 'high water' in the Act and frequent references in contemporary documents to the tide at the bridge, only a few years later a court, on application by riparian owners who wished to prevent anglers from fishing in the Thurne, solemnly held that there was no tide there, although the rise and fall was and is clearly visible. The court's decision was difficult to understand. But the Judge apparently thought that the rise and fall of water (which many witnesses said was the tide) was due respectively to rainfall and evaporation, as other witnesses said. It was an extraordinary situation that Parliament in the Act authorising the railway should in effect declare there was a tide, and that the court should decide the opposite a few years later.

After the case riparian owners prosecuted anglers, many of whom came to Potter Heigham station to fish in the river, often taking special 'fishing and boating' railway tickets (see page 63). Some defied the ban and fished, but many were deterred, so the passenger traffic to Potter Heigham, Catfield and other stations near the river and broads was affected by the court's decision. The whole matter caused great indignation in the district, which was still felt thirty years later.

The Bure flows into the Yare near Vauxhall station and no M & GN line was built across it until over twenty years later when the Lowestoft extension was made.

THE LYNN & FAKENHAM RAILWAY

The Lynn & Fakenham was authorised from a junction with the Hunstanton & West Norfolk at the Gaywood Road, about 1½ miles from King's Lynn terminus, eastwards through Massingham to another junction, facing south towards Dereham, with a GE line south of the latter's Fakenham station. Running powers were granted over the H & WN to the junction with the GE's own metals outside King's Lynn and thence into the GE passenger and goods stations. Further powers were granted for traffic to the King's Lynn dock line and into the GE's Fakenham station. Lord Townshend, of a famous Norfolk family, was the first chairman, and the other two directors were Sir W. A. Browne-Folkes MP of Hillington and Mr Walker. The capital was £150,000 and the borrowing powers £50,000. Wilkinson & Jarvis were also the L & F's contractors.

As the line was to connect with the GE at each end, it might have been expected that the GE would make some attempt to take it over or at least work it; but it did not. Had it done so, it might have saved itself a great deal of trouble and expense, as the L & F and its successor, the Eastern & Midlands, were aggressive concerns.

At a shareholders' meeting in October 1878, it was announced that good progress was being made; 2¾ miles of rails had already been laid and the line was expected to be ready as far as Massingham by the end of the year. The capital was fully subscribed. Sir Edward Lacon and Mr Aldred had joined the board and Lacon and Youell were the company's bankers. Mr Nicolson was secretary and engineer. The GE was not helpful, at one time refusing to allow material to pass over the Gaywood Road Junction, so that it had to be carted

OPENING TO MASSINGHAM

In fact the line, which was single, was not completed to Massingham until July 1879. The Board of Trade inspected it, but there were further delays and it was not opened until 16 August. The directors announced at the shareholders' meeting in September that 'certain traffic had been lost in consequence'. It was also stated that Mr Pepper had been appointed manager, all necessary materials had been delivered and it was expected that the line would soon be extended to Rudham. From Gaywood Road Junction the country was at first easy but then became more difficult with several stretches of 1 in 100. It is not always realised how hilly much of West Norfolk is—with its deep lanes it is rather like the west country. The distance to Massingham was 12 miles. There were stations at Grimston Road and Hillington not far from Sandringham, which had become a royal residence some years before. The temporary terminus was really at Little Massingham, over a mile from Great Massingham village.

Four passenger trains each way were provided on weekdays only, with an extra on Tuesdays, and took about 40 minutes for the whole journey. The fares were first and 'gov' only. In the beginning Wilkinson & Jarvis had to undertake operation. A small 0–4–0 tank engine which had worked on the construction of the line, an 0–6–0 tank transferred from the Y & NN, and a 4–4–0 tank *Hillington* were at first the only engines available (see Chapter 10).

AMALGAMATION PLANS FAIL

The L & F and Y & NN were now so closely associated that they desired to connect the two systems and to amalgamate. In 1879 the Y & NN presented a Bill for a further extension from North Walsham through Aylsham to a junction with the L & F at a spot called Pudding Norton, south-east of the town of Fakenham, just south of the intended junction of the L & F and GE. A junction with the GE at North Walsham and what

THE PREDECESSORS IN THE EAST 41

was called a tramway into Yarmouth to connect with the existing GE tramway on the quay were also proposed. The Bill further sought authority for the L & F and Y & NN to amalgamate. But the GE and East Norfolk opposed and put forward a Bill for an extension of the latter's authorised branch from Wroxham to Aylsham to the spot later called County School on the GE Dereham—Fakenham line, a route almost parallel to the Y & NN's proposed extension. The parliamentary committee approved the East Norfolk scheme and rejected the Y & NN's Bill, except for some minor deviations of the lines already authorised.

OPENING TO STALHAM

After this disappointment the Y & NN was encouraged by the completion of the final 2-mile section of its original line from Catfield to Stalham on 3 July 1880. The station, described as 'on the east side of Staithe Road', was at the north end of the village by the main road to Norwich. The word 'staithe' is Scandinavian and in Norfolk and Yorkshire speech means a landing place. Stalham and Sutton staithes are where tributaries of the river Ant rise, giving access to the fine Barton broad and to the Bure. Sutton is a small village close to the line between Stalham and Catfield. Hickling broad, which is reached by the river Thurne, was about 1 mile from Catfield station and is the largest real broad, as Breydon Water near Yarmouth is regarded as only a wide stretch of water in a tidal river.

Six trains each way were provided daily between Stalham and Yarmouth and three each way on Sundays, taking generally 50 minutes overall. The whole line was of course single, and many level crossings, which became so characteristic of the M & GN, were provided; one referred to in the Act was on behalf of the Admiralty to provide access to a Royal Naval Reserve battery north of Beach station. There were engine sheds and small workshops at Yarmouth. All track was of Vignoles flat-bottom type without chairs, and rails were 70 lb per yard. A 4 per cent dividend had again been declared

MIDLAND & GREAT NORTHERN JOINT RAILWAY

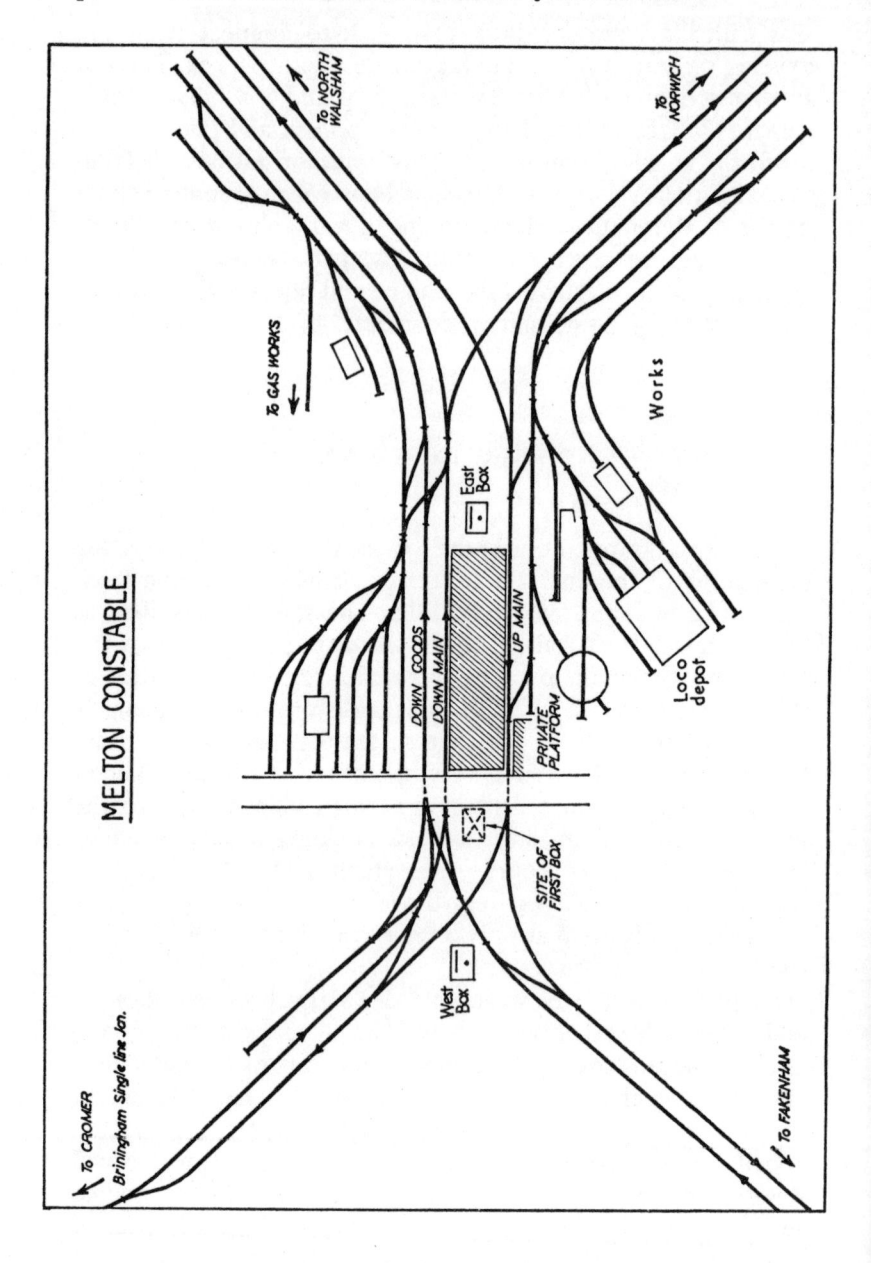

MELTON CONSTABLE

THE PREDECESSORS IN THE EAST

for the second half of 1878 but for the first half of 1879 it was only 1 per cent owing to increased expenses.

THE YARMOUTH UNION RAILWAY

The grandly named Yarmouth Union Railway, authorised on 26 August 1880, might have been expected to do something to remedy the strange situation at Yarmouth, which now had three termini, all completely isolated from one another, Vauxhall and South Town GE, and Beach Y & NN. Despite its fine title, it was only a short line, 1 mile 2 chains; with a long Act which authorised the 1879 plan for access to the quay by a route from a junction just outside Beach station platforms (facing north), then west across the Caister road, followed by a complete change of direction due south back into the town and into the street by the White Swan Inn, where for about a furlong it had to be described as a tramway. Then it made a junction with the existing tramway belonging to the GE, which extended the line from Vauxhall goods station through the streets and along the principal quay on the Yare, there known as the harbour. Mr Wilkinson and Mr Jarvis, the contractors, and Mr Pinn were the first directors. The capital was £20,000 and the borrowing powers £5,500.

AMBITIOUS PLANS

Meanwhile the L & F had received authority by an Act of 12 August 1880 for an elaborate programme of extensions. The chief of these was the long desired separate route to Norwich through Melton Constable (henceforth called Melton), Whitwell and Drayton. From this line at Melton there was to be a branch through Holt, Kelling, Cley and Wiveton to Blakeney Harbour. At Fakenham the new line would begin at Pudding Norton (mentioned on page 40) and pass under the GE line. At Themelthorpe, west of Whitwell, the line was to cross the GE's East Norfolk extension from Aylsham to County School, by this time under construction. The GE had opposed the L & F's Bill and put forward a counter scheme to build a line to Blakeney itself. To appease the GE the Act contained elaborate provisions for facilities for GE traffic from

Themelthorpe to Blakeney, and corresponding facilities for L & F traffic from Themelthorpe to Aylsham; but strangely enough it gave no authority for a junction at Themelthorpe, nor was one built there for eighty years. The junction for the Holt and Blakeney line at Melton faced west, convenient for through traffic from the Norwich direction but involving a reversal for traffic from the west. This was to cause trouble later.

The same Act also provided for a line into King's Lynn, which was authorised to leave the H & WN at Salters Road only 120 yards south of Gaywood Road Junction, by means of a junction facing south, branch off westwards, cross the dock line with a junction, cross the 'Loke' in Lynn and terminate at Austin Street near Garland's Yard, where there was to be a goods and later a passenger station about ¼ mile north of the GE station. 'Loke' was an inappropriate word for a road in a town, as in Norfolk speech it generally means a country lane.

MORE OPENINGS

In the midst of the parliamentary proceedings the L & F was much encouraged by the opening of the Massingham—Fakenham line on 6 August 1880. The line ran slightly north-east to Rudham and Raynham Park and then followed the Wensum valley, crossing the little river several times, to a station at Fakenham south-west of the town, a good half-mile from its centre but duly named Fakenham Town. The GE station was nearly a mile away. The section was 9 miles long. Near Rudham the gradients were again steep, including 1 in 90–100. At King's Lynn the GE provided a new bay platform and a separate booking office, partly at the L & F's expense. There were six passenger trains each way on weekdays and one on Sundays, taking from 55 minutes to an hour from Lynn to Fakenham. Small locomotive shops were established there, and Mr G. R. Curson, an experienced GE man, was made superintendent of the railway. Rudham became East Rudham in March 1882.

The Y & NN's extension from Stalham to North Walsham was opened on 13 June 1881. The route was at first northwest and then west, north of the river Ant, here canalised as the North Walsham & Dilham canal, to a station west of Honing village, which was not ready until August 1882. It was known as Honing for Worstead, as the latter, with its own GE station, was only about 1¼ miles to the south. The line then bridged the Ant and continued north-west until it ran parallel with the GE East Norfolk line for nearly a mile to a separate station in North Walsham about 100 yards from the GE station. As it was just that distance nearer the town it was named North Walsham Town. Stalham to Honing was level but the line then rose at 1 in 100 to North Walsham. Authority for a junction there had been refused but, as the companies' properties adjoined, a temporary connection was laid in October, over which another of the 4-4-0 tank engines arrived; owing to the growing hostility between the companies, however, this junction was not retained for long. The same number of trains ran after the extension was opened, save that one Sunday train from Yarmouth did not run further than Martham and back. The overall time from Yarmouth to North Walsham was 1 hour 10 minutes. It was hoped that completion of the extension would have a good effect on the financial position of the company but the expense of the works had swallowed up most of the receipts. At the meeting early in 1881 it was stated that the profits earned were quite insufficient for a dividend to be declared.

MELTON—NORTH WALSHAM LINE SANCTIONED

The L & F and Y & NN again attempted to obtain authority to have their lines connected, this time with success. For the 1881 session they promoted a Bill for a line from Melton via Aylsham to North Walsham. The GE, whose East Norfolk extension through the district was approaching completion, opposed. There was another competitor in the field, the Central Norfolk, which having reappeared in rather a different form now included a Melton—North Walsham line in its proposals and even acquired a quantity of material. It did not obtain an Act however, and the L & F and Y & NN had their line sanctioned on 11 August. In the same Bill the L & F sought powers to build another branch from Kelling through 'Sherringham' (sic) and Runton to a point 'near Cromer cemetery', the future Beach station. Despite GE opposition this line was also authorised. By the same Act the Y & NN, in anticipation of the expected connection with the L & F and the outside world generally, ceased to be a light railway. This was just as well, as under the Board of Trade regulations it had only been allowed to run trains at not more than 25 mph and the weight of rolling stock was restricted. The Y & NN and L & F also obtained specific power to make working agreements.

YARMOUTH UNION COMPLETED

The works of the YU, the short line with the long Act, had not begun, so the three companies obtained fresh powers which the Y & NN was to execute. Supervising construction was a young man called Marriott, who had recently joined Wilkinson & Jarvis after serving articles with Ransomes & Rapier, and after a short period with the GN; he was to become one of the most important figures in the whole history of the M & GN. Under his direction the works were pushed forward energetically so that the line was opened to the junction with the GE tramway on 15 May 1882. The elaborate provisions for operating the tramway section in the original Act were not required, as the trucks were hauled by GE tram engines, 0–4–0 tanks and later 0–6–0 tanks, specially constructed for the purpose. The advantage was access to the fish quay but the traffic could not be substantial or conveyed for long distances until the North Walsham—Melton link was ready.

In view of the financial position of the L & F and Y & NN at this stage, their extension programmes showed considerable courage. The L & F had declared a 1 per cent dividend in 1880; for the half-year ending 30 June 1881 it could only announce the same on 'shares issued in respect of the line opened for traffic', and that it had been necessary to raise money by issuing debentures. The Y & NN, which had the expensive North Walsham extension to pay for, had to report for the half-year ending 31 December 1881 a 'small loss on working' and was also issuing debentures.

TOWARDS NORWICH

Great things were expected of the Norwich extension, which

THE PREDECESSORS IN THE EAST 47

was opened in short sections. The first portion, 14 miles from Fakenham to Guestwick, was opened on 19 January 1882. From the Town station it crossed the Wensum, went under the GE and followed the river for a mile to Langor Bridge, where later there was a siding. Then it struck north-east up 1 in 100 past Thursford station to Pigg's Grove summit, 312 ft above sea level, the highest point reached on the M & GN; there the line crossed the Holt road, went due east to Melton and then nearly south, partly down 1 in 100, through Hindolvestone to Guestwick.

The next section, 6½ miles to Lenwade, was opened on 1 July. This continued the descent, over the GE again near Themelthorpe village through Whitwell and Reepham station to a level portion. There were five trains each way on weekdays between Lynn and Melton and four on the Melton—Lenwade section, with variations on Tuesdays. On Sunday there was one each way between Lynn and Melton only.

MELTON WORKS ESTABLISHED

Before the line was built Melton had been a small village but it was appreciated that it could become an important junction. It was there that Mr J. W. Mann (a Fletcher man from the North Eastern), who was appointed locomotive superintendent of the L & F in 1880, built locomotive shops and houses for the men. So Melton became the engineering headquarters of the Eastern & Midlands and of the M & GN; the original shops at Fakenham became sheds for the goods department. The authorised junction there with the GE was not built and the powers lapsed.

MORE PLANS FOR LYNN AND BLAKENEY

The L & F and Y & NN now decided that what was really wanted was a complete amalgamation of their lines with the YU, the M & E and the PW & SB. After negotiations with the GN, the Midland, the Waring family and other interested parties, a Bill was presented for the 1882 session. Success of the combined concern would require better connection between the lines east and west of Lynn. There was a proposal (renewed later more than once) for a line from South Lynn goods station over the GE and on to the authorised L & F station at Austin Street. The land for the branch there had been acquired, levelled and fenced, and the station buildings begun. But if this arrangement had been adopted, trains between east and west would have had to reverse at Austin Street, as they did at the GE station, and a short section of GE metals between Salters Road and Gaywood Road would still have intervened. The L & F board approved a different scheme for a direct line from South Lynn eastwards for 4 miles to join the L & F main line, to avoid using the GE line altogether for east-west traffic. A Bill to authorise the 'Lynn loop' as it was called was also presented.

The L & F still had great hopes for Blakeney. The same Bill sought to acquire the harbour company there, provide more lines on the quay, and build an extension for 3 miles to Stiffkey (pronounced Stewky), a village near the shore well known for its cockles. Powers were also sought for a Dereham branch from Lenwade, and an extension from a point west of the authorised Norwich station round through the north of the city to a central station at King Street, and a further extension to the GE east of Thorpe station.

AMALGAMATION AUTHORISED

An Act for the Lynn and Blakeney lines passed on 11 August but the Norwich central clauses, which had encountered opposition from the dean and chapter in relation to some of the land to be acquired as well as from other quarters, were withdrawn; the Dereham scheme also failed. The amalgamation Act, creating the Eastern & Midlands Railway Company followed on 18 August. The amalgamation was to be in two stages. First, on 1 January 1883 the L & F, Y & NN and YU were to combine to form the E & M. Shares were generally to be transferred into E & M stock but L & F and Y & NN debenture and preference holders were to retain priority rights in respect of the earnings of those sections of the line. Second, the M & E and PW & SB were to be amalgamated with the E & M as from 1 July 1883 but the GN and Midland were to continue to operate those lines under the existing arrangements. The E & M

THE PREDECESSORS IN THE EAST

was only to run trains with its own engines on the former PW & SB with Midland consent and on the Bourne—Lynn with both GN and Midland consent. The former stocks of the M & E and PW & SB were necessarily to be kept separate, as the collection of receipts for meeting obligations under them would largely remain dependent upon continuing the working arrangements and financial agreements with the GN and Midland.

Considerable through traffic was expected to develop to and from the GN and Midland. The GN at this stage was not very pleased with its Bourne—Lynn responsibilities, what with the floods and the failure of the Sutton Bridge docks scheme. But it was delighted with an association with the E & M, which would at last give it access to a route right into Norfolk, particularly at a time when it was likely to lose traffic between the North and East Anglia owing to the completion of its joint line with the GE, giving the latter its long desired route to the North.

Pending complete amalgamation, the L & F agreed to work the Y & NN for 55 per cent of the gross receipts, and in anticipation of the completion of through routes and the need for faster passenger and goods trains it ordered a series of 4–4–0 tender engines, four of which began work in 1882 (see Chapter 10). It had taken over direct operation of its trains from Wilkinson & Jarvis in 1881 and the engines and stock had become its own property at that time.

NORWICH REACHED

The final 10¼-mile section from Lenwade to Norwich, fulfilling hopes dating back to the 'Norwich & Spalding' and earlier, was opened on 2 December 1882. It began with a further climb of 1 in 100 to beyond Attlebridge and then descended at the same gradient to Drayton, but the rest along the Wensum was level, with bridges over the river near Drayton and Hellesdon stations. The Norwich station was in the north-west, near the river and a quarter of a mile north of the Dereham road. It was not quite complete, nor was it really nearer the city centre than the GE Thorpe and Victoria stations; but it was called City from its completion in 1883 and was to become the largest station in area on the M & GN. On the opening day a special train from Kings Cross brought a large party of guests and the proceedings included a banquet in St Andrew's Hall worthy of a celebration of a railway opening in early days.

CHAPTER FOUR

The Eastern & Midlands Railway

TROUBLE ON THE BOARD

Under the amalgamation Act five directors elected by the L & F and Y & NN shareholders were to hold office until the first general meeting after the first amalgamation. They were Lord Townshend, chairman, Sir W. Folkes, Lord Hastings, Sir Edward Lacon and Mr Aldred—the same board that the L & F had before amalgamation. At the meeting they could be re-elected. At the second amalgamation one director each was to be elected by the former M & E and PW & SB shareholders respectively; but one of the existing five would have to resign so that there would be a total of only six.

However, shortly before the first meeting on 24 February 1883 Lord Townshend and Sir W. Folkes resigned; and at the meeting Mr Read (who had been expected to be the nominee of the M & E at the second amalgamation) and Mr Otway were elected directors in their place. Mr Aldred was made chairman.

It appears that soon afterwards serious disagreement occurred on the board. The landowning and banking element, by now only represented by Lord Hastings and Sir Edward Lacon, clashed with the financial and contracting element, represented particularly by Mr Read. Mr Wilkinson and Mr Slade (a director both of the M & E and PW & SB) were made directors at the second amalgamation, and Lord Hastings and Sir Edward resigned. The way was left clear for Mr Read's rash and elaborate schemes for further expansion, which Mr Wilkinson as a contractor would support and which are described in this chapter. If Sir Edward Lacon, for example, had remained on the board, policy might have been different and the later financial troubles avoided. The Warings did not join the new board, but concentrated on their activities with the Somerset & Dorset and elsewhere. From the autumn of 1883 there were still only five directors instead of the authorised six.

Mr Tait, manager of the Y & NN, was made general manager of the E & M. Mr Curson was his assistant and Mr Alfred Aslett, a GN man who was born at Peterboro', was accountant, all with offices in King's Lynn. Mr Mellett, engineer, and Mr Mann, locomotive superintendent, were at Melton but Mr Syms, the secretary, at first had his office in Yarmouth.

Although the Lynn loop had been sanctioned, the board announced that it intended to complete the Austin Street depot, reminding the shareholders that rent at King's Lynn and other payments to the GE and H & WN absorbed a large proportion of profit and the payments could be considerably reduced.

MELTON—NORTH WALSHAM COMPLETED

The Melton—North Walsham section, where Mr Marriott was in charge as resident engineer, involved heavy works including several bridges and cuttings. Some of the material acquired by the defunct Central Norfolk was taken over and used. The work was so energetically undertaken that this important link, 17 miles long, was opened on 5 April 1883. From Melton the line was downhill; it then passed the upper reaches of the Bure to Corpusty and Saxthorpe station, and from there its course lay through Bluestone, parallel with the GE East Norfolk extension (see Chapter 3) which was only about a third of a mile to the south; Blickling park was close by to the north. Aylsham station was to the north of the town where the line crossed the Bure, but was duly named Aylsham Town. The GE station was over a mile to the south. Then the line went east, through Felmingham, with up and down stretches of 1 in 100, and culminated in a steep curved rise at 1 in 64 under the GE line and up to North Walsham Town. A 4–4–0 tank, No 9 *Fakenham*, took the first train through from Lynn to Yarmouth. Holiday passenger traffic to Yarmouth could now be developed, while on the freight side, as well as fish, valuable cattle traffic was obtained.

Page 53 *Interesting expresses 1930-1940:* (above) *Cromer—Kings Cross express at Wisbech North about 1932. Note ex-*LNW *non-corridor bogie coach;* (below) *Saturday Cromer—Manchester express approaching Nottingham Midland about 1934*

Page 54 (above) *Characteristic* M & GN *(ex-*GN*) six-wheeled coach;* (centre) *Sutton Bridge 1937;* (below) *old four-wheeled tender off ex-Cornwall Minerals engine used for water storage and conveyance to local stations, late 1940*

The report for the first half of 1883 stated that the situation compared with the corresponding period in 1882 was satisfactory. Working expenses were high and there had been unremunerative mileage on the Yarmouth section. Norwich City and Melton—North Walsham had only been completed during the half-year so that their earnings were not yet an indication of their capacities. Gross receipts were £21,671, brought in by 223,688 passengers, 28,285 parcels, 59,110 tons of general goods and coal and 53,472 head of cattle. The directors said: 'It was wiser to establish a service calculated to encourage growth of traffic rather than merely to keep pace with it'.

A LAVISH SERVICE

The passenger service that summer comprised six trains each way on the Lynn—Melton section, seven on the Melton—Norwich (mostly through from Lynn but one from Fakenham only) and six on the Melton—Yarmouth (five through from and to Lynn). Several omitted some stations, and one from Lynn to Yarmouth and three in the opposite direction were described as expresses. There was also an early local from Lynn on Tuesday and another each way from Fakenham to Norwich on Saturdays. The Sunday service was so arranged that it was possible to spend a day in Yarmouth from almost every station. This was done by running a Lynn—Yarmouth train, with Norwich line connections at Melton, and a Melton, a North Walsham, and a Martham train to and from Yarmouth, besides a Lynn—Norwich each way. On weekdays there were good connections with GN and Midland trains at Lynn but no Sunday passenger trains were provided by those companies on the lines to Peterboro' and Bourne.

EXTENSION SCHEMES

A Bill to revive the schemes for a Central station in Norwich, the connection with the GE at Thorpe and the Dereham branch, was presented in the 1883 session but without success. It also contained two further interesting schemes. One was to provide the company with its own route from Yarmouth to

Norwich by a line from Martham, crossing the Bure near Thurne mouth and the GE East Norfolk line between Whitlingham and Salhouse, to a junction with the proposed Norwich central line near the Magdalen Road. But the GE had already obtained authority in 1879 for a direct Yarmouth—Norwich line through Acle to Brundall, in addition to its old route through Reedham, and this line was completed on 1 June 1883; the E & M scheme therefore failed. The other proposal was to make an extension north-westwards from Bourne to Edenham and then use the track of Lord Willoughby D'Eresby's little private railway (opened in 1856 and closed in 1873) from Edenham to its junction with the GN at Little Bytham; but these powers were also refused. These schemes were part of Mr Read's and Mr Wilkinson's policy of further expansion, but only caused expenditure on Bills which did not pass.

Authority was, however, obtained in 1883 and 1884 to increase the capital and enlarge the borrowing powers. By the latter Act time to build the authorised extensions was increased. In the half-yearly report on 31 October 1884 the board stated that construction of the Lynn loop would begin immediately. Great importance was attached to it, as it would not only relieve the company of increasing payments to the GE but would also remove factors which checked traffic development.

LITIGATION WITH THE MIDLAND

Although it had been agreed that the Midland should continue to work the Peterboro'—Lynn traffic, the E & M became dissatisfied with the amount of goods it received from the Midland by that route. Early in 1884, therefore, it applied to the Railway and Canal Commissioners for redress, alleging that the 1863 working agreement was still in force, and that the Midland was under an obligation to develop the 'through traffic' of the route. What the E & M wanted the Midland to do was to hand over at Lynn the traffic to Norwich, Yarmouth and other places where the E & M now had its own line. The Midland contended firstly that through traffic included traffic to the Peterboro'—Lynn line which came anyway, and secondly that the obligation stemmed from the old promise to make a junction with the GE at Wisbech and send traffic east by GE from there. Pages of the argument and decision are concerned with this, which seems unrealistic, as the junction had never been made; a junction with the GE at Lynn had existed for eighteen years and the route would not have been direct. But the crux of the matter was the third Midland contention, that it was handing most of the traffic, including Irish cattle, to the GE at Peterboro' instead of sending it by Sutton Bridge and the E & M, because when it went by the GE it reached, for example, Norwich about midday, in time for delivery to the consignee that day. If it went via Sutton Bridge and Melton, it would not arrive until the evening, too late for delivery before next morning. It was pointed out how competitive the traffic was; it might come by the LNW and GE via Peterboro'; it might come almost entirely GE, by the new GN–GE joint; in both cases it would reach Norwich at midday. If it came by the GN and Spalding, this was the only chance for it to reach Norwich by E & M at a time reasonably competitive with the GE. The commissioners said that the L & F and its successor, the E & M, were strangers to the original agreement, and that they could not take into account the fact that the lines west and east of Lynn were now in one ownership. They held that the matter of prompt service to customers, especially where traffic was competitive, was paramount over any 'agreement to develop through traffic' and refused to interfere. At the E & M's request they 'stated a case' for the High Court's opinion but the E & M did not take the matter further. The practice of having a High Court judge as chairman of the commissioners, with provision for appeal to the Court of Appeal (like appeals from the Transport Tribunal nowadays) was only introduced later.

CHANGES ON THE BOARD

Mr Aldred died in October 1884 and Mr Read, as deputy chairman, took the chair at future shareholders' meetings. Soon afterwards he was also styled 'Managing Director' and continued in charge in these capacities. He officially became chairman in 1887; by this time there were only three other directors, Mr Wilkinson, Mr Slade and Mr Otway.

OPENING TO HOLT

Work on the section from Melton towards Blakeney and Cromer was proceeding slowly. The 5-mile portion as far as Holt was opened on 1 October 1884; a difficult line, it first went steeply down and then up, including 1 in 80 and 1 in 90 gradients. One thousand and forty pounds was paid on account of the purchase price to the Blakeney harbour company, but nothing was done towards construction of the line from Kelling.

'SEPARATE UNDERTAKINGS'

Despite the amalgamation of all the companies as the E & M, the Lynn loop and the Cromer line were constituted 'separate undertakings' by Acts of 1884-5. The idea of this statutory schizophrenia was to make it easier to raise the money. The undertakings had power to issue guaranteed preference stocks, which sounded very fine, but the guarantee had to be on the rest of the eastern section, the Lynn to Norwich and Yarmouth lines. This caused a great deal of trouble later.

THE LYNN LOOP

The land for the Lynn loop was secured by January 1885. The line was ready for goods traffic on 2 November and was opened for passenger traffic on 1 January 1886. As it included cuttings, embankments and bridges, two over GE lines, in the 4½ miles, this was a creditable achievement. It was double track, with a public goods siding at Hardwick Road and a passenger station at Gayton Road. A new passenger station, South Lynn, was provided close to the old goods station. Thereafter most of the trains for the east used South Lynn, connecting there with GN and Midland trains. The latter continued to run into and out of King's Lynn, and the E & M also provided its own shuttle service between there and South Lynn. A summer express for Yarmouth started at King's Lynn and reversed at South Lynn. But the great advantage was that traffic could move direct between west and east, instead of running over and paying toll to the GE, often an unfriendly company, and without reversing at King's Lynn. The line from South Lynn to the harbour junction with the GE was doubled. The old line from Gaywood Road Junction to Bawsey was closed. The junction at Gaywood was taken out and the lines at the Bawsey end became sidings. But for a considerable time the rails on the section were left in place, as there was still a possibility that the GE might want to take over the eastern section of the E & M. The old passenger station at West Lynn, west of the Ouse bridge, was closed on 1 July 1886 and dismantled. In GE, L & F, and E & M timetables, King's Lynn had long been known as Lynn, but the E & M called it Lynn Town after the opening of South Lynn. The Austin Street depot at King's Lynn was never opened as a station but the general offices of the company were established there.

The passenger and fish traffic developed well but the middle eighties were a period of agricultural depression, aggravated sometimes by bad weather and foot-and-mouth disease. The directors' reports referred frequently to these troubles, which reduced chances of prosperity for the line in a mainly agricultural district, and to produce economies some reduction in staff was made. Acts in 1884-6 authorised £340,000 new capital, and £33,000 loans by debentures. Mr Mann left and Mr Marriott became locomotive superintendent as well as engineer. Mr Aslett was made traffic manager.

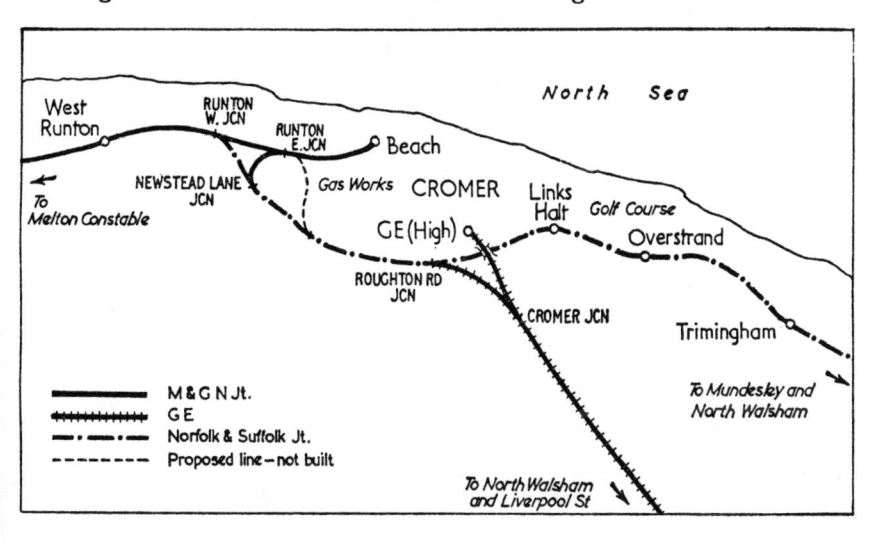

OPENING TO CROMER

The works beyond Holt had become almost derelict but despite the financial difficulties the directors decided to complete the line to Cromer. By employing his own men instead of contractors Mr Marriott found he could carry out the work more cheaply, and the section was opened on 16 June 1887. From Holt the line went north to the intended junction with the Blakeney branch near Kelling Heath, then east, steeply down at 1 in 80, over a road three-quarters of a mile from Weybourne village, then north-east towards the shore. Thereafter it was always only about half a mile from the cliffs, with stations at the growing resort of Sheringham (still spelt with two 'rr's'), and a small one at West Runton (not opened until September) to Beach station, 10 miles long in all. Beach is not on the sea front but is less than a quarter of a mile from it and is close to some of the best hotels, while the GE station was on a hill above the town. Much cutting and embankment work was required in hilly 'Poppyland'. Thanks to the Lynn direct line a through express from Kings Cross to Cromer ran for the first time in August. The Prince of Wales (later King Edward VII) was an early traveller on the line when visiting Lord Hastings. Mr Marriott had to make special arrangements for the royal party's safety, as it was a time of serious trouble in Ireland and an attempt to wreck the royal train was a possibility. In the half-yearly report ending 31 December the directors said that thanks to the Cromer line, passengers had increased by 96,953 to a total for the year of 413,277.

BLAKENEY SCHEME ABANDONED

Meanwhile the directors had wisely decided, concerning the authorised Blakeney and Stiffkey line, 'that the traffic of the district between Kelling and Blakeney would not be sufficient to justify the expenditure of the capital required'. By an agreement of 28 December 1886 it was arranged, subject to parliamentary sanction, that the harbour company should keep the £1,040 which the E & M had paid, that the agreement to acquire the harbour would be rescinded and the powers to build the line repealed. Parliament authorised this by an Act of 28 June, 1888, but the E & M had spent money to no purpose. Ticket stockbooks issued by the L & F contained pages headed with the names of Kelling, Cley, Salthouse, Blakeney and Stiffkey although such stations never existed, and some of the books remained in use as long afterwards as 1946. On 4 February 1901 sidings were established at the intended junction at Kelling for the purpose of obtaining ballast.

MORE LITIGATION WITH THE MIDLAND

Encouraged by the completion of the Lynn loop and the Cromer line, on 12 May 1887 the E & M again complained to the commissioners that the Midland was not handing over a proper amount of goods traffic via the Peterboro'—Sutton Bridge line. It also alleged that the Midland was sending little traffic by the Bourne—Sutton Bridge route, which was true. Grinling's *History of the Great Northern Railway* records that the E & M further complained that such traffic as the Midland sent that way was more than it sent via Peterboro' and Wisbech, that it was 'starving' that route in order to make up its share of the guarantee with the GN on the Bourne—Lynn line. If Mr R. S. Wright, the E & M's counsel relied seriously on this, it was soon brushed aside. The old difficulty of the junction at Wisbech that was never made was mentioned, but the commissioners again decided that the Midland was not under an obligation under the 1863 agreement to send the through traffic by the PW & SB; it could deal with it in the 'best interests of the traffic' which meant, in practice, that it could hand it to the GE at Peterboro' if it reached the consignees more promptly than it would by E & M. The complaint about the Bourne line was equally unsuccessful, as it was held that the Midland was under no obligation to send through traffic that way, via Stamford, at all, the Cheshire Lines type of clause wording being merely permissive (Chapter 2, page 25), 'empowering not compelling' the Midland to send the traffic. The commissioners added that the best access to the M & E was via Peterboro' under the 1863 agreement, which was earlier in date. They said that the valuable traffic between the E & M and Burton upon Trent could best be handled by co-operation between the GN, Midland and E & M.

KINGS CROSS TO CROMER

A happier feature was the Kings Cross—Cromer through service, which at first ran in summer only. For the first time, E & M engines worked regular passenger trains on their own line between South Lynn and Peterboro'. In the summer of 1888 there were two trains each way over E & M metals from Peterboro' to Cromer, 84 miles, in an average time of 2 hours 50 minutes, 29½ mph inclusive and 35½ mph exclusive of stops, but the best train took only 2 hours 45 minutes, 30¼ mph inclusive. There were seven or eight regular stops besides two or three conditional. As the whole route was single except for the Lynn loop there were many slacks for tablet exchanging.

Foxwell's *Express Trains* published the next year included 'honourable mention' of the service, although it did not attain the book's standard for an express of 40 mph. The GN was concerned to play its part well. In the down direction the two expresses conveying the through coaches from Kings Cross were the 10.10 am Leeds and Manchester which reached Peterboro' in 90 minutes, and the 2 pm Manchester, one of the best trains on the line, which slipped them at Peterboro'. This was the best overall service, reaching Cromer in 4½ hours, with stops on the E & M at Wisbech, Sutton Bridge, South Lynn, Fakenham, Melton, Holt and Sheringham regularly, and at Hillington, Massingham, Thursford and West Runton conditionally. From Peterboro' the two corresponding up services used expresses from Newcastle and Manchester which reached Kings Cross at 5 pm and 7.55 pm respectively. The GN provided the coaches, generally its standard six-wheelers of the period; they were dual-fitted, as the E & M used the Westinghouse brake and the GN the automatic vacuum. The E & M engines were the Beyer Peacock 4-4-0s. Reversal was necessary at Melton, but connections were made there with Norwich and Yarmouth trains. The best GE service at this period was 3½ hours from Liverpool Street to Cromer. In the summer of 1889 there were the same two down services between Kings Cross and Cromer but three in the up direction.

Trains on the Cromer line were arranged so that passengers could have a day at Yarmouth, and through trains were run, in competition with the GE, so that Norwich people could have a day in Cromer. This service operated on Sundays too, and some trains ran through Melton without stopping. 'Fishing and Boating' tickets were issued for people visiting the broads, particularly to Potter Heigham and Ormesby. All these were summer facilities.

MORE EXTENSION SCHEMES

Despite the failure of the Blakeney scheme, and the financial difficulties, the board was interested in further extensions. One proposal at the end of 1887 revived the 1883 scheme to provide the company with its own route from Yarmouth to Norwich. This time the line was to start a short distance on the Yarmouth side of the Thurne bridge at Potter Heigham (with a curve both towards the latter and in the Martham direction), cross the Bure near Thurne mouth, and then follow the same course as the 1883 plans to the west of the city of Norwich. A Bill was deposited but the E & M wisely took the matter no further. The GE's direct line via Acle had been open since 1883.

Another extension, eventually more fortunate, was proposed at the same time from North Walsham to Mundesley, a small seaside resort. The GE opposed, as it was also interested in the district and had arrangements with a Mr Palmer, who provided horse-buses, what GE publicity called 'conveyances'. For the present the GE was bought off with running powers and the branch was authorised on 20 June 1888.

ALLIANCE WITH THE MIDLAND

The board was so interested in through goods traffic from the Midlands that it now joined with the Midland, with which it had had such acrimonious disputes (and which had even sent a seaside train from Leicester to Yarmouth by the GE route), in reviving the 1866 scheme for a direct line from Bourne to join the Midland near Saxby. The line proposed in a Bill for the 1888 session would have gone further south than that eventually constructed; it would have crossed the GN main line south instead of north of Little Bytham station, and would have continued to an end-on junction with a Midland mineral branch at Cottesmore. This was to be adapted for passenger traffic, so that the trains could run west and join the Syston—Peterboro' line at Ashwell, 4½ miles from Saxby. By an agreement on 16 March the E & M would construct the double-track line as another 'separate undertaking' out of capital (presumably the Midland would provide most of this). In the next session the Midland would apply for powers to take over the whole 'western section', the M & E as well as the PW & SB. The companies made an intimate traffic agreement in respect of the E & M's eastern section, under which traffic between places on the E & M east of Lynn and every competitive place in the country (except London) was to be 'hypothecated'—directed whenever possible to the Midland route.

SAXBY—BOURNE LINE AUTHORISED

It was extraordinary conduct for the E & M board to risk a serious quarrel with the GN at this stage when it felt that the Midland had treated it shabbily over through goods traffic. The GN had shown it was a better friend by the trouble it took over the Cromer service, and by sending freight traffic. If the Bourne—Lynn line were taken over by the Midland, the GN would presumably retain its powers as joint lessee. But the direct line to the Midland, and the traffic agreement, would have a serious effect on GN traffic and prospects. The GN opposed the Bill vigorously. The new route was authorised on 28 June but the GN's counsel had persuaded the committee to prevent the objectionable traffic agreement being scheduled to it, and a junction between the line and the GN at Little Bytham was sanctioned.

In the report for the half-year ending in June the E & M board stated it had given the Midland the option of building the line from Bourne to Cottesmore, and that the Midland would apply next year for powers to do this and to take over the whole western section. Mr Read's other activities as a director of the Somerset & Dorset and of the Kettering, Thrapston & Huntingdon made him inclined to be more favourable to the Midland than the GN.

GN AND MIDLAND JOINT OWNERS OF WESTERN SECTION

However, wiser counsels prevailed, and that autumn after some negotiation the GN, Midland and E & M boards reached accord. The Midland would present a Bill for construction of the line from Bourne on a more northerly course, leaving the authorised line at Witham-on-the-Hill, passing through South Witham, avoiding the mineral branch and joining the Midland at Saxby. If the GN so desired (and later it did so desire), the line would be joint GN and Midland from Bourne to the point where it would cross the GN north of Little Bytham, and thence wholly Midland. There would be a connecting junction, GN property, at Little Bytham if the GN wanted it. The whole of the western section would be transferred absolutely by the E & M to the Midland and GN and become their joint property. Former PW & SB and M & E debenture and preference holders would receive equivalent Midland shares but the ordinary shareholders would get only £47 per £100 worth. Later the GN would assume half these responsibilities. E & M directors would no longer be eligible for election by these former PW & SB and M & E shareholders but could be re-elected by the others. A Bill to effect all this was presented for the 1889 session. On 8 January it was stated that the PW & SB line, as well as the Bourne & Lynn, would be regarded as joint GN and Midland from 1 January, pending the passage of the Bill. This was at the last meeting of the Bourne & Lynn Committee, and the magic words, Midland & Great Northern Joint first appeared when the new committee of that name met at Kings Cross on 5 March; thereafter it controlled the western section. The Act passed on 24 June. In practice, however, all this was still little more than a change of name. An M & GN committee working the system with its own engines and carriages was still four years ahead.

FINANCIAL CRISIS ON THE E & M

At this moment financial disaster came to the E & M. The

ordinary shareholders of the eastern section had received no dividends for several years. The western section shareholders, especially the preference holders, had received small dividends thanks to the GN and Midland guarantee. The company's borrowing powers were exhausted and many debts were owing. The matter came to a head thanks to an unsatisfactory arrangement for hiring passenger carriages, a method of hire-purchase and payment by instalments. The company defaulted in payment to Mr W. Jones, who had hired carriages to it on this system. He brought an action to which there was no defence and obtained judgment for his money on 27 June 1889. Next day he applied to the Chancery Division of the High Court for the appointment of a receiver and manager of the company.

In consequence of the 1866 financial crisis, when so many railways were in financial difficulties, an Act of 1867 provided for the situation when a railway company could not meet its obligations. On a creditors' petition, the court would appoint a receiver and manager whose duties were to get in receipts, if possible keep the line working in its proper function as a public carrier for the benefit of creditors, apply takings to meet reasonable working expenses, and use any profit towards meeting creditors' claims. Later, he would prepare a scheme of arrangement, which the court could invite creditors and shareholders to accept. The usual practice in such cases was for the company's manager to be appointed receiver, and Mr Read was duly appointed on 10 July.

At the shareholders' half-yearly meeting on 15 November it appeared that the company owed £3,416 to the Railway Clearing House, £49,867 on 'sundry outstanding accounts', and £55,434 on working stock leasing accounts. There was also an item called 'debit balance on revenue' of £71,645, which included unpaid interest on debentures and arrears of guaranteed dividends on preference stocks issued by the Lynn and Cromer undertakings. The King's Lynn Dock & Railway was also in a receiver's hands from March 1890, adding to creditors' and shareholders' anxieties.

On 2 May 1890 an indignant meeting of E & M debenture holders was held, when Mr Read and the board were accused of mismanagement, too high working expenses, obtaining rolling stock on hire without the means to pay for it, and paying dividends out of capital. The meeting resolved that application be made to remove Mr Read from the receivership. Some trustees, who were holders of Lynn shares, complained that under a deed executed by authority of a shareholders' meeting the company had promised to pay dividends charged on gross receipts out of a separate account, prepared so that the money subscribed should be applied to build the Lynn loop, that the cash had been supplied, and the line built. They asked the court to order Mr Read to treat their claims as working expenses, and give them preference over other creditors.

IN CHANCERY

Before Mr Justice Kay on 28 June 1890 counsel for Mr Read argued that working expenses meant what it said. Counsel for other creditors supported, and added that arrangements between stockholders could not affect creditors; dividends could only be paid on profits, not on gross receipts. Counsel for the debenture holders said that the validity of some of the hiring arrangements for supplying carriages, especially Mr Jones's, which had caused the receiver's appointment, was doubtful, and the court should ascertain whether claims under these were justified. The judge said that the purpose of the Act was to keep the line working for everybody's benefit, when possible, and to prevent creditors from stopping it working. The receiver must first apply money to meet real working expenses, even though the guaranteed dividends and interest on debentures were charged on gross receipts, and in consequence the applicants were not entitled to the preference they claimed. But he added that working expenses would include instalments due and overdue for hire of rolling stock. He said he was surprised at the argument of doubtful validity of the hiring agreements. Had he heard of the sharp practice about hire-purchase agreements so rife in later years, he might have been less surprised. The debenture holders then applied to the judge on 4 July to remove Mr Read from the office of receiver, but were unable to show he was not carrying out his duties properly.

The trustees appealed to the Court of Appeal on 31 July. But the Lords Justices said robustly that there was really one railway all the time, just a separation among shareholders, and dismissed the appeal. Nevertheless money had been spent in resisting these claims and applications which would have been better devoted to paying creditors generally.

A GOOD SERVICE UNDER DIFFICULTIES

In the circumstances it was remarkable that the company continued to provide as good a passenger and freight service as it did. Fortunately the Midland was more interested in developing through goods traffic now that it was committed to the construction of the direct Saxby—Bourne line. The GN as joint owners of the PW & SB, had the route from the south to Lynn and Norfolk generally which it had wanted since 1850. An all-year-round through service between Kings Cross and Cromer was introduced in 1891. The down train was the predecessor of the 3 pm from Kings Cross, which was to run for many years. The E & M engines continued to work the expresses on the Peterboro'—South Lynn section. The best runs in the summer of 1891 were Melton—South Lynn, $31\tfrac{3}{4}$ miles in 55 minutes (66 minutes in the opposite direction), and South Lynn—Fakenham, 24 miles in 36 minutes. Unpunctuality, always serious on the long single sections, remained a problem. But the safety record was good. Except for experiments on the Cockermouth, Keswick & Penrith, and on the Caledonian, the E & M was the first company to adopt Tyer's electric tablet system. Mr Aslett left the E & M in 1891 for a successful career on the Cambrian, and later on the Furness. Mr Curson took over his duties with the title of superintendent of the line, so he was in charge of operation of the services.

ECONOMIES

Replacement of iron rails on the old Y & NN section, progress of which had been reported at the 1887 autumn meeting, and again to cheer up the unhappy meeting in November 1889, had to stop for economy reasons. Construction of the Mundesley branch was postponed, and an Act in 1891 granted an extension of time for its completion.

HOW TO OBTAIN ROLLING STOCK?

The problem of providing rolling stock was serious. Mr Read prepared a scheme to consolidate all the hiring agreements, intending to concentrate the company's liabilities under them and obtain more rolling stock. He proposed that the rolling stock obtained in future should involve the company in the same rights and liabilities as it had in respect of stock obtained under the consolidated agreements. He reached agreement with some trustees representing suppliers of rolling stock who were creditors, and with some new subscribers who would provide £100,000 for the trustees to pay amounts due to the suppliers and to obtain more rolling stock under fresh hiring agreements. The trustees would have power to seize such stock if there was default in payment. At this period some of the engines had Mr Read's name on them to discourage creditors from trying to seize them.

On 11 April 1891 Mr Read applied to the court for approval of these complicated arrangements to obtain stock. Unfortunately a Mr Rucker, who represented many debenture holders, was still not satisfied about the validity of the hire-purchase agreements. On his application Mr Justice Kekewich ordered an inquiry into them, and Mr Read's application had to be postponed. The contract between the E & M and some suppliers called Whadcoats was taken as a test case. Mr Rucker's counsel argued that the agreements were not hire-purchase at all but merely loans on the security of the rolling stock, and part of the Whadcoats transaction looked rather like this. However, on 7 November the judge decided that the hire-purchase agreements were valid. On 24 November the judge heard Mr Read's application, and on 5 December approved his scheme, saying it was proper for him to obtain rolling stock.

IMPROVEMENTS ON THE JOINT LINE

Meanwhile the new M & GN committee was improving the line. In December 1889 came developments, especially in signalling, at stations and yards: new crossing places were provided at Holbeach and Terrington, which were completed in May 1891, and more sidings at South Lynn. With lavish Midland money work on the Bourne—Saxby line proceeded. In order to improve the route further a Midland Act on 25 July 1890 authorised a direct line at Spalding to enable through passenger and goods trains to avoid having to reverse there. The same Act sanctioned a slight further deviation near Toft, west of Bourne. In January 1892 the committee authorised doubling of the existing line for $3\frac{1}{2}$ miles from Bourne to Twenty. On 28 June 1892 an Act authorised a new road and rail bridge at Cross Keys, Sutton Bridge, to replace the old one. Hopes for the docks there were not abandoned, as the dock company obtained fresh powers in 1895. The route between there and Peterboro' was also improved by doubling the line from Wisbech for nearly a mile westwards to Barton Lane box, completed in August 1891, and about the same distance eastwards to Horse Shoe Lane Junction (where the goods trains to the harbour got in the passenger trains' way), completed in October 1892. The words Midland & Great Northern Joint first appeared in the timetables, including Bradshaw, in 1890. In consequence of the GN's abolition of second class (except in the London district) such bookings disappeared from the Lynn—Bourne section on 1 November 1891.

Meanwhile, the Spalding avoiding line was under construction with Mr H. P. Le Mesurier (later engineer of the Bengal—Nagpur railway) as resident engineer. It left the Bourne line at a point called Cuckoo Junction, passed over the GN line from Peterboro', and the GN—GE joint line from March, and joined the Sutton Bridge line just east of the river Welland, so that a new bridge over the river was needed and the junction was called Welland Bank. It was $1\frac{1}{4}$ miles of double line. The old single line from Cuckoo was doubled and extended parallel to the GN, so that it joined it just south of Spalding station. The single line from Welland Bank to the station was also doubled, and an additional platform provided. The doubling between Bourne and Twenty was carried out. All these works were brought into use on 5 June 1893 but for the present the avoiding line was only used for goods traffic. The Bourne—Little Bytham Junction—Saxby line had made such progress that goods trains could use it from the same day, 5 June, but its

Page 71 (above) *Little Bytham end-on junction with the Midland;* (below) *a very minor halt—Potter Heigham Bridge*

Page 72 *The effect of the* LNER: (above) *Yarmouth—Leicester express headed by ex-*GC *4-4-0 near Bourne in about 1937;* (below) *local train headed by ex-*GE *Claud 4-4-0, at Norwich City in 1939*

THE EASTERN & MIDLANDS RAILWAY 73

opening for passengers was not until nearly a year later (see Chapter 5).

A JOINT OFFER

In the autumn of 1891 the GN and Midland indicated that they were interested in acquiring the rest of the E & M—the eastern section, the Lynn loop, the Cromer undertaking and all. The Midland at first showed signs of wanting to take over the E & M by itself but from November 1891 until July 1892 there were negotiations between the GN and Midland boards over the terms to be offered by them to the E & M. The Midland suggested to the GN that the GE had a 'moral claim' to be brought in as a third partner of a joint system, like the Cheshire Lines. But the GN would not agree, saying the GE would divert traffic to its own routes, and anyway the GE in June 1892 declined to have anything to do with such a proposal. In October 1892 the GN and Midland agreed substantially on terms for absorption of the E & M jointly, and that a Bill should be presented in the 1893 session to authorise this.

Meanwhile a scheme of arrangement between the E & M and its creditors was prepared; it was approved at a meeting of ordinary shareholders, and by a committee of 4½ per cent debenture holders. Although terms between the GN and Midland were not by then quite complete, the directors and shareholders of the E & M petitioned the court to approve the scheme of arrangement on 16 August 1892.

The terms of purchase whereby the scheme would be implemented, and the Midland and the GN would aquire 113 miles of railway, were finally decided. The consideration was £1,200,000 Midland and Great Northern rent/charge stock, entitled to a fixed dividend of 3 per cent per annum, which was to be paid primarily from the gross receipts of the lines acquired. This liability of £36,000 per annum was not to fall immediately on the purchasing companies. The stock would be divided into £748,000 'A' stock, the holders of which would get £1 10s per cent in the first year and thereafter 3 per cent, and £452,000 'B' stock, the holders of which would get no dividend until June 1897 and thereafter a progressive improvement reaching 3 per cent in 1901. The 'A' stock would be allotted to holders of Lynn loop 4½ per cent debentures and 5 per cent guaranteed preference at par value, to holders of Cromer undertaking 5 per cent guaranteed preference at 85 per cent of their holdings, and to holders of eastern section 4½ per cent debentures at 75 per cent and 5 per cent debentures at 70 per cent of their holdings. Twenty-four thousand pounds 'B' stock would be allotted to the GN and Midland as consideration for their assuming responsibility for rent charges on lands payable by the E & M. The balance of 'B' stock would be issued to liquidators of the E & M, who were given wide powers to use it to pay E & M debts and liabilities; they could allot shares to meet creditors' claims, and could sell shares and pay creditors in cash. Any residue would be allotted to the remaining preference and ordinary shareholders, a preference holder being entitled to receive twice as much as an ordinary holder, according to the amount of his holding. The Midland and GN would acquire the rolling stock, machinery and surplus lands by a separate cash payment after a valuation.

The Bill was duly presented. On 19 November the petition to approve the scheme came before Mr Justice Kekewich, supported by counsel for the 4½ per cent debenture holders. The judge said that the scheme appeared to be for the benefit of the parties concerned but the absorption on which the scheme depended had yet to be sanctioned by Parliament, and it was not possible to anticipate statutory authorisation. The interests of unsecured creditors still had to be considered. He added that opposition in Parliament (from the GE) might cause rejection of the Bill. In our own day, for similar reasons, judges have approved agreements for increased wages when a Bill was pending in Parliament to forbid them. So the judge said he could not approve the scheme before the Bill passed.

Under the Bill the M & GN committee would become a corporation, with its own seal, so that it could hold property and bring and defend legal proceedings. The Bill recited the constitution of the committee under the Norwich & Spalding amalgamation Act of 1877. The committee would manage all the old E & M, western and eastern alike, as one system, under the title of the Midland & Great Northern Joint Committee.

The Midland and the GN made a further agreement on 12 May 1893. The cash payment for E & M rolling stock, machinery and surplus lands was fixed at £160,000. The companies agreed that the joint line should be run on equality, without any preference or priority. Neither company would enter into any agreement with another party which could prejudice eastern section traffic without the other company's consent. Traffic from the eastern section to the GN or Midland and beyond would be arranged by the companies by routes and in proportions to be agreed; disputes to be, if necessary, determined by an arbitrator. The agreement was scheduled to the Bill which became an Act on 9 June. Perhaps fortunately for the promoters, the GE only opposed it in respect of minor matters which were soon settled. As for the Mundesley scheme, the GN and Midland wished to abandon it, but Parliament refused to allow this. The Act transferred the powers to the M & GN committee and imposed a penalty if the line were not completed within the time permitted in 1891.

THE M & GN IS CONSTITUTED

The committee was incorporated as from 9 June and the E & M was vested in it as from 1 July 1893. The staff became servants of the committee of course, and the Lynn offices were chosen as the committee's general offices. At the time of handing over, there were, including stock on hire, 39 engines, 104 carriages, 718 trucks and 5 miscellaneous vehicles. The engines were the same as those of the E & M in 1889 but the number of carriages and trucks was less owing to the need for economy and the difficulty of obtaining rolling stock.

Thus the E & M had an independent existence of just over ten years. Certainly the purchasing companies acquired it at a low price but they were taking over a concern which lay mainly through agricultural country, which was in a serious financial situation, and whose routes were generally competitive with the GE. In the circumstances the terms for the shareholders were probably the best obtainable.

Coat of Arms

CHAPTER FIVE

The Committee from 1893 to 1914

ALLOCATION OF RESPONSIBILITIES

Under the new arrangements the Midland supervised the locomotive department and the GN the permanent way and signalling departments. But the committee owned the rolling stock and operated the trains. All this was similar to the Somerset & Dorset Joint, in which the Midland was a partner and which provided a useful precedent. The neighbouring GN and GE Joint, where each company ran its own trains, was quite different, and the Cheshire Lines, in which the GN and Midland were also interested, was different again; there the other partner, the Manchester, Sheffield & Lincolnshire (later the GC), provided the engines but the joint committee owned the carriages, and each company also ran its own trains. As some of the M & GN directors were on the Cheshire Lines committee too, M & GN committee meetings were for a few years sometimes held at Manchester.

Mr Marriott acted as resident engineer and locomotive superintendent. It was at first doubtful whether the committee would appoint him, and it was only through the intervention of Mr Wilkinson and of the Midland's solicitor that he obtained the position. Early in 1894 the committee insisted that he gave all his time to his railway duties and did not engage further in private practice as an engineer.

THE LOCOMOTIVES

Mr Johnson provided a series of inside-cylinder 4-4-0s with 6ft 6in drivers, and some 0-6-0 goods engines, both similar to his current standard designs on the Midland. Some old E & M engines were scrapped but others remained in service. At first some GN and Midland engines remained in use on the western section, and others were sent to Yarmouth and elsewhere to assist. But as soon as the committee had enough engines of its own, it took over operation of nearly all trains on the joint system (see Chapter 10).

BOURNE TO SAXBY

The Bourne—Saxby line was opened for passenger traffic on 1 May 1894 and was 13 miles long from Little Bytham box to Saxby. It left the GN Essendine line 9 chains west of Bourne station and went up a gradient of 1 in 100 to Toft tunnel, also known as Bourne tunnel, 330 yards long and the only tunnel on the M & GN. Then came a viaduct and more 1 in 100 ascent, followed by a descent crossing the route of the old Edenham and Little Bytham Railway (see Chapter 4) to the end-on junction at Little Bytham box, by the bridge over the GN main line, adding just over 5 miles to the M & GN. The purely Midland section, all single, rose through Castle Bytham and South Witham stations to a summit at Pains siding and then descended through Edmondthorpe and Wymondham station to Saxby. The tracks continued to a junction point just west of the station, and two new platform faces were provided on them. Ground was prepared for a curve to enable traffic going south to run direct and avoid reversal, but no track was laid. Also not built was the junction with the GN at Little Bytham. On the same date the Spalding avoiding line was brought into use for passenger trains. In December 1895 a private siding was provided into Lacon's brewery, Yarmouth, from a point on the old Union line close to the junction with the GE tramway. Sir Edward Lacon, of course, was an original promoter and director.

TRAIN SERVICES

Through expresses from the Midland appeared in July 1894 and for some years ran in summer only. For the first two or three seasons there were two eastbound expresses and one westbound between Birmingham and Leicester and Yarmouth, generally with through Norwich and Cromer carriages. Sometimes they ran combined with Kings Cross—Cromer trains between South Lynn and Melton. The best train in 1896 was the 9.25 am from Birmingham, 10.45 am from Leicester, which reached Yarmouth at 3.30 pm. The trains used the Spalding avoiding line but at first made regular or conditional stops at Holbeach. In the summer of 1898 there were two trains in each direction, one daily and the other on Mondays, Fridays and Saturdays only. By the end of the century there were' two daily in each direction, and the best run was Bourne—South Lynn non-stop, 34 miles in 48 minutes, at an average speed of 42.5 mph.

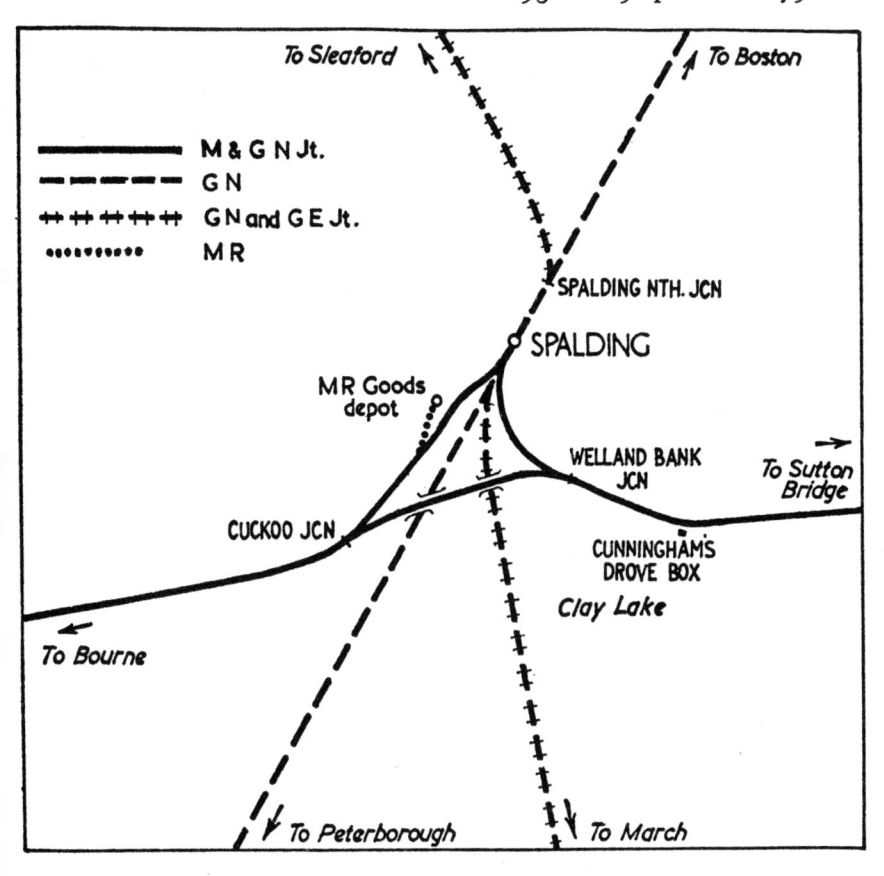

The local passenger service between Bourne and Saxby was only three trains each way but the goods traffic developed well. Midland engines worked cattle trains on some days of the week as far as Lynn, and another Midland engine stationed at Spalding worked a regular goods train to Somers Town, St Pancras, reversing at Saxby. The value of the line was enhanced when in 1898 the Holwell Iron Company opened a mineral branch from near South Witham to iron mines at Buckminster. But this traffic mainly flowed westwards over the Midland, rather than over the M & GN. For a number of years some trains still ran to and from the Peterboro' GE station. Through stopping trains ran between Peterboro' and Norwich, Cromer and Yarmouth. Peterboro' GN—Norwich coaches were attached to the Kings Cross—Cromer expresses from 1895.

COAST EROSION

A severe storm in March 1895 caused damage and sea encroachment at the California cliffs between Caister and Great Ormesby, which was to remain an anxiety for many years.

STAFF CHANGES

At first there were separate traffic managers, Mr Madden with offices at Spalding and Mr Curson at Lynn, for the old western and eastern sections respectively. In January 1895 the separate office at Spalding was abolished, Mr Madden went to the GN and Mr W. Cunning (from the Portpatrick & Wigtownshire Joint) was appointed traffic manager of the whole system; in January 1896 Mr Curson became his assistant. The committee decided that Mr Curson would not be a suitable manager for the whole line, but the minutes of the meeting when this decision was reached record no reason for it; and Mr Curson seems to have been an efficient officer.

TRACK AND SIGNALLING IMPROVED

The influence of the new committee soon began to be apparent in the equipment on the line. It carried out a sub-

Fig 1

stantial programme of relaying, using a standard M & GN 85-lb bullhead chaired rail, while the old 70-lb flat-bottomed rails were removed from the running lines and only survived occasionally in sidings. GN somersault signals were installed widely. Often they were very tall, with the signal arm much

Fig 2

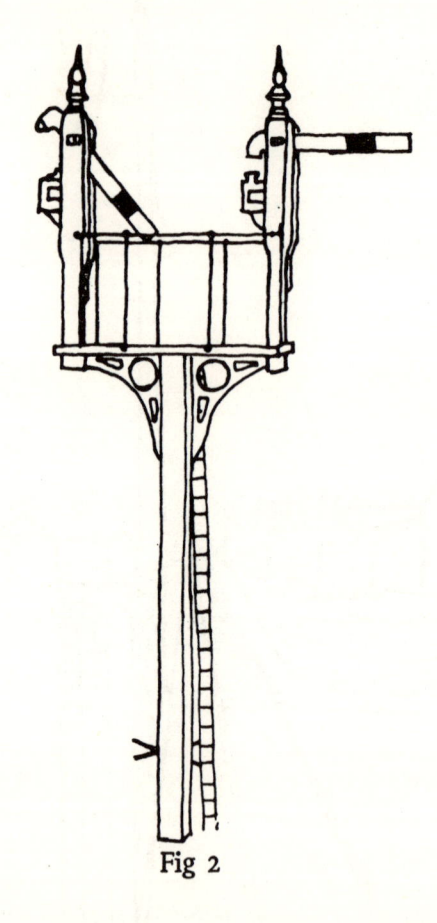

higher up the post than the lamp, and the arm swung down so much that it was nearly parallel to the post (Fig 1). The old E & M type of signal survived at Cromer and other places for a few years (Fig 2), as did some standard Midland signals at Sutton Bridge and between there and Peterboro' for much longer (Fig 3). Tyer's tablet system was brought into use on all single sections, both on the part of the eastern section where it had not previously been adopted and on the western section, generally in replacement of staff and ticket.

Fig 3

MORE EXTENSIONS

From this time on, when the M & GN required parliamentary powers, the general but not exclusive practice was for the Midland or GN to obtain the Act. On 20 July 1894 a Midland Act gave extra time for the Mundesley branch and sanctioned acquisition of more land for doubling the line for a short distance east of Spalding. This was from Welland Bank Junction, where the avoiding line joined the Sutton Bridge line, eastwards for a mile to Cunningham's Drove box. This was completed on 10 April 1896 and made it easier for trains to enter and leave Spalding and the avoiding line without getting in each other's way. There was a siding between Welland Bank Junction and Cunningham's Drove called Clay Lake.

Further battles with the GE now impended about schemes to extend the line into fresh districts. The GE was dissatisfied with the continued delay in building the Mundesley branch and considered applying for powers to build it itself, or at least make sure of powers over it. The GE also proposed a line from Mundesley southwards along the coast through Bacton to Happisburgh (pronounced Haysboro'). There was also the quiet country between Mundesley and Cromer around Overstrand, but a more important area in dispute was between Yarmouth and Lowestoft. The GE had had its so-called direct route with through trains via the Haddiscoe curve for many years but it wanted a line along the coast. The M & GN wanted to serve Lowestoft, and the rising resort of Gorleston, on the coast just south of the mouth of Yarmouth harbour. The GE wanted to serve Sheringham, hitherto an M & GN preserve. On 21 May 1896 the GE obtained powers to make a line 3 furlongs long from its North Walsham station to join the authorised M & GN Mundesley line at the Antingham Road. Meanwhile the M & GN had asked for tenders for the construction of the line. Mr Mousley's was accepted and work began in December, though there was difficulty in getting some of the land. By a Midland Act on 7 August the M & GN was authorised to extend the line from Mundesley through Overstrand under the GE just south of its Cromer station and curve round almost in the opposite direction to join the Melton line three-quarters of a mile west of Beach station, at a point later called Runton East Junction.

Also in 1896 the GE board considered a scheme to extend its proposed Happisburgh line southwards along the shore through Palling and Horsey to Yarmouth. This coast was a quiet district and long remained so. The shore, unlike Cromer cliffs, was sand dunes (called denes in Norfolk), covered with marram grass and having sandy beaches. It was hoped that the coastal villages would become seaside resorts and that golf links would be made for which marram grass (like the original links in East Scotland) would be suitable. The Yarmouth course, one of the first in England, close to Caister station, had been opened about twenty years before. The Broads would be served at Hickling and Horsey.

This scheme might have caused the M & GN committee much anxiety, as it would have been parallel to its main line about 4 miles off, close to the coast, and would have catered for Cromer—Yarmouth traffic, which the M & GN already carried via Melton, and was proposing to carry via Mundesley and

North Walsham. Fortunately for the M & GN, the GE board decided that potential traffic would not justify such a line and for the present sought powers only for the line from Mundesley as far as Happisburgh.

In the autumn Bills for the competing Yarmouth—Lowestoft lines were deposited. At Lynn there was a dispute between the companies about extension of the GE goods station for M & GN traffic. So the M & GN proposed a line from Hardwick Road to Austin Street, in order to use that place as a separate goods station after all.

THE NORFOLK & SUFFOLK JOINT

In view of the violent competition at the time for London—Cromer and other traffics, the spirit of co-operation now displayed was extraordinary. On 18 March 1897 the GE and M & GN reached agreement about the proposed extensions. The M & GN would not oppose the GE Yarmouth—Lowestoft Bill. The M & GN's proposed line would be cut down to the section from Caister Road (where it was to leave the old 'Union' line) to the west side of the GE East Suffolk main line into South Town; an extension over this line to join the Yarmouth—Lowestoft line (to be authorised to the GE) in Gorleston would be proposed the next year. The M & GN would have running powers into Lowestoft station from the junction of the new line at Coke Ovens. The M & GN would not oppose the GE Mundesley—Happisburgh Bill. Application would be made next year for a junction between the Mundesley—Cromer line and the GE, and, if found practicable, for a further junction to give the GE access to Sheringham, running powers to be accorded. A new committee, the Norfolk & Suffolk Joint Railways Committee, was to be formed, incorporated with its own seal, to control: the North Walsham—Mundesley line from Antingham Road Junction, the Mundesley—Cromer line, the Mundesley—Happisburgh line, and the Yarmouth—Lowestoft line from the junction at Gorleston. This new joint system, GE and M & GN, would have four GE and four M & GN directors. The dispute about Lynn goods station was to be referred to arbitration and the M & GN Bill for the line from Hardwick Road withdrawn, so that Austin Street's chances of becoming a busy goods station again receded. Larger offices for the committee's headquarters had been provided there in April 1895.

Accordingly the GE's Bill passed on 3 June 1897. The M & GN's, for a line which was short but important since it included a viaduct over Breydon Water, followed on 6 August; it also gave still more time for the completion of the North Walsham—Mundesley line.

POPULARITY OF 'POPPYLAND'

In the late 1880s and early 1890s Norfolk became increasingly popular as a holiday area. The Grand Hotel was opened at Cromer in 1891, the Metropole in 1894, and royal patronage followed, when the Princess of Wales (later to become Queen Alexandra) and the Duke and Duchess of York (later King George V and Queen Mary) stayed there in April 1897. Cromer and the neighbourhood was 'discovered' by the London press as 'Poppyland' and written up in the warmest terms. The principal enthusiast was Mr Clement Scott of the *Daily Telegraph* who described Cromer as the 'perfect watering place' and even went so far as to write a lyrical poem, *The Garden of Sleep*, about an ancient churchyard on the coast near there. The Broads, too, became popular for boating holidays in yachts and converted wherries.

The result was that competition for passenger traffic to Cromer and the Broads became intense. The GE improved its service in the summer of 1896 by sending its best trains via the Wensum curve (avoiding Norwich Thorpe, opened in 1879). The fastest train each way took 3 hours between Liverpool Street and Cromer with stops at Ipswich and North Walsham, with another train allowed 3 hours 10 minutes down and 5 minutes more up. The GN and M & GN had introduced the 3 pm from Kings Cross to Cromer via Peterboro' in 1894, an all-year-round service, allowed 4 hours 40 minutes in the winter. In the summer of 1896 there were three Kings Cross—Cromer through services each way, with stops at Finsbury Park for the GN 'Northern Heights' suburbs and at Hitchin. The best train was the 3 pm down, which took 4¼ hours. In October the Cromer Urban District Council congratulated the M & GN on its service.

THE COMMITTEE FROM 1893 TO 1914

LONG NON-STOP RUNS

In July 1897 the GE accelerated its best trains, the 1.30 pm down and corresponding up, to a 2 hours 55 minutes overall London—Cromer schedule, running for the first time non-stop between Liverpool Street and North Walsham and including a restaurant car. To counter this the GN and the committee arranged for the midday train from Kings Cross to leave at 1.10 pm, reach Peterboro' in 92 minutes with a stop at Finsbury Park, and then run non-stop to Melton, 68¼ miles in 95 minutes, 43.1 mph. After reversal at Melton and a stop at Sheringham, Cromer Beach was reached in 3¾ hours; a corresponding up service with a similar schedule was also put on. The Peterboro'—Melton run, with many slacks for tablet exchanging, was most creditable, and the Johnson 4-4-0s generally accomplished it punctually. The load was at first about eight GN six-wheelers with semi-corridor lavatory accommodation, but vestibuled bogie stock appeared after a few years. The 3 pm down and corresponding up train often loaded to twelve or fourteen coaches. The best runs on these were Peterboro'—Sutton Bridge in 42 minutes, 27½ miles, and South Lynn—Melton in 55 minutes, 31¾ miles, with a one-minute stop at Fakenham. Despite the longer distances of its routes, 20 miles in the case of London—Cromer, the long single-line stretches, and the Melton reversal for the Sheringham and Cromer trains, the M & GN had several advantages. Kings Cross then, and long afterwards, was regarded as far more accessible from much of London, including the West End, than Liverpool Street. Moreover, though the GE Cromer station on the hill had a fine situation from the scenic point of view—Sir William Acworth said it was the best in the country—it was a mile from the town and beach, a long cab drive or walk. Beach station was in a much more convenient position. Passengers going on the Broads at Potter Heigham or Stalham could join the connecting train on the same platform at Melton, instead of changing from one station to another at North Walsham. The 3 pm down train retained its quicker schedule for the 1897 winter service.

MORE BLAKENEY SCHEMES

Proposals for a Blakeney line appeared again in 1896 and 1899, when local people asked the committee to support a light railway to be built there from Holt. But the board, knowing what the E & M had lost over Blakeney in the 1880s, refused to help, and a further scheme intending to build a line on to Wells also failed. In 1897 there were also proposals for connecting light railways near Sutton Bridge, and to Crowland, but nothing came of them.

DEVELOPMENTS AT SUTTON BRIDGE AND ELSEWHERE

The new Cross Keys bridge at Sutton Bridge was opened on 18 July 1897. As well as carrying both road and rail traffic, the latter single line and controlled by tablet, it also swung for shipping. It was of the steel girder type, with the swinging span on the west side, 176 ft long, and the two shorter fixed spans on the east side. The swinging span was worked by hydraulic power, provided from a power house with stationary engines.

The new bridge was south of the old, so the rail approaches at each end were diverted and the passenger station was altered again. By this time sixty to eighty trains crossed the bridge daily, and it was opened for ships about five times a day in summer and once or twice a day in winter. The designer was Mr J. A. McDonald, the Midland's engineer, and Handysides were the contractors. The cost was £80,000. Early in 1902 road tolls on the bridge were given up and the committee was relieved of the heavy obligations of maintaining the approach roads.

Further powers for re-opening Sutton Bridge docks were obtained in 1895. The matter was mentioned in 1897 to the committee and the company continued to exist for a long time, but eventually the docks were abandoned. Later there was a golf course on the site, with one of the dock sides forming a bunker. But the little branch remained in use for many years, as it served a short quay on the river where small ships with timber could berth.

Page 89 *Station scenes 1:* (above) *Hillington for Sandringham, April 1936;* (below) *Sutton Bridge, May 1937*

Page 90 *Station scenes 2:* (above) *Lenwade, a single platform station but with block post;* (below) *Hindolvestone in January 1959; both views facing towards Melton Constable*

THE COMMITTEE FROM 1893 TO 1914 91

In September 1897 Bourne station was enlarged at the joint expense of the committee and the GN, and the old Elizabethan house became a private residence. In October, owing to traffic development, the committee decided that more of the main line from Peterboro' to Yarmouth should be doubled. Work was completed from Fakenham to Langor Bridge on 1 July 1898, and from Terrington to west of Lynn bridge on 15 December. Terrington to Wingland siding, a mile east of the new Cross Keys bridge, followed on 27 March 1899. Later the line was doubled to the east end of Cross Keys bridge.

OPENING TO MUNDESLEY

The Mundesley branch was opened for goods on 20 June 1898, and for passengers on 1 July. The M & GN line from Town station and the GE connecting line to Antingham Road Junction were double, but the rest was single. There was a bridge over the canalised Ant about a mile from North Walsham, and an intermediate station, non-crossing, at Paston and Knapton. The whole distance was $5\frac{1}{2}$ miles. A generous passenger service was provided in summer, nine GE and seven M & GN trains in each direction on weekdays and three by each on Sundays. It was agreed that goods, if not specifically consigned by GE or M & GN, should be sent by each in alternate months. Tickets were interavailable. As the M & GN was to maintain the line, its type of bridge was adopted, somersaults were installed, and tablets used. Unfortunately, a through M & GN train from the west had to reverse at North Walsham Town. Antingham Road Junction provided an indirect connection between the GE and M & GN. The committee suggested a more direct connecting line in November, but without success.

THE NORFOLK & SUFFOLK JOINT APPROVED

The GE and M & GN Act establishing the Norfolk & Suffolk committee passed on 25 July 1898. Two connecting lines at Cromer were sanctioned. One was to leave the GE just south of its station, where the GE crossed the authorised line to Mundesley (now to be N & S), and curve sharply round to join this line on its south side near the Roughton road. The other left the Cromer—Mundesley line near the Fakenham road and went across to the M & GN Cromer line at a point just east of where the Mundesley—Cromer line was to join this at East Runton. These lines would be GE, arranged so that a GE train, after reversing at its Cromer station, could run direct to Sheringham. Outside Yarmouth the short M & GN line over the GE East Suffolk line, joining the authorised Lowestoft line in north Gorleston, was also authorised. The N & S committee was constituted in October. Mr Jackson and Lord de Ramsey of the GN, and Mr Paget and Mr Starkey of the Midland, were the first M & GN members. The committee had its own staff and stationery.

COAST LINE PROPOSED AGAIN

There was talk of reviving the scheme for the coastal line south of Happisburgh as an N & S line to connect the authorised lines more closely. At the southern end the line would have joined the M & GN near Ormesby. But under these circumstances the M & GN would only have obtained half the receipts from a line which would be near its own, and which would have carried the Cromer—Yarmouth traffic. Indeed, it was extraordinary that the M & GN should have considered such proposals, as furthermore the route from Liverpool Street would have been much shorter than that from Kings Cross. There would have been danger from coast erosion and flooding—the old church tower at Eccles, near Palling, had recently disappeared under the sea, like Dunwich in Suffolk—and there were serious floods at Horsey in 1938, and Palling in 1953.

Powers to divert the section to Happisburgh further inland near Bacton were obtained in 1898, but nothing more was heard of the scheme and the powers for the Happisburgh line were repealed in 1902. However, golf courses were opened at Sheringham, Runton, Cromer, Mundesley and Gorleston. Period return tickets for golfing holidays were issued for many years, and as early as 1896 trains stopped specially at Hellesdon, for golfers on the Norwich course.

Further alterations to the Mundesley—Cromer line were authorised. By a Midland Act of 13 July 1899 the line was deviated between Trimingham and Overstrand closer to the shore for nearly 2 miles. By a GE Act the authorised line from the Fakenham road to the M & GN was abandoned and replaced by a short N & S line; this left the Mundesley line about three-quarters of a mile further west at Newstead Lane and joined the M & GN three-quarters of a mile east of West Runton station, so forming a triangle; as the junction was laid for through running towards Sheringham it shortened the distance by about a mile.

CROMER EXPRESS SERVICE CHANGES

The best expresses from Kings Cross and Liverpool Street both had the same schedules in the summer of 1898. But thereafter the 3¾-hour schedule to Cromer was not kept up, although the Peterboro'—Melton non-stop run was made each summer and the best GE express schedule was unaltered; the latter also had through coaches to Mundesley. In 1899 the 1.10 from Kings Cross took 3 hours 50 minutes to Cromer and in 1901 4 hours 5 minutes; the corresponding up train took 3 hours 50 minutes. For several seasons from 1902 the best train from Kings Cross took 3 hours 50 minutes, but left at 2 pm (combined with a Manchester portion) which was too close to the popular 3 pm departure. Also from 1902 there was a departure from Kings Cross at 5.45 pm on Mondays and Fridays only, which took 4 hours, and in the 1904 season the 10.20 am from Kings Cross was accelerated to the same time. As if to show that the faster schedules were not difficult a special from Cromer ran up to Kings Cross in 3¾ hours on 8 June 1901.

STATION CHANGES

On 1 July 1901 a new station complete with crossing loop was opened at Weybourne between Holt and Sheringham; it had been refused by the committee in 1897 but sanctioned in 1899. The second 'r' in Sheringham had disappeared from the books in 1894, Lynn became officially King's Lynn in 1888, and Martham became 'for Rollesby' on 1 November 1897. Caister became Caister-on-Sea on 1 January 1893 but on the GE Lynn did not become King's Lynn until 1 January 1911.

LIGHT RAILWAY SCHEMES

Although so much trouble had been taken to authorise the Yarmouth—Lowestoft direct line, and work was about to begin, a concern called The Drake & Gorham Electric Traction Company proposed an electric tramway (sometimes called the East Anglian Light Railway) from the Yarmouth trams at Gorleston to Lowestoft along the main road. The company applied to the Board of Trade for an order permitting construction under the Light Railways Act, 1896 (see Chapter 3). At a public inquiry held at Lowestoft on 12 May 1899 the Light Railway Commissioners, in view of strong opposition from the N & S, summarily rejected the application for the tramway from Gorleston to the Lowestoft borough boundary. Work on the new railway began soon afterwards.

There was another proposal, by an independent concern, for a line to Dereham from Hellesdon in 1900, but the committee was not interested, and an application to the commissioners was rejected on GE opposition.

ACCIDENTS

On 13 July 1900 there was a buffer-stop collision at Sutton Bridge, and two people were injured. On 17 August, two goods trains collided in South Lynn yard. There were several collisions with level crossing gates left across the line in these years, more than once at Catfield.

A CHANGE OF MANAGERS

In 1898 the M & GN committee wished to appoint a successor to Mr Cunning as traffic manager. Mr Marriott had strong claims to the office and, with the support of the Midland's chairman, he was nominated by Sir Henry Oakley, formerly GN general manager and now a director both of the GN and of the committee. But on this occasion, the committee decided to appoint Mr J. J. Petrie, a Midland man, who had been manag-

THE COMMITTEE FROM 1893 TO 1914   95

ing the Severn & Wye joint lines. Mr Curson remained as assistant and Mr Marriott continued as engineer and locomotive superintendent.

MORE DOUBLING

Work on doubling continued. Thorney—Eye Green was completed on 27 February 1900, and the stretch to the junction with the Midland metals at Wisbech Junction, Peterboro', on 24 June. Fakenham—Raynham Park was opened on 18 June. In the Melton area, one mile towards Cromer, to a point called Briningham Junction, was completed on 17 June; as far as Corpusty, the first station towards Yarmouth, on 20 May 1901, and westwards to Langor Bridge, east of Fakenham, on 2 June 1901. On this last section near Thursford the old line was abandoned and a new double line built on a fresh alignment. Briningham Junction was not really a junction, but might have become one if a Melton avoiding line for Cromer trains had been built. The great advantage of these double lines was that trains could approach and leave Melton from several directions without getting in each other's way. Murrow to Barton Lane, Wisbech, (see Chapter 4) was also doubled on 19 February 1901, while Honing, between North Walsham and Stalham, became a crossing station on 23 June.

MIDLAND EXPRESSES IMPROVED

The through services from and to Birmingham and Leicester, which became known on the line as the 'Leicesters', were becoming very popular. In the summer of 1902 they were improved and given through Derby and Nottingham portions. The departure from Birmingham about 1.55 pm, and from Leicester about 2.50 pm, and the corresponding morning westbound service leaving Yarmouth about 9 am, which operated for many years, were all introduced in this year. In October this service began to run all the year round. An M & GN Johnson 4-4-0 stationed at Norwich, for the first time in regular service ran the morning train through to Leicester, returning on the afternoon one. Connections from Liverpool and Manchester were made at Derby, and from Sheffield at Nottingham. The trains competed with a Birmingham—Yarmouth train by the LNW–GE route, and with Liverpool, Manchester and Sheffield trains by the CLC–GC–GE route, which included a through Cromer service. In view of this, a through Midland and M & GN Manchester—Yarmouth service, eastbound only, was introduced in the summer of 1903. Next summer, 1904, one Midland train in each direction had Manchester—Yarmouth through coaches, and another had Liverpool—Yarmouth and Manchester—Cromer coaches. When the Lowestoft line was opened, all these through services for Yarmouth had through portions for Lowestoft included.

From 1919 the departure of the principal train eastwards out of Leicester was made later, at about 3.20 pm; this was done again from 1946. It was such a convenient time after weddings that the train was sometimes called 'the honeymoon express'.

OPENING TO LOWESTOFT: BREYDON VIADUCT

Completion of the Lowestoft line was delayed by difficulty in acquiring some of the land, and by trouble in building the embankment between the south end of Breydon viaduct and the bridge over the GE, where the ground was very soft and absorbed quantities of material poured into it to make a foundation. The extension was fully opened on 13 July 1903. The pure M & GN section left the old Union line, the gradient of which was modified, at the site of the Caister Road crossing, where the crossing was replaced by a bridge; it then crossed the Bure, the Norwich road and the GE from Vauxhall. It was at first double but became single for the Breydon viaduct, the most important engineering work on the system. Breydon water, crossed where it narrows to river width, is a large tidal extension of the Yare on both sides of the channel and has considerable rise and fall of tide. There is a busy traffic of yachts and commercial vessels on it, and it is a well-known Broadland centre for bird life. The viaduct was 800 ft long and comprised four fixed spans (three to the north and one to the south) with a double swing span on a central pier between them. Opening power was provided by a gas engine, and hydraulic adjusting gear at the central pier was operated from a cabin. The whole machinery was in duplicate, as with strong winds both engines were needed to turn the span. Mr Marriott was responsible for its design and construction. On 8 July, as a test, six engines ran over it coupled together. After the viaduct the line became double again, and three-quarters of a mile farther on crossed the GE East Suffolk line to join the GE curve from South Town at Boundary Road, renamed Gorleston North Junction, where the N & S section began. Gorleston North station, half a mile farther south near the Beccles Road, was rather far out, but the next station, Gorleston-on-Sea, was well in the town and only about a third of a mile from the beach. Keeping fairly near the sea, the line passed through Hopton and Corton stations to the edge of Lowestoft where it turned inland to Lowestoft North station; it joined the GE at Coke Ovens Junction where the railway is north of the harbour. Lowestoft Central station and the north quays are half a mile farther on. The total distance of new line was about eleven miles. A further station was added in July 1914 when, by agreement with the proprietors of the golf course, Gorleston Links halt was opened between Gorleston-on-Sea and Hopton. GE type signals with plain finials were installed on the N & S section; notices at stations on the N & S lines were generally on behalf of the N & S committee, but at station entrances it was usually indicated that it was a station of the GE and M & GN.

The M & GN had its own agent and carting facilities at Lowestoft. At first there were four M & GN trains and three GE trains to and from Lowestoft Central; the M & GN trains used Yarmouth Beach and the GE trains South Town. In addition four southbound and three northbound M & GN trains ran to and from Lowestoft North, as there was a dispute with the GE about stabling M & GN carriages at Central. Several M & GN trains (besides holiday expresses) were through from Peterboro' and elsewhere. The extensions at Yarmouth Beach were opened on the same day, 13 July; an extra track was provided from the junction into the station. Nevertheless, the latter had its drawback, in that it was yet another reversing station on the M & GN.

FISH TRAFFIC

Since the M & GN now served Lowestoft as well as Yarmouth it began to handle increased fish traffic. From 1898 the steam trawler and drifter replaced the old sailing smack, increasing the catch and bringing it more quickly into port. This traffic was very competitive with the GE, which generally obtained a larger share, although the M & GN held its own, conveying about 5,000 tons a year from Lowestoft alone. There were disputes with the GE in 1903-4 about the sidings on Yarmouth quay. A few years later, there were, in the season, a train at about 3.50 pm to Peterboro' connecting with a GN express goods for Scotland, two at about 5.30 pm for Lancashire, Yorkshire and the Midlands, and two at about 7.10 pm, one for London traffic where the M & GN competed despite the long route, and the other to Grimsby for transmission to the Continent. Fish was also conveyed by ordinary passenger trains for intermediate stations. Some operations meant carriage at 'passenger train or similar service' rates, but others for salt fish could be at goods rates. Larger consignments were loaded in Yarmouth and Lowestoft into fish vans but smaller ones were carted to the stations.

A valuable ancillary service to the fish traffic was the conveyance in September and October of Scots fisher girls to carry out bloatering and kippering processes on the herrings. They generally came from the Aberdeen and Peterhead districts, sometimes from as far away as Wick, and, not including male workers, often numbered about 4,000. Special trains were run both by the GE and M & GN routes. At first ordinary passenger stock was used but later Mr Bloxham, the popular stationmaster at Yarmouth Beach, arranged corridor trains for their long journeys, and entertainments for them in Yarmouth. They could be seen returning in their special trains, carrying presents for relatives in Scotland.

NO M & GN AT PETERBORO' GE

The GE contended that M & GN engines owned by a separate corporation were not covered by Midland running powers

THE COMMITTEE FROM 1893 TO 1914 99

into Peterboro' GE, and required rent. The Midland suggested a payment of £275 per annum but the GN refused to agree, and the few M & GN trains into Peterboro' GE, which were no longer well patronised, were withdrawn on 1 October 1904. Separate Midland sidings were retained at Wisbech M & GN.

N & S PROGRESS

The committee decided to proceed with construction of the Cromer—Mundesley line and obtained extended powers in 1903. By a GE Act of the same year a short line was authorised giving a direct run from the North Walsham direction to the authorised connection from the GE Cromer station to the Mundesley line. There was difficulty in getting some of the land and heavy compensation had to be paid in one case. The contract was let to Mr Finnegan on 18 November and work began early in 1904. The GE then decided it would be better to run its Sheringham service direct by the newly-authorised connection instead of reversing at Cromer GE, and so by an Act of 1904 the short curve into that station was abandoned. By the same Act the authorised GE line from Newstead Lane to the junction with the M & GN just east of West Runton station was transferred to the N & S committee. There were warnings even at this stage that the line, in such quiet country and near other lines, would not pay, and that the money would have been better spent on a joint Cromer station or on an avoiding line to save reversal at Melton. Time perhaps proved them right, as the Mundesley—Roughton Road section was the first to be closed, in 1953.

A WEST RIDING EXPRESS

In July 1903 the GN introduced a new through summer express to the M & GN. The main train left Leeds Central at 11.5 am, called at Wakefield (Westgate and Kirkgate), Doncaster and Retford, ran round the Barkstone (later Barkston) north curve to Sleaford, reached the M & GN at Spalding, and then ran non-stop to Melton. There were through carriages for Cromer, Yarmouth (due 4.28 pm) and Lowestoft. A through portion from Manchester Victoria (L & Y) was attached at

Wakefield Kirkgate, giving a service from several Lancashire and West Riding towns. There was a Sheffield connection at Retford, and at Sleaford through coaches from Derby Friargate and Nottingham Victoria were added, in competition with the Midland trains. There were corresponding services in the opposite direction. In the summer of 1902 the GN had tried for a while a through Manchester Central—Cromer carriage, which was detached from a Manchester—London train at Peterboro'; but this service via the L & Y ran for several years and L & Y vehicles sometimes ran through to Cromer. From the 1908 season onwards, through carriages from Bradford Exchange to Lowestoft were included, and from the 1909 season a restaurant car was provided from Leeds Central to Yarmouth.

LACK OF SUNDAY SERVICES

Generally, the committee, unlike the E & M, did not provide a Sunday passenger service in the winter. For some years there was a Stalham—Yarmouth service on Sundays in October, as day trips to Yarmouth were popular, but this ceased after 1905 as part of the general policy of no Sunday passenger trains except in summer.

THE N & S COMPLETED: GE AT SHERINGHAM

The Cromer—Mundesley line was opened in two sections in the summer of 1906. On 23 July were opened the GE line giving direct access from the south, from a point which became known as 'Cromer Junction' to Roughton Road Junction, the N & S line from there to Newstead Lane Junction, the N & S west side of the triangle from there to Runton West Junction, and the pure M & GN east side of the triangle from Newstead Lane to Runton East Junction; these were mainly for the benefit of the GE Sheringham trains. The N & S Roughton Road Junction—Mundesley section followed on 3 August for passengers, but goods trains did not run until 1 March 1907. From Mundesley station, which was provided with three through platforms and an up bay, the line ran closer to the sea, and then went north-west, about half a mile from the cliffs, through Trimingham and Overstrand, which were both crossing stations with island platforms. Next it turned due west, more inland, to pass under the GE line and was joined at Roughton Road by the connecting line. To attain Cromer Beach the line had to proceed north-west through wooded country, down steep gradients including 1 in 80, and turn nearly east again to join the Melton line at Runton East Junction, throwing off the spur at Newstead Lane to Runton West. The curves both from Newstead Lane and from Cromer Junction to Roughton Road were double but the rest of the line was single. The total length of new lines was about 12 miles.

In anticipation of the additional traffic the M & GN made the up platform at Sheringham an island and put in a bay at Cromer Beach on the south side of the existing single platform. In October 1905 and April 1906 respectively, the line was doubled from Runton East to the connection with the Cromer Gas Works siding (leaving a short single section between there and the Beach station), and from Runton East to Runton West Junction.

In view of more serious GE competition for Sheringham, the committee considered doubling more of the main line, particularly from Thorney to Murrow, in order to accelerate the trains, but decided only to provide a new crossing place on that section at Wryde. The GE put on four down and three up Liverpool Street—Sheringham through services, detaching the coaches at Cromer Junction in the down direction, and reversing them into Cromer GE in the up. The best service, off the 1.30 pm from Liverpool Street (the North Walsham non-stop) reached Sheringham at 4.43 pm. To compete with this the 1.10 pm from Kings Cross was reinstated, reaching Sheringham at 4.43 (just as the GE train was due from the opposite direction) and Cromer Beach at 4.50 pm, the best Kings Cross —Cromer service ever operated. This, and the corresponding up train, had a restaurant car throughout. A balancing up service to the evening 5.45 from Kings Cross (by now Fridays only) was provided at 7.45 am from Cromer on Mondays and Tuesdays and allowed 4 hours. The 3 pm from Kings Cross and the corresponding up train received through Mundesley carriages, reversing at Cromer Beach.

On the Mundesley line, there were seventeen trains each

way daily between North Walsham and Mundesley, about two-thirds GE and one-third M & GN. GE trains ran to and from Mundesley or Overstrand, and some M & GN trains ran between North Walsham Town and Cromer Beach. Other M & GN trains ran between there and Mundesley, so there were almost as many trains on one side of Mundesley as there were on the other. On Sundays in the summer there were, each way, three GE trains between North Walsham and Overstrand and two M & GN between there and Cromer Beach, largely for visitors to gardens near Overstrand which were open to the public.

There were disputes with the GE about the number of its trains into Sheringham; the M & GN alleged there were more than had been agreed and that they were causing congestion. Next year the GE agreed, on condition of being allowed to run eight trains in and out of Sheringham, to admit into Lowestoft Central the M & GN trains which had not been running further than Lowestoft North. Thereafter there was nearly an hourly service between Yarmouth and Lowestoft, and tickets were interavailable. The GE also claimed to carry local Sheringham—West Runton passengers, which was agreed on payment of a small sum for working expenses.

FRUIT TRAFFIC

Fruit traffic was very important at this period, as from the 1890s the Wisbech area had become one of the principal fruit-growing areas in the country, producing apples, pears and plums in orchards (which covered nearly half the cultivated land), strawberries, raspberries, red and black currants and gooseberries. The stations mainly concerned were Terrington, Walpole, Sutton Bridge, Wisbech itself, Wisbech St Mary, Murrow, Long Sutton, Gedney and Holbeach. The principal destinations were the Midlands, the North and Scotland. The traffic was largely conveyed in special trains, up to sixty trucks from one station alone at the height of the season at 'passenger train or similar service' rates. The favourite container was the 4-lb chip basket, originally introduced in this district, which needed less handling than the smaller baskets previously used, an important factor. This traffic became one of the most valuable which the M & GN had. As its busy season partly coincided with holiday passenger traffic, it presented quite a serious problem.

A POOLING AGREEMENT

In November 1905 a pooling agreement was made with the GE in respect of parcels from Norwich (except local carryings) and goods, including fish by goods train, on the basis of three years' earnings ending 30 June 1905.

POTATO TRAFFIC

Another traffic to increase at this time was that of potatoes, especially from Long Sutton and Holbeach, which were situated in the potato-growing area around Spalding mainly served by the GN. Concessionary rates were granted to encourage growers to bring potatoes to the stations and in the season up to eighty or ninety trucks daily came from M & GN stations to Spalding for transport by GN routes to London, the South, the Midlands and the North.

NORWICH GOODS TRAFFIC: COAL, CATTLE AND BRICKS

Freight traffic from Norwich, besides the well-known Colman's mustard and starch, included machinery, boots and shoes, electrical appliances, ironwork, beer, mineral water, vinegar and seeds. The inwards traffic in general goods included military stores for the barracks. Coal and cattle traffic were always important; Norwich cattle market was the largest in the area. The Peterboro' area produced mainly agricultural machinery and bricks. A large brick works at Eye Green, later the source of much traffic, was first established and siding connected in July 1897, and another at Dogsthorpe between Eye Green and Peterboro' followed in 1899. At Peterboro' M & GN goods trains generally used either Nene sidings near the junction with the GE, or Crescent sidings by North station, both Midland owned. In east Norfolk small brick kilns, not necessarily near the line, were common and some of the brick traffic went by wherries.

THE BEST YEARS

The late 1900s were probably the greatest days of the M & GN. The committee had provided better engines and carriages, replaced the track with modern rails, proceeded with doubling the line in several places, and improved many stations. Good through services were operated to and from the parent companies' lines. The gross revenue increased steadily from £275,823 in 1900 to a record of £341,527 in 1907, which was a good year for the coal and agricultural traffic. After 1906 the committee undertook no more extensions of doubtful value. Renewed proposals for a Wells and Blakeney line, and schemes for a branch to Hunstanton and an independent Norwich—Wisbech line, were all turned down.

Unpunctuality on the long stretches of single line, especially at busy holiday periods, remained a serious problem. But the safety record was good. No black day of collision on single line, like Thorpe, Radstock, or Abermule, is to be found in the annals of the M & GN.

BALLAST

Ballast and stone for the line were mainly obtained from pits and quarries near Holt station and at Kelling siding. Flint and other stone from there were used all over the system. In later years most of the line was reballasted with slag over the stone. But the old method could long be seen in places which had not been reballasted, such as Long Sutton and near Toft tunnel.

AN AMALGAMATION SCHEME THAT FAILED

In 1907-9 there occurred some remarkable events in the railway world, which might have brought great changes to the M & GN but in the outcome affected it very little. On 3 December 1907 the GN and GC, wishing to end the fierce competition between them which had existed since the GC extension to London in 1899, made an agreement that their systems should be administered by a joint committee. The companies would continue to exist, and some receipts would still be credited to them individually, including to the GN dividends and interest on the GN holding of M & GN rent/charge stock (by now amounting to £54,000), and in the moribund Sutton Bridge dock company. The agreement which purported to be made under the old GN–MS & L '50 years agreement' (authorised by an 1858 Act) was subject to the approval of the Railway and Canal Commission. But when it came before that body in February 1908 there was strong opposition from many parties, especially the Midland and the GE, which argued that the GN and GC could not make such an agreement under the 1858 Act. The commissioners so held, and did not go into the merits or public advantage of the agreement. The GN and GC sought allies from the opposition; and it was announced in the summer that the GE had joined them and that a Bill to authorise a working union of the three companies would be presented the next year. It was believed that the Liberal government of the day was in favour of eventual nationalisation and would prefer to deal with a few big amalgamated companies (as the government had to do in 1947) instead of with many.

The three companies began making arrangements to reduce wasteful competition between them. Their Bill proposed a joint committee to operate the three systems, but the companies (like the existing South Eastern & Chatham, and the earlier GN–GC proposals) would remain separate. But it was sought to repeal the 1893 GN and Midland agreement (scheduled to the Act which constituted the M & GN). Of course, the GN and GE had nearly amalgamated more than once before, and the fact that they had not was a reason for the existence of the M & GN. It was presumed that under the new combination the GN would transfer traffic from M & GN to GE routes, and that the M & GN lines would be handed to the Midland. But if this were done much of the alleged advantage of the new combine, the reduction of wasteful competition, would be considerably less. Competing services from Kings Cross to Norfolk might disappear; but Midland and M & GN lines would still provide routes to the North and Midlands which would be in direct competition with GC–GN–GE routes. Within Norfolk there would also still be competition in many places. The best interests of Norfolk and the railways generally would probably, in the long run, have been promoted by retaining a GN share in the M & GN lines, and bringing about co-operation with GE services, as occurred later in LNER days, avoiding transfer difficulties and waste.

Under the 1893 agreement the GN and Midland promised to pay the M & GN two-thirds of payment received for a passenger or parcel conveyed between specified points on the parent lines and places east of Lynn served by the M & GN, if the passenger or parcel was not conveyed by an M & GN route. The GN had of course been sending such traffic by M & GN as much as possible; but if it sent the traffic by GE route instead, it would be liable to make the payments. Negotiations were opened with the Midland to try to alter the obligations. It was even suggested that the Midland might be asked to join the combination of the three companies. Alternatively, it was thought that the Midland might retaliate by promoting a line from the London, Tilbury & Southend to join the M & GN at Norwich.

When the Bill came before the House of Commons in the early spring of 1909 (with lukewarm government support) there was much opposition. Many members said that amalgamation would cause monopoly and that the railways would be able to increase rates and fares easily, to the disadvantage of the public. Abstract questions of nationalisation and grouping of railways were discussed at length, instead of the merits or otherwise of the Bill's proposals. The 1909 House was very different from that of 1921, which passed the Bill to group the railways, including these three into the LNER. Sir Frederick Banbury, a director (later chairman) of the GN, who often sat on the M & GN committee, made a spirited speech in favour of the Bill. Eventually the House, on the suggestion of Mr Winston Churchill (as he then was), President of the Board of Trade, referred the Bill to a committee, which 'would consider all matters concerned with this Bill'. In practice, this would mean long discussions on the abstract questions at the three companies' expense, instead of getting on with the Bill's merits; the companies therefore withdrew it.

Thereafter, the three companies co-operated somewhat by combining agents' offices and cartage arrangements, and extending interavailability of tickets, in some cases in the M & GN area. On 10 August 1911 the GN and Midland agreed to

Page 107 *The last years 1:* (above) *Yarmouth—Leicester express leaving Bourne early 1950s, headed by* GE *rebuilt Hill B12/3 4-6-0 61533;* (below) *Aylsham North, showing H. G. Ivatt 2-6-0 with Yarmouth Beach—Peterboro' train*

Page 108 *The last years 2:* (above) *crossing the Ouse at West Lynn.* LMS 0–6–0 *44231 with Chesterfield—Yarmouth Beach train;* (below) *one of the last trains,* GN *2–6–0 61763, on eastbound Leicester train, leaving Saxby, February 1959*

cancel some of the clauses of the 1893 agreement, which prevented either party from making arrangements which could harm M & GN traffic without the consent of the other, and hindered the dispatch of some of the traffic other than by M & GN route. In future, such traffics could be sent by a GE route if it was more suitable. A Midland Act of 1912 sanctioned the new agreement.

The high 1907 level of M & GN receipts was not maintained, and the committee considered economies and incentives to traffic. From May 1907 return tickets at reduced fares, for periods between one month and twelve, were introduced from Kings Cross to many M & GN stations. Day and weekend excursions were run from London, even sometimes in winter. The question of good advertising was often before the committee. Large posters about 'Poppyland' and 'Broadland' were well displayed.

THE THROUGH EXPRESSES, 1907-14

The pattern of the principal summer through trains altered comparatively little between 1907 and 1914. The regular Leicesters (morning westbound and afternoon eastbound) had Manchester Central—Cromer and Liverpool Central—Lowestoft through carriages. In the summer of 1907 there was a restaurant car working from Manchester to Lowestoft eastbound and back to Derby westbound, but in the summer of 1908 the car was operated only between Nottingham and Cromer. Some of the Cromer coaches were run to and from Mundesley from 1907, but this facility was not advertised in the timetables until 1913. In the summers of 1908-10 the GN, thanks to its better relations with the GC, operated a Manchester London Road—Yarmouth carriage (besides the Manchester Victoria through coaches) which served Sheffield Victoria, was attached to Derby coaches at Nottingham Victoria and to the through Leeds train at Sleaford. In the 1911-14 seasons this service was only to and from Sheffield.

Competition for London traffic, despite better relations with the GE, remained keen. In the summer of 1907 the GE named its crack train, the 1.30 pm from Liverpool Street, the 'Norfolk Coast Express', provided new rolling stock for it, and extended its Mundesley through carriage to Overstrand. The competing 1.10 pm from Kings Cross, which had a load of seven or eight large bogies, was allowed 86 minutes to Peterboro' with a Finsbury Park stop, and was sometimes hauled over this section by a Stirling 2-2-2 or Ivatt 4-2-2 7 ft 7 in single. From the 1909 season onwards the train was altered to leave Kings Cross at 1.5 pm combined with a Scarborough portion but was decelerated by 8 minutes to a 3 hours 48 minutes run from Kings Cross to Cromer. The best up train was allowed 3 hours 55 minutes. On the morning services the GE had an advantage, as its trains took 3 hours and the Kings Cross trains 4 hours. The Friday evening through coach from Kings Cross disappeared after 1909 (a connection was available) and the corresponding up early morning service was on Mondays only. In the last three summers up to 1914 there were three down and four up through services daily between Kings Cross and Cromer, of which two each way had Mundesley, and one each way Norwich City, coaches. On the latter through passengers were rare but it was a useful facility for passengers for stations between Melton and Norwich. In the summers of 1908-9 there was a Sunday evening train from Yarmouth Beach, stopping at Caister and North Walsham, which attached a portion from Cromer and Sheringham and made a Norwich connection at Melton through to Kings Cross. This seems to have been the first advertised Sunday train, except for excursions, on the old western section, and the only train advertised in the timetable ever to operate from Yarmouth to Kings Cross. From 1907 to 1914 the GE had seven or eight Sheringham trains daily each way in the summer, and three on Sundays.

STRIKES AND FLOODS

The fine coronation summer of 1911 brought increased traffic; but there was a sudden strike of railwaymen all over the country for a few days in August and increases in wages were made. In March 1912 there was a national coal strike for a month, and services were reduced, though the GE, which had laid in extra stocks of coal, was not affected.

On 3 December 1911 a winter storm caused flooding of the line between Bourne and Twenty, where it had been flooded in 1880. Special trains brought ballast from Holt and the line was re-opened on 9 December. In July 1912 coast erosion near Caister caused anxiety. But the worst troubles at this stage were caused by an appalling summer storm on 26/27 August, causing disastrous floods all over East Anglia. The M & GN lines were among the worst hit. Several bridges between Melton and North Walsham were washed away, leaving a train marooned at Aylsham with bridges collapsed on either side. The main line was also flooded near Fakenham and at Potter Heigham, land near the broads becoming great stretches of water. At Hellesdon the Melton—Norwich line was flooded to such a depth that a boat sailed through the yard to the platform. The crisis occurred at the peak of the summer holiday and fruit traffic, and at a particularly unfortunate time for Mr Marriott as he was ill with ptomaine poisoning. The North

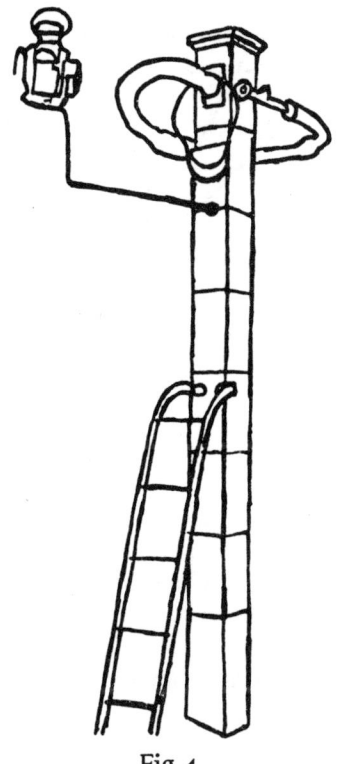

Fig 4

Walsham—Mundesley—Cromer line was also affected but by 11 September it had been sufficiently repaired for trains to pass at restricted speed. One Sheringham—Yarmouth and three Cromer—Yarmouth trains were run in each direction by that route, the water at Potter Heigham having gone down; they connected at Sheringham and Cromer with Leicester and Kings Cross trains, as the break at Fakenham had by now been repaired. Holidaymakers had to return by unusual routes, particularly by the GE via Norwich, Wymondham, Forncett

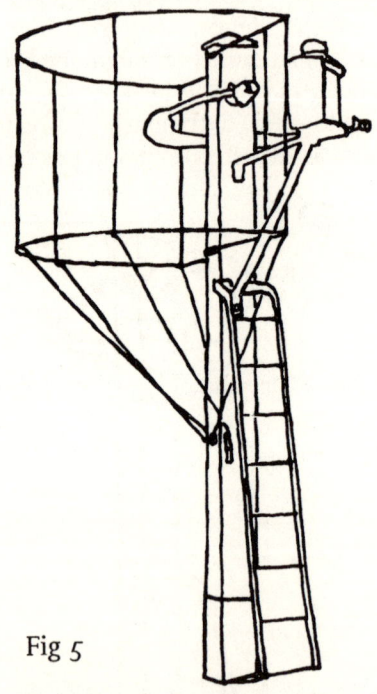

Fig 5

and Ipswich, which entailed several reversals. The M & GN freight trains, and the fisher girls' specials, also went via Mundesley until 1 October, when the Melton—North Walsham section was reopened. The cost of repairs was £20,000.

THE WHITAKER TABLET EXCHANGER

A great improvement in the operation of the single line sections occurred in these years thanks to the introduction of the mechanical tablet exchanger. For some years before 1906 the signalman or porter handed the tablet for the next section to the fireman as the train passed at a very slow pace. The tablet for the previous section was received on the ground by means of the apparatus shown in Fig 4. As the train passed, the fireman placed the ring of the pouch containing the tablet

Fig 6

on the curved bar, which was bound with cord to slow down the movement of the ring. Often, the apparatus was surrounded with a wire-guard, especially near level crossings, where a dropped tablet could cause danger to the public (Fig 5).

Since these methods of exchanging tablets could cause injuries to the men, the Highland, and Great North of Scotland had for some years used a mechanical exchanger. But Mr Whitaker, locomotive superintendent of the Somerset & Dorset Joint (where fast trains ran on long single stretches, as on the M & GN) did not consider it satisfactory. After an injury to a fireman, he invented his own apparatus and introduced it on the S & D. In 1905 a Board of Trade circular recommended its adoption. On 17 August that year an M & GN fireman was injured at Massingham when using the old method, and in May 1906 the com-

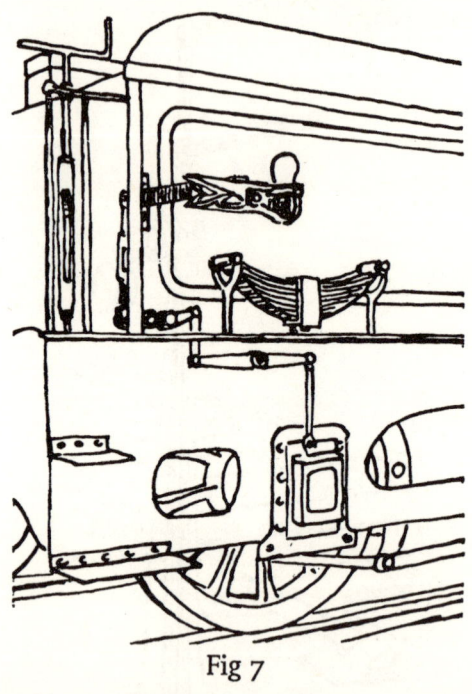

Fig 7

mittee adopted the Whitaker apparatus. The lineside part is shown in Fig 6. It stood parallel with the line, and when about to be used the upper portion was turned at right angles to face the approaching train. The ring of the tablet to be picked up was hung on the lower arm. The upper arm had a metal jaw, > shaped, to catch the tablet's ring on the engine's apparatus. The latter was similar (Fig 7), having a jaw to pick up the lineside tablet and holding the ring of the tablet to be dropped at a slightly higher level to correspond with the jaw on the lineside. When not in use the engine apparatus was turned flat against the tender, but when an exchange was to be made the fireman turned it outwards at right angles, like the lineside apparatus. The momentum of the tablet received from the passing engine was sufficient to swing the lineside apparatus parallel to the rails again, where it was then locked by a swing catch. To allow for any inequality of the road, and consequent vertical movements of the tender when the train was running at high speed, an equalising arrangement of a system of levers raised or lowered the position of the apparatus on the tender when it was swung out. The exchange could be carried out at speeds of 40-50 mph, with hardly any danger to enginemen and signalmen. Forty-two complete exchangers

Fig 8

were installed, besides twenty-five receivers (Fig 8) and twenty-five deliverers where single line became double. The apparatus was generally sited as near the signal cabins as possible. All engines (except a few shunters) were so equipped, as were a few GE tanks working to Sheringham. The only passenger line not equipped was the N & S Mundesley line, where there were hardly any trains which did not stop at all stations, and the old type of receiver remained in use for many years. It was calculated that there were as many as 350,000 exchanges in a year, of which one in 5,000 was dropped. The cost of the equipment, made under licence in the Melton shops, was amply justified, not only by the reduction of danger to the men but also by the reduced coal consumption as trains were now able to maintain a more constant speed. The boxes containing the tablets were always kept in the signal cabins, and the tablets were issued and replaced by the signalmen, which diminished the danger of misunderstandings such as contributed to the Abermule accident.

Between many of the crossing stations there were non-crossing stations provided with signals as block posts. If a train left a crossing place with a tablet, another train could follow, also with a tablet, subject to block control. But no tablet for that section could be issued from the next crossing station until the box there contained all the tablets issued at the first crossing place. When there were trains following each other at short intervals as at busy holiday times, the advantages of this were considerable.

SIGNALS AT LEVEL CROSSINGS

Another unusual feature on single lines arose from the practice of equipping level crossings with their own protecting distant signals for each direction of running. When the gateman put his gates across the road and cleared the way for a train, he pulled a lever which put both distants at 'clear'. The use of one lever saved expense, and avoided the chance of an inexperienced gateman pulling a wrong lever, if each signal had its own lever. But the appearance of signals down for both directions of running was strange. A further complication sometimes occurred when one of the signals protecting the crossing was near an ordinary signal, controlled from a cabin, and relating to the opposite direction of running. In these circumstances two signals, both showing 'clear' for opposite directions, could be quite close together. This could be seen at Catfield (Fig 1). The M & GN drivers were of course familiar with the sight, but a visiting driver on a holiday train from

THE COMMITTEE FROM 1893 TO 1914 117

one of the parent companies would need careful instruction if he was not to find such signals very confusing.

TOWN HOLIDAY AND EXCURSION TRAINS

Characteristic of summer Saturday operation at this period were the additional through trains put on for town holidays in the North and Midlands, 'wakes' as they are called in the North, and 'Bowlingtide' at Bradford. Shorter runs on some days in the summers of 1912-14 were from Yarmouth, Sheringham and Cromer to stations near the rivers, such as Potter Heigham, for trips on the Broads; excursions to more distant destinations were sometimes operated, including one all the way from Norwich to Aberystwyth on Whit Monday in 1912.

FASTEST AND LONGEST RUNS

In the summer of 1911 the fastest run on the line was made by the 12.20 pm from Peterboro', which reached Wisbech, 20.8 miles, in 28 minutes, at 44.5 mph. The long Peterboro'—Melton runs were unaltered at 43.1 mph but were now easier to operate since more line was doubled and the Whitaker exchangers were in use. Other Kings Cross trains were timed over the same course at 40.5 mph, excluding stops. The best Leicesters at this period ran non-stop between South Lynn and Bourne at 40.8 mph, between Bourne and Leicester at 40 mph, and between South Lynn and Yarmouth at 39-40 mph, excluding stops. The through Leeds train was allowed 2½ hours from Spalding to Yarmouth, 98¼ miles at an average speed of 39.3 mph, excluding stops at Melton and North Walsham.

THE STAFF

The staff were nearly all local men, and generally had characteristic Norfolk voices. Passengers often got to know them well. The practice on the afternoon eastbound Leicester was for M & GN guards to take over at Saxby, and we used to look out to see if 'Lubbock' or 'Sam' came on the train. They were very loyal to their employer, the committee, and sometimes this trait caused some embarrassment to passengers.

Connections at North Walsham, where there was much interchange between GE and M & GN, were often awkward, and M & GN—and GE—porters were very reluctant to carry luggage for the short distance between the stations.

WINTER SERVICES

In winter, in the years before the 1914-18 war, there were two down and three up Kings Cross—Cromer through services, including the 3 pm down and one up with Kings Cross—Norwich vehicles. The afternoon eastbound and morning westbound Leicesters ran. On the Mundesley line the M & GN share only amounted to one North Walsham Town—Cromer Beach and one Mundesley each way, besides several between Mundesley and Cromer.

SUNDAY SERVICES

The pattern of summer Sunday trains remained much the same, but the lack of trains on winter Sundays caused some public discontent. At Easter and Whitsun a National Sunday League excursion was run, leaving Kings Cross for Cromer early in the morning. Journeys which could be made by GE on Sundays in winter were Peterboro'—Wisbech—Lynn, Fakenham—Norwich, Cromer—North Walsham—Norwich, and Yarmouth—Lowestoft by the Haddiscoe curve. For a time, one GE train ran to Sheringham on winter Sunday evenings, partly to provide stock for Monday morning. But the lack of Sunday services was one of the reasons for the development of local buses later. The only trains regularly booked on winter Sundays were goods trains between Peterboro' and King's Lynn, Peterboro' and Sutton Bridge, Saxby and South Lynn, and Spalding and King's Lynn. An early morning Peterboro'—King's Lynn goods train conveyed mails on weekdays and Sundays.

TICKETS

First-class tickets were generally white and third class were green. Some first-class tickets for special purposes had blue bands across them, and some third-class tickets were grey. Single tickets were generally headed 'Mid. & G.N. Joint Committee', but returns generally had 'Mid. & G.N. Jt. Comm.' on each half. Some examples of tickets are shown below.

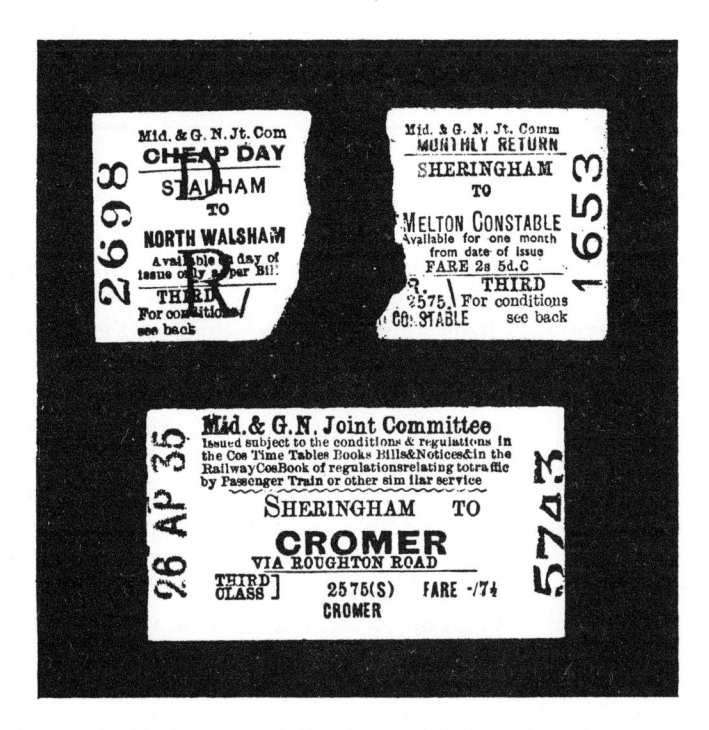

(Above left) *Stalham—North Walsham third-class cheap day return half, issued 25 March 1940, a rare facility in wartime;* (right) *Sheringham—Melton Constable third-class monthly return outward half, issued 26 August 1946;* (below) *Sheringham—Cromer* (GE) *third-class single, issued 26 April 1935. An unusual ticket: it is for a journey which for many years could not be made in the reverse direction, it is routed via Roughton Road, which was a junction in open country, not a station, and it is an* M & GN *ticket for a journey which could only be made by an* LNE *train (before 1923, a* GE *train)*

CHAPTER SIX

The Committee from 1914 to 1936

WARTIME CHANGES

The outbreak of war on 4 August 1914 was at the Bank Holiday weekend, the height of the summer traffic. Army mobilisation, bringing Territorials from summer camps, which on the M & GN included the Norfolks and the 5th Essex, and the movement of military stores, put a great burden on the railways. Members of the staff who were reservists and Territorials of course left at once, and others volunteered for the army, so that the committee was short of 160 men by the end of September. Norfolk was very much the invasion coast of the war, so the 6th Regular Division was at first stationed there, and only went to France in the autumn. The influx of troop trains brought 'foreign' engines on to the M & GN, among them some from the Great Western.

Like the other railways, the M & GN was controlled on behalf of the government by the Railway Executive Committee, composed of the president of the Board of Trade and the general managers of the principal lines. It had been expected that the war would cause a reduction of passenger travel but this did not occur for some time. The summer service, save for cancellation of excursions and other extras, was maintained in September and the usual winter service was then provided. Cheap bookings, excursions, period returns and luggage in advance were gradually suspended but this had little effect; passengers travelled for business and pleasure much as usual. Fish traffic declined as so many of the fishermen and their trawlers were minesweeping and the North Sea of course was very dangerous for fishing boats. But goods traffic increased, partly for war purposes and partly due to the diversion to rail of seaborne traffic to Yarmouth, Lynn and Wisbech. Moreover, grain, potatoes, fruit and other foodstuffs were being produced in greater quantities to make good the shortage of imported food caused by the activities of German submarines against merchant shipping.

PASSENGER SERVICES REDUCED

In March 1915 the Kings Cross—Cromer through service was reduced to one train each way and through Lowestoft coaches ceased to run on the Leicesters. Despite the war, many holidaymakers continued to arrive in the summers of 1915-16. The pre-war winter service was then operated, except for the above withdrawals, and passenger traffic held up so well that extra coaches had to be provided on some trains. For security reasons and to restrict travel, a system of permits was introduced for some adult civilian travellers under the Defence of the Realm Act. Bluestone station which was little used was closed permanently for passenger traffic on 1 March 1916, though the goods sidings remained in use. A blizzard on 26 March 1916 caused serious interference with the train services.

In December 1916 the Railway Executive Committee said that the railways could only carry on if drastic reductions were made in ordinary services; among other problems locomotive coal was in very short supply. The Lloyd George coalition government which had just taken office agreed and on 1 January 1917 passenger services were reduced all over the country. The 3 pm from Kings Cross to Cromer and its return service were taken off. On the N & S lines the M & GN provided the only Yarmouth—Lowestoft service, three trains each way, but M & GN trains between North Walsham Town and Mundesley disappeared for six years. The Leicesters continued to run but were decelerated. The Sunday morning delivery of mail to Wisbech and Lynn by goods train was also suspended. Interavailability of tickets was increased but reservation of seats, compartments and saloons for private parties ceased. Common use of wagons, introduced in 1916, was extended. To equate shares between railways the country was divided up into twelve groups, in each of which operations were directed by a principal company. The M & GN and the N & S were in the GN's group. Further reductions of service took place in May 1918. The through Yarmouth coaches on the Leicesters were taken off but connections were available. Gorleston Links Halt was closed.

NAVAL BOMBARDMENTS AND AIR RAIDS

Norfolk's first direct experience of the war came on 3 November 1914 when German warships shelled Yarmouth. Little damage was done and they soon withdrew. A similar raid occurred on 25 April 1916 when both Yarmouth and Lowestoft were shelled but after the Battle of Jutland at the end of May no further raids took place. In any case they caused little direct damage to the M & GN. A far more serious threat was presented by air raids carried out by Zeppelins, the German airships, which were only faced with a short flight to the Norfolk coast from their bases in west Germany and German-occupied Belgium. The first raid on 19 January 1915 damaged a M & GN train, fortunately empty, at King's Lynn, and caused a number of casualties at Yarmouth and Cromer. Many such raids followed and the committee took out a special policy of insurance against damage both by air raid and bombardment. However, from 1916 several Zeppelins were shot down in the area and defence against them and the bomber aircraft which succeeded them so improved that air raids almost ceased in the last few months of the war.

Many army units trained in the area and guarded the coast, and beach defences with wiring and mines were set up at many points. An armoured train, built by the London & North Western at Crewe and hauled by a GN 0–6–2 tank engine, patrolled the lines nearer the shore.

WAR WORK AT MELTON

Mr Marriott and his depleted staff at Melton, who often carried on night and day, and several times during air-raid alerts, like factories in 1940, undertook much special war work. They made roller bearings and parts for aircraft construction firms as well as machinery and other articles for the munitions

THE COMMITTEE FROM 1914 TO 1936

committee and the War Office. To assist Derby and Doncaster they repaired engines and trucks for the Midland and trucks for the GN, and they built new trucks for the latter. Some M & GN trucks went overseas.

USE OF CONCRETE

An important development, for which Mr Marriott's skill and experience were responsible, was the application to railway work of concrete; this proved an excellent substitute for brick, wood and steel, which were in short supply owing to the war. He had introduced concrete fencing posts in 1909, and had patented and registered inventions and designs numbering in all 135, using both concrete and reinforced ferroconcrete. These included signal posts, telegraph posts, girders, gateposts for level crossing gates, fittings for gatehouses, platform walls, sleepers, bridging blocks and station buildings and name boards. Tests were carried out at Melton and at the factory of Messrs Ellis at Leicester, and from June 1916 to May 1917 concentrated particularly on signal posts. Concrete signal posts made at Melton were later supplied to the GN, GC and Midland. Concrete sleepers first appeared on running lines in June 1916 at Melton. The use of concrete of course produced savings both in labour and maintenance.

M & GN STAFF IN THE FORCES

Although many railwaymen remained at their jobs since they were of national importance, as many as 560 of the staff had joined the forces by November 1916 and the committee was frequently concerned in making payments to these men's families. Mr Petrie's and Mr Marriott's sons were serving. Second Lt Stanley Marriott, Mr Marriott's youngest son, who had been at Gresham's School, Holt, and was his father's pupil at Melton, was killed in action in 1916. Altogether 829 of the staff joined the forces of whom 115 were killed, or died of wounds or sickness. The great majority of the others returned to the railway in 1919-20. Twenty-six N & S staff joined up, of whom five were killed.

MR MARRIOTT BECOMES MANAGER

Mr Petrie died on 18 October 1918, and on 1 January 1919 Mr Marriott was at last appointed traffic manager as well as engineer and locomotive superintendent. He had been with the committee and its predecessors since 1880 and owed much to his training and experience with Messrs Wilkinson and Jarvis, who were both very capable men. He had had full responsibility as engineer of the E & M from September 1883 and also as locomotive superintendent from 1884 when he was still a young man. Since the difficulties over his appointment by the committee as resident engineer and locomotive superintendent in 1893, his relations with his employer, the committee, were always particularly cordial, despite the way he was passed over for appointment as traffic manager in 1898. It was fitting that he should now become manager after long and faithful service. The M & GN owed much to his ability and personality. Among other things he was responsible for the design of many stations, including Mundesley, which was regarded as one of the most attractive in Norfolk.

POST-WAR PROBLEMS

When the Armistice came on 11 November 1918, the railways generally were in a very difficult position. Rolling stock was often in need of maintenance and repair, and track relaying was much in arrears. Many troops still had to be moved, largely for demobilisation, and the restoration of normal services and facilities took a considerable time; government control continued until August 1921.

Very soon there were serious industrial disputes. From 26 September to 5 October 1919 there was a general railway strike. The M & GN was able to run a few trains with some volunteer assistance. Lorries (often old army ones) were largely used to transport goods. This event, coupled with the General Strike seven years later, was a major contributory cause of the later decline in freight traffic, as so many people realised for the first time how goods could be sent by road instead of by rail. A large increase in railway goods rates, ordered by the

Page 125 E & M 0–6–0T No 16 (formerly Ormesby) at Melton about 1888. Note headcode

Page 126 (above) E & M 2–4–0 No 43 (ex-LNW) at Norwich about 1890; (below) Beyer Peacock 4–4–0 No 34 in original condition at Cromer Beach 1896

Ministry of Transport in January 1920, also contributed to the growth of competitive road transport.

RESTORATION OF PASSENGER SERVICES

The 3 pm from Kings Cross was restored in May 1919 with a fair schedule, 4 hours 28 minutes to Cromer, and soon regained its popularity, but the restored up train was very slow. The Leicesters' through coaches to Yarmouth reappeared at the same time. Large numbers of holidaymakers took advantage of the first post-war summer, and were generally dealt with by longer trains and reliefs, without increasing the advertised service, though there was much overcrowding. But more M & GN trains ran between Yarmouth and Lowestoft, and the GE trains there were restored. More GE trains ran between North Walsham and Overstrand, and one M & GN train ran through from Lynn to Mundesley. Gorleston Links Halt was re-opened on 11 August.

A morning eastbound and afternoon westbound Leicester reappeared in the summer of 1920, and through Lowestoft carriages were restored. Sometimes the Yarmouth and Lowestoft portions were made up into trains of over twenty carriages, Midland bogies and Midland and M & GN six-wheelers. The West Riding GN train was restored on Saturdays only and provided a through service from Bradford and Leeds to Cromer, Yarmouth and Lowestoft.

From April to June 1921 there was another national coal strike and services again had to be reduced. The policy of running only M & GN trains between Yarmouth and Lowestoft via Gorleston, as in 1918, was again adopted, but there were a few GE trains via the Haddiscoe curve. Soon after the strike a good summer service was again provided. Eight- and fifteen-day excursions were offered to Cromer and other destinations with departure from Kings Cross on Saturday mornings. The West Riding train ran on Saturdays, conveying a Nottingham Victoria—Lowestoft portion which was attached and detached at Sleaford. The last Cromer—Overstrand service would run on to Mundesley and North Walsham if there were passengers off the Leicester and Kings Cross trains. This practice was later adopted at Easter and Whitsun also.

The GN West Riding train did not reappear in the summer of 1922, and for a year or two Yorkshire passengers to the M & GN fared rather badly. But the up Cromer—Kings Cross train was improved; it now left at 12.10 pm, since 1921 had been attached at Peterboro' to a restaurant car express from Newcastle, and arrived at 4.30 pm. Manchester Central—Lowestoft through carriages ran daily by the Midland route.

MUNDESLEY ROUTE IMPROVEMENTS

The service on the Mundesley line was increased. In April the GE, which had been providing all North Walsham—Mundesley trains since 1917, agreed that the M & GN should run most of the locals through from North Walsham to Cromer Beach. These used the GE station at North Walsham, where M & GN engines had previously been a rare sight. The GE still ran its Liverpool Street—Mundesley and Overstrand through carriages, and one of the Overstrand trains ran on empty to Cromer GE, reversing at Roughton Road and Cromer Junctions. The M & GN instituted a number of economies in the operation of these trains. As they were all-corridor, tickets were issued on board, and the booking offices at Overstrand, Trimingham and Paston were not required. The equipment for the conductor-guard was designed by the accountant, Mr Doughty. Furthermore the signalboxes at Trimingham and Overstrand were closed, making one tablet section from Roughton Road to Mundesley, though the station loops were still maintained for goods and emergencies.

FRUIT AND FISH TRAFFIC

In the years after the war the fruit traffic was again very considerable, particularly in the hot summer of 1921. Agricultural light railways, one from Spalding to Sutton Bridge north of the existing line, and another from Whaplode to Crowland, were proposed in 1919; they might have been useful feeders for the fruit and potato traffic but nothing came of the schemes. The fish traffic, with the restoration of normal conditions after the war, was also substantial.

SIGNALLING DEVELOPMENTS

Although the tablet boxes were always in the signal cabins (see Chapter 5), in 1921 there were still fourteen cabins where the tablet system was not interlocked with the signals, which could be raised and lowered independently, irrespective of whether the tablet had been issued. Mr Marriott had this defect remedied, though interlocking of this kind was far from general on other companies' lines at this time.

A development of a different kind had taken place in February 1916, when a device called an occupation key was installed at Kelling sidings. This enabled a ballast train to move along the single line to the sidings and, when the train was clear of the running line, insertion of the key in the box there enabled the signalman at Holt or Weybourne to release a tablet for another train.

THE M & GN AT THE GROUPING

Just four days after government control of the railways ceased on 15 August 1921, Parliament passed the Railways Act, 1921, which effected the grouping of the railways. This took place on 1 January 1923 but made comparatively little difference to the M & GN for some time, although the long-discussed amalgamation of the GN and GE was now accomplished. The M & GN was still a joint line, London Midland & Scottish and London & North Eastern, with its committee of three directors from each company, and its own staff. Mr Marriott still had his traffic manager's office at Lynn and his engineer's office at Melton. Mr Tatlow, the secretary, was still at Derby. The N & S had its secretary, Mr London, at Liverpool Street. Engines and stock retained their characteristic livery and M & GN lettering; and notices in towns directed passengers 'to the LNE station', and 'to the M & GN station'.

PASSENGER SERVICE DEVELOPMENTS

In July 1923 the LMS introduced one of the best trains to run on the line in the summers between the wars. This connected

Liverpool Lime Street and Manchester London Road with Yarmouth and Lowestoft; it also provided a through service between Manchester and Cromer. The Liverpool and Manchester portions joined and divided at Stoke, and the train was routed via the North Stafford line (stopping at Uttoxeter), and via Willington Junction to Nottingham, so avoiding Derby. A LNW twelve-wheeled restaurant car worked between Liverpool and Lowestoft, and the Manchester—Yarmouth schedule was 6 hours 25 minutes.

The longest non-stop runs in 1923 were made by the Leicesters between Bourne and South Lynn, 34 miles in 50 minutes, 40.8 mph. The fastest runs were by Norwich portions of the Leicesters between Melton and Drayton, 16.8 miles in 22 minutes, 45.7 mph. But in the summer of 1925 the longest non-stop run was by the Liverpool train between Melton and Yarmouth, 41½ miles in 62 minutes, 40.2 mph, and the fastest run was Peterboro'—Wisbech, 20.8 miles in 26 minutes, 48 mph.

A new halt at Cromer Links, between Roughton Road Junction and Overstrand, which had been suggested for some years, was opened on 9 July 1923. As it was unstaffed, it was served by the conductor-guard trains. That summer one train ran each way on weekdays between Cromer Beach, Mundesley and North Walsham Town, the first advertised passenger train to use the section between there and Antingham Road Junction since 1916. In the following summer this was increased to two trains each way. Stopping trains, with M & GN engines, ran through between Spalding and Nottingham Midland regularly from 1923 onwards.

The up train from Peterboro' to Kings Cross with the through Cromer portion became so heavy that from the summer of 1923 until 1932, all the year round, the Cromer and Grimsby carriages were run daily in front of the main train as an unadvertised relief, due at Kings Cross at 4.20 pm, and known as 'The Ghost'. In summer this gave the best Cromer—Kings Cross service run between the wars, 4 hours 10 minutes, generally with restaurant car from Peterboro'. At the end of the summer of 1923, Mr Marriott was able to report a considerable improvement in punctuality.

Through carriages from Leeds to Yarmouth and Lowestoft,

but run by the Midland route, reappeared in the summer from 1924, generally on each weekday. This service never seemed to get the same publicity as the old GN train had. In practice, through coaches often ran in the reverse direction but in some summers were not mentioned in the public or working timetables, and even if they were they were sometimes shown only as running back as far as Sheffield. Midweek in the summer of 1927, for example, the timetable showed no return service to the West Riding, although the westbound morning Leicester included through Sheffield carriages, duly labelled. Sometimes the eastbound service was shown only as 'except Saturdays', passengers on Saturdays having apparently to rely on an unadvertised relief or town holiday train. In the summers of 1927-8 the LMS worked the Leeds coaches from Harrogate, and from the summer of 1929 from Bradford.

Also in the summer of 1924 the Birmingham coaches on the principal Leicesters (afternoon eastbound and morning westbound) began to work to and from Gloucester and Cheltenham. These trains had a Leicester—Lowestoft restaurant car from the summer of 1927.

MR MARRIOTT RETIRES

Mr Marriott retired on 31 December 1924. Mr Walker became traffic manager, Mr Newman mechanical engineer, and Mr Langley civil engineer. Mr Marriott died in 1944.

DECLINE OF 'POPPYLAND' TRAFFIC

In the 1920s there was not so much good class holiday traffic to 'Poppyland' as there had been before the war. London passengers were mainly directed to the shorter GE route, but the Liverpool Street—North Walsham non-stop train, which had been restored, ran only three times a week in the summer from 1924. Large numbers of people continued to go on the Broads, especially after motor cruisers had developed, but both these traffics were subject to competition from the private car.

In the summer from 1925 onwards there was a through train each way on weekdays between Cromer Beach and Yarmouth Beach via Mundesley and North Walsham Town.

In the summer from 1927 a similar train left Yarmouth in the morning on Tuesdays, Wednesdays and Thursdays (it was 'except Saturdays' from the summer of 1933) and returned from Cromer in the evening, enabling passengers, according to the advertisement, to spend 5½ hours in 'Poppyland'.

THE GENERAL STRIKE

The General Strike on 4 May 1926, following a stoppage of the coal mines three days before, had a drastic effect on the services, some being run with volunteer assistance. It lasted for only ten days but the miners did not fully return to work until December, and much railway coal had to be imported. The M & GN ran a holiday service from late July but the Liverpool and Manchester train and the Leeds train were not operated. However, special trains were provided in July for the Nottingham cycle works' outing to Yarmouth. Unfortunately, the strike again demonstrated that when the railways were in difficulties much traffic could go by road.

From 1927 the Liverpool and Manchester summer trains ran on Mondays, Fridays and Saturdays only, but were well patronised. The Manchester portion had an unusual route, as after Macclesfield it ran by the old North Stafford Churnet Valley line, stopping at Leek, and joined the Liverpool portion at Uttoxeter. The same route was used in the other direction.

TOWN HOLIDAY AND EXCURSION TRAINS

The LNE did not run regular timetabled services from the North and Midlands to M & GN destinations, as it had available purely LNE routes. But on summer Saturdays in the late 1920s and 1930s town holiday and excursion trains, from places on the old GN in the West Riding and Nottinghamshire, were frequently run to the M & GN. At first they were often composed of GN semi-corridor six-wheelers but later were generally bogie corridor stock. As the carriages waited at Yarmouth from one Saturday to another before returning, they were sometimes used on the through trains to Cromer. Sunday excursions to Yarmouth from North Walsham, Stalham and Potter Heigham reappeared in the summer from 1927. Extra locals 'except Saturdays' ran between Yarmouth and Potter Heigham to compete with the buses. Sunday excursions from King's Lynn to Matlock ran again from 1928, and in 1929 there was an excursion from King's Lynn to Stratford-on-Avon. Sunday excursions from King's Lynn and Wisbech to Kings Cross ran outside the summer period, sometimes composed of LMS stock when LNE coaches were not available. Some Yarmouth— Lowestoft trips were operated by LNE Sentinel-Cammell railcars for a time from 1928.

MORE MUNDESLEY DEVELOPMENTS

On the Mundesley line the conductor-guard North Walsham —Cromer Beach service was worked alternately by old GE and M & GN engines and stock for three-year periods. From 1927 some of the Cromer coaches on the principal Leicesters worked to and from Mundesley in the summer but as in 1907 this facility was not publicly advertised. From 1935 the westbound service actually started at North Walsham GE, after the coaches had worked there empty from Sheringham via Cromer Junction.

THE KINGS CROSS—CROMER EXPRESSES

The LNE continued to give high priority to the Kings Cross— Cromer trains. In the winter of 1931 the down train was given an extra stop at Huntingdon, running there from Hitchin at 57.9 mph, the fastest on the old GN at that time. The up train, 'The Ghost', was at last shown separately in the 1932 public timetable, with a schedule of 78 minutes from Peterboro', 58.8 mph (76 minutes 60.2 mph from 1934), but the overall Cromer—Kings Cross schedule was not altered. The popularity of these trains was largely maintained because they gave a good service between Kings Cross and intermediate stations, such as Wisbech and Fakenham; in some years, through Kings Lynn coaches were operated. A further improvement to the service would have been a restaurant car on the 3 pm down— the tea trolleys on Peterboro' platform were always most welcome. Another useful London connection was provided by the Mundesley and Cromer to Peterboro' carriages, which were attached to the westbound Leicester morning train as far as South Lynn; they then stopped at Wisbech and connected at Peterboro' with an up Leeds express. Even in 1935 passengers from Cromer Beach were still using this service for London.

In July of that year a change occurred in the Cromer—Liverpool Street service. The breakfast car train was altered to start from Cromer Beach and ran via Mundesley to North Walsham, where it attached the Sheringham portion.

MORE EXCURSIONS

Beginning in 1930 day excursions were run in summer to Hunstanton, via Spalding and King's Lynn, from old GN stations and later from Nottingham Midland. Excursion trains were also operated once again on summer Sundays in the 1930s from King's Lynn and almost all stations eastward to Cromer and Yarmouth, and from Norwich City to Cromer; they began in June and continued until mid-September. In the summer of 1933 the facilities offered for a 'half-day' outing to Yarmouth and Cromer were almost as good as in the summers up to 1914. But the trains in the 1930s were always by special notice, and were not shown in the ordinary timetables. The lack of such trains in the early 1920s is believed to have been due to Mr Marriott's disapproval of Sunday operations.

An idea of the intense service on a busy summer Saturday can be given by the figures for August Bank Holiday Saturday 1932, when twenty-four through trains left Yarmouth Beach between 8 am and 4.30 pm, seventeen for LMS destinations and seven for LNE. Even more would be coming inwards, so very careful control and use of the passing places on the single sections were necessary. More of the relief Saturday trains were by this time shown in the timetables.

HOLIDAY CAMP SERVICES AND HALTS

Holiday camps, of the type which have become common in recent years, were established at Caister and Hemsby in 1933. Partly to serve these, miniature halts were opened on 17 July 1933 at Newtown, between Yarmouth Beach and Caister, at

Caister camp, at California cliffs, and Scratby, between Caister and Ormesby, at Potter Heigham Bridge, close to the yachts and riverside bungalows (which the station was not) and at Sutton Staithe, between Catfield and Stalham (see page 41). The halts were generally open only in the summer and were served by conductor-guard locals. A Sentinel-Cammell car worked the service for a short time. Through trains were run at Easter and on summer Saturdays between Liverpool Street and the camp halt at Caister, which they reached by reversing at Antingham Road Junction. Sutton Staithe halt was only used in the summer of 1933.

SUNDAY TRAINS

The first Sunday passenger trains since 1914 to be shown in the ordinary timetables appeared in the 1934 summer timetable. They were LNE trains between Norwich Thorpe and Sheringham via Mundesley and Runton West Junction and ran for a short period in August; they continued each summer from 1935 to 1939.

Another Sunday summer train which began in 1935 was one from Sheringham to Cromer GE.

MORE SATURDAYS ONLY SERVICES

The Liverpool and Manchester trains became bi-weekly in the summer of 1932 and Saturdays only in 1934, but on the Saturdays the Liverpool and Manchester portions ran separately throughout, both with a restaurant car. Also part of the summer service was a train between Manchester Victoria and Yarmouth by the old Midland route, outwards on Friday night and returning on Saturday. Other summer Saturday services connected Halifax, Nuneaton and Northampton with Yarmouth by Midland routes. Excursions to Skegness from M & GN stations, and from former Midland stations via Saxby and Spalding, were operated at this period. Excursions were even operated in these years from Scotland to Yarmouth, to enable relatives and friends to visit the Scots fisher girls working there.

GOODS TRAFFIC; DEPRESSION; ROAD COMPETITION

In the 1920s freight traffic declined significantly. Besides industrial depression there was also agricultural depression, and much land which had been under corn during the war now reverted to pasture. The M & GN, in a mainly agricultural district, was seriously affected.

Another serious problem in the twenties and early thirties was the growth of road competition—from the lorry, the local bus, the private car, the char-a-banc, and later the road motor coach. The railways were heavily rated, and the money so raised was partly spent in improving roads, helping the railways' competitors, an injustice which was not corrected until 1928. The distances over which the M & GN conveyed much of its traffic made it particularly vulnerable to road competition. It was not far for people in Norfolk towns and villages to take a char-a-banc outing to Yarmouth, and such trips soon began from places like Leicester. A bus could go from the centre of a village to the centre of Norwich. The lorry was in some ways more serious, as it could run from the farm or orchard direct to the market, for example from near Wisbech to Leicester, and so cartage to and from rail (often required at both ends) was avoided. The fruit and potato traffics were especially affected. Furthermore, allegations of bad handling and consequent damage, and of delay in rail transit were often made. Such charges, of course, lost nothing in the telling and were frequently quoted without any reference to the large proportion of traffic safely and promptly conveyed by rail. Unlike the railways, the road hauliers were not subjected to controls over the rates they charged.

In 1928 the four main railway companies obtained wide powers from Parliament to operate their own road passenger services. The LMS and LNE could now run buses in any district to which access was afforded by the system of any railway committee on which they were represented, which included the M & GN and the N & S. But the policy of running railway-owned buses to connect with trains, previously adopted by the Great Western, the Great North of Scotland and the GE, was not followed. In the M & GN's district the Eastern Counties

Omnibus and Lincolnshire Road Car companies operated the buses. Large LMS and LNE investments were made in these concerns, which often proved profitable, but the buses did not necessarily connect with the trains, or even start from the stations.

The industrial and agricultural depressions were at their worst in 1931. As well as the losses due to road competition, the fruit traffic was seriously affected by the dumping of fruit from abroad. This was particularly unfortunate as the production of soft fruit had developed significantly both in east Norfolk and in the Wisbech area of the old western section. To some extent these losses were made good by the growth of sugar beet traffic, a crop which was assisted by government subsidy. Some growers of potatoes went over to sugar beet, which was fortunate for the railway, as the potato traffic was suffering from road competition while sugar beet was mainly conveyed by rail under what were called 'farm to factory' arrangements made by the M & GN. Factories were established at South Lynn and Spalding, and the tonnage conveyed rose from 10,000 in 1929 to 40,000 in 1934.

Protective duties on imported foreign fruit stopped the dumping in 1932, and home-grown wheat was also favoured by legislation. Moreover, the Road and Rail Traffic Act, 1933, which introduced the system of licensing goods road vehicles, did much to protect the railways from unrestricted road competition, though the basic fact that the lorry could go direct from the farm or orchard to the market remained. Nevertheless, the fruit traffic made a considerable recovery. The fruit vans were improved with specially constructed insulated containers, and fruit was sent all over the country, even to Ireland. In 1934 a collection service by railway lorry was introduced mainly for strawberries, and in the 1936 season 300,000 chips were despatched. Other valuable traffics in the 1930s, mainly from the old fenland western section, included cabbages, broccoli and lettuces for both London and provincial markets, and flowers, especially daffodils, narcissi, hyacinths, chrysanthemums and tulips. For these, special trains of vacuum-fitted stock ran from Sutton Bridge and Holbeach to Spalding, from where they were worked forward by LNE and LMS routes.

Additional sidings were provided at South Lynn in 1932 to cater for freight traffic originating locally. There were several firms with private sidings in this area, which contributed valuable traffic.

SOME SHORT-DISTANCE GOODS SERVICES

From 1923 to 1936 the M & GN undertook the goods service on the N & S Yarmouth—Lowestoft line, with two or three regular trips each way in addition to fish trains. In 1919 there had been one GE goods between South Town and Gorleston 'when required'. As late as 1936 the 6.48 am from Yarmouth Beach to Lowestoft was mixed, passenger and goods. On the Mundesley line, there had also been mixed trains (GE operated) in 1919-22. In the 1920s there was for some years a daily GE goods between North Walsham and Mundesley, which connected there with a M & GN goods for Cromer Beach. But in the 1930s the LNE provided the daily pick-up which ran between North Walsham and Sheringham via Mundesley, Newstead Lane Junction and Runton West Junction.

The Union Line in Yarmouth was worked by the simple train staff system, one engine in steam, between Caister Road Junction and White Swan Junction, the special ex-GE tram engines hauling the trucks between there and the quays. In 1919 there had been six or seven regular trips each way, with one 'when required' on Sunday morning, but in the 1930s there were generally only three each way on weekdays only.

M & GN engines made regular goods trips on the King's Lynn harbour line, which was also worked with the staff on the one engine in steam principle. Traffic on the M & GN Wisbech harbour branch was always regarded as valuable, and was sometimes greater than that on the old GE harbour branch there.

For some years after the war, there were still Sunday morning goods trains between Saxby and Bourne (one ran on to Twenty 'when required') but not to Spalding or Sutton Bridge (see page 118). But a Sunday morning goods train between Peterboro' and Lynn continued to run throughout the period. The LNE withdrew the passenger trains between Sleaford and Bourne on 22 September 1930, but the line remained in use for goods traffic (part of it until 1965, see chapter 9) in association with the Spalding—Bourne line.

MORE SIGNALLING DEVELOPMENTS

On 19 May 1928, by means of a system of track circuits, tablet operation over Breydon viaduct was replaced by block working. The points at either end of the single-line section over the viaduct were remotely controlled by Caister Road box, and the north and south boxes at the viaduct were abolished.

The special occupation key device at Kelling sidings was replaced by operating the siding points by the ordinary tablet-controlled ground frame in April 1935, and the sidings were not used after August 1939.

From 1923 the passage of M & GN trains between the signalboxes at Westwood Junction and Wisbech Junction, north of Peterboro', was controlled by unusual signalling arrangements. There were no block instruments, trains being offered and accepted on a bell; the points interlocked so that no conflicting movement was possible and so that no signals were put at clear until the signalmen in both boxes operated them.

The name Cunningham's Drove for the signalbox where the double line became single, a mile east of Welland Bank Junction, was changed in 1932 to Clay Lake, the name of the siding a short distance to the west (Chapter 5, page 83).

ACCIDENTS

The standard of safety remained high. The only serious mishaps in this period were a collision between a M & GN passenger engine and an ex-GE goods engine in Spalding yard in 1923, and a collision between two goods trains at the Murrow level crossing of the former GN–GE and M & GN in very frosty weather in February 1927, fortunately with no fatalities.

THE STAFF; STATION GARDENS

Co-operation between the joint staff and the old GE staff was general, very different from the old days, but some anomalies persisted. As late as 1927, a return ticket from Liverpool Street to the Lynn district was not available back to Kings Cross via the M & GN and Peterboro'. Care and good appearance of the stations were encouraged by competitions for the best kept station. Stalham was the winner in 1931, and Whitwell, Aylsham, Caister, Hindolveston, Lenwade, Martham, Sheringham, West Runton and Weybourne were commended. Gayton Road won in 1934.

A RECORD RUN

A remarkably fast run, one of the fastest ever on the M & GN, was made early in the morning of 15 November 1935, with newspapers giving general election results. No 53, a rebuilt 4–4–0, hauled a load of one LNE bogie van which had been detached from a Kings Cross train at Peterboro'. The emergency schedule to King's Lynn with a stop at Wisbech was 48 minutes, but No 53 reached Wisbech, 20.8 miles, in 21 minutes, and then ran on to King's Lynn, 18½ miles, in 23 minutes, including slacks at the bridges. The overall time was 46 minutes.

THE LATEST NEW HALT

A new unstaffed halt at Sidestrand, between Overstrand and Trimingham, was opened on 25 May 1936, the last station to be provided while the old M & GN organisation existed.

THE FINAL MILEAGE

On 30 September 1936 the true M & GN lines comprised 183 miles 33 chains route mileage (109 miles 18 chains single, 74 miles 14 chains double). The N & S lines were 22 miles 22 chains (11 miles 66 chains single, 10 miles 36 chains double).

CHAPTER SEVEN

The LNER Regime

THE COMMITTEE

In 1935 the LMS and LNE agreed that the local administration of the M & GN should be taken over by LNE officials. The new arrangements, part of a general policy of co-operation and agreed division of responsibility adopted by the LMS and LNE, came into force on 1 October 1936.

The committee of directors continued to meet. Since the 1890s, the usual practice had been that the committee consisted of six members, three appointed by each parent company from its own board, but sometimes the full complement of six was not appointed. In the 1930s, however, there were as many as seven or eight official appointments, as the joint LMS and LNE committee for the M & GN also controlled a group of other joint lines owned by the two companies. Other groups of these lines were controlled by other committees. The groups were numbered, and in 1936 the M & GN was in group 1.

CHANGES

In consequence, the LMS was still concerned with policy through its representatives on the committee. But under the new scheme, administration was undertaken by the LNE southern area with headquarters at Liverpool Street, and covered the N & S lines as well as the M & GN. The LMS continued to supply the passenger stock on the Leicesters and other through trains from its line, and to send and receive considerable freight traffic. Mr Walker, the last separate traffic manager of the M & GN, retired, and the locomotive department, so long directed at a distance from Derby and locally from Melton, was placed under Stratford.

Even before this there were indications that the old methods were changing. The comparatively small number of goods vehicles owned by the committee had been distributed among the parent companies. Carriages belonging to several of the constituent companies of the LMS and LNE, not just to the GN and Midland, were being used regularly on the M & GN. Many ex-GN, GE and GC engines soon appeared, and many M & GN engines were withdrawn (see Chapter 10). Melton shops were closed, except for small repairs, in December 1936, but the gas works long remained in use. The staff affected were found other jobs, but there was some local discontent as the works were an important industry in a quiet district. The civil engineering department showed more signs of LNE influence. When the somersault signals became due for replacement, standard LNE upper quadrants were installed, but a large number of somersaults remained in use.

At this time a scheme was proposed for effecting economies at Yarmouth by closing one of the stations and concentrating traffic at the other two. Beach and Vauxhall were small and cramped, and communications between them, and with South Town, were indirect. But owing to the intervening rivers connecting lines would have been expensive to construct, and the passenger congestion was only serious in the summer, so no action was taken. However, a comprehensive scheme of improvement and modernisation was carried out at King's Lynn station.

FISH TRAFFIC

The fish traffic had declined, partly because of road competition, though the LNE checked some of this by litigation preventing lorries from entering quays except on the railway's terms. But in any case many of the fish had moved away from the best fishing grounds off Yarmouth and Lowestoft and there were now more trawlers and drifters than the trade could afford. Often on busy days, if a boat could not reach the quay and be unloaded quickly, the catch could not be sold, and eventually a system of licensing the boats was introduced by

Page 143 (above) *Johnson 4-4-0 No 78 as first rebuilt with an extended smokebox about 1907;* (below) *4-4-0 tank No 9 (formerly* Fakenham) *at Mundesley*

Page 144 (above) *Johnson 0–6–0 No 65 at Melton about 1925;* (centre) *0–6–0T No 93 at South Lynn about 1935;* (below) *H. A. Ivatt (type) 0–6–0 No 92 at Spalding, 1929*

legislation. As a result, in 1936 there was only one train daily exclusively for fish, the 3.15 pm from Lowestoft, which stopped conditionally at Gorleston-on-Sea for fish brought direct from the Yarmouth south quays by road, left Yarmouth Beach at 4.7 pm, and stopped only at Melton and South Lynn to Peterboro'. However, extras were still put on at the height of the season, and the Scots girls still came in their special trains, from as far away, in 1935, as Kyle of Lochalsh.

THE PASSENGER SERVICES

The Saturdays only Liverpool—Lowestoft through train did not reappear in the summer of 1936, as the long established service by the old GC–GE route was still in operation. The Saturday Northampton train ran by the GE route. In the 1935 summer timetable Aylsham had a Sunday train to Yarmouth for the first time since 1914 but it ran via the GE. In the summer of 1937 a through service was introduced between Melton and Liverpool Street. Leaving Melton at 7.11 am, the through portion was attached to a breakfast car train at Cromer GE; it returned on the 5.16 pm restaurant car train from Liverpool Street. It was the first additional daily through service to and from London for Melton and Holt passengers (besides the 3 pm from Kings Cross and the 12.10 pm from Cromer) since 1915, and it ran all the year round. Advertised summer Saturday trains between Nottingham, Leicester and Hunstanton via Saxby, Bourne and King's Lynn appeared at the same time, and in the summer of 1938 there was one from Bedford via Leicester. The 3 pm from Kings Cross at last received a buffet car as far as Peterboro' and the 3.29 am newspaper train from Kings Cross now had a portion for Wisbech M & GN and King's Lynn.

In Bradshaw the M & GN timetable was not put near the LNE ones until 1939, and even then the service west of Bourne was a long way off among the LMS tables, which made the through trains by that route difficult to look up.

In the late 1930s the practice developed of running nearly all the through holiday trains on Saturdays only, largely as a result of public habits changing to suit the requirements of hotel proprietors and landladies. In the summers of 1938-9 the only through daily expresses were the principal Leicesters (morning westbound and afternoon eastbound), still with their Gloucester and West Riding through carriages, the 3 pm from Kings Cross and its return train the 12.10 pm from Cromer, and the new Liverpool Street—Melton service. There was also a through stopping train from Norwich City to Nottingham. More of the Saturday trains now began to run in June, instead of early July and town holiday trains were still popular; in July 1939 the return Coventry train went through from Yarmouth with an LMS engine and LNE stock. The out-of-season excursions from Lynn and Wisbech to Kings Cross continued, sometimes with old M & GN coaches, and excursion facilities were well provided until the outbreak of war, including the summer Sunday excursions which often came from Leicester and the Midlands. On Whit Monday 1938 an excursion was provided from Norwich to Matlock.

In the summers of 1938-9 Mundesley and Sheringham had one train on Sundays from Whitsun onwards, as well as the three or four run from July to early September. Another Sheringham development was an 8.42 am departure on weekdays, conveying two portions as far as Cromer Junction; then the first portion ran to Norwich and Liverpool Street with a breakfast car, and the second backed into Cromer GE and ran slow to Norwich.

THE HINDOLVESTONE ACCIDENT

An accident, which might have been serious but in fact caused no loss of life, occurred near Hindolvestone on 20 August 1937. A morning train from Leicester to Norwich, consisting of ex-GC 4-4-0 No 6013 and three LMS bogie corridors, which had left Melton 14 minutes late on a 42 mph schedule, was running at high speed on a falling gradient when the tender and coaches became derailed on a 60-chain right-hand curve. Of the sixteen passengers, two were slightly injured. Major Wilson, the inspecting officer, reported that the leading tender axle derailed first, and that the road could have been burst by the next pair of wheels, the remaining wheels being derailed by the bursting. He could not find the cause with certainty but thought that there had been rolling and lateral oscillation, and perhaps partial relief of weight on the leading tender wheels due to the high speed. Contributory factors might have been a slight irregularity in the level of the track, and the poor condition of one of the carriages.

MILITARY TRAFFIC

Events which indicated the renewed danger of war, the conflict between Italy and Abyssinia 1935-6, the Munich crisis in 1938, the doubling of the Territorial Army and the introduction of National Service in 1939, brought much more military traffic to the line. In 1936 a large anti-aircraft practice camp was established at Weybourne, close to the sea, and another one was set up soon afterwards at Stiffkey, which was served from Holt station. Quantities of steel, cement and other materials were transported for air-raid precautions purposes.

WAR AGAIN

In anticipation of the war which broke out on 3 September 1939, the railways including the M & GN and the King's Lynn dock lines were taken over on 1 September by the government, acting again through a railway executive committee. The full ordinary passenger train service was maintained for a short time to get holidaymakers home and soldiers to their units, and as before there were many troop trains. But drastic reductions of services, particularly on the M & GN, were made on 11 and 25 September; all the through expresses were withdrawn, the 3 pm from Kings Cross, and the corresponding return train, ended their long careers, the all-year-round Leicesters, which had run throughout the 1914-18 war, were suspended until 1946, and the new Liverpool Street—Melton service was taken off. Besides the need for economy in fuel and staff, lines had to be available for military traffic and there was the immediate danger of severe air attack, although this did not in fact occur until the summer of 1940. The M & GN, unlike lines to the south and west, had few 'evacuees' to carry from town to country districts. The halts between Potter Heigham and Yarmouth were closed, but those on the Mundesley line remained open. Many cheap ticket facilities, all excursion trains and reservation of seats and compartments were again suspended. But luggage could still be sent in advance, a great boon on long wartime journeys. Many other changes, characteristic of the previous war, occurred again. Provision of more home-grown food was vital, so that the grain, vegetable and fruit traffics increased, goods were again diverted from sea to rail, and fish traffic diminished. Shortage of fuel was also a serious problem, made worse by several hard winters, especially in February 1940, while there was again a staff shortage, as so many joined the forces.

The south rather than the east, was the invasion coast from the summer of 1940, but the east coast was dangerous enough. Many troops were in training and on coast defence in Norfolk and Lincolnshire, and beach defences, with wire and mines, were again built. Streets in Yarmouth near Beach station were blocked with barricades, and piers were damaged to prevent landings on them. After the German conquest of Holland in May 1940, when troop-carrying seaplanes alighted on canals, the Navy patrolled some broads in motor-launches and mined others. This duty was later taken over by the 9th Battalion, Royal Norfolk Regiment, mainly men from the district, including ex-M & GN employees. As in the previous war, civilian passengers in and out of the area were subjected to restrictions. The consequence of all this was that few holidaymakers came in the wartime summers of 1940-4, compared with 1915-18, as there were so few beaches and broads they could safely visit, and there were no through trains to bring them, as there had been in the previous war.

AIR RAIDS

From the summer of 1940 there were many air raids. German planes coming over the sea were difficult to detect and intercept, especially in thick weather, though fortunately there was a large radar station south of Mundesley. Norwich City and Thorpe stations were both severely damaged by bombs, and there was also considerable damage to rolling stock. Even worse hit was Gorleston North station which was so badly damaged in 1941 that it was eventually closed; rather out of the town, it had suffered from tram and later bus competition, and closure took place from 5 October 1942. The raids also affected the working of trains, which often had to be diverted when lines were damaged by bombing, or when there were unexploded bombs near the line; and operation was difficult enough already with the increased freight traffic. Heavy trains were run to convey ammunition to be stored under hedges and in woods in quiet districts so as to reduce the danger of explosions, and there were several large RAF stations, such as Horsham St Faith near Norwich, which received their supplies of aeroplane parts and stores by rail.

WARTIME PASSENGER SERVICES

The number of stopping trains was about the same as in 1917-18, but there were trains from Yarmouth South Town to Lowestoft via Gorleston in addition to those from Yarmouth Beach, as the service via the Haddiscoe curve had disappeared some years before. Stopping trains between Lynn, Spalding and Nottingham were for some years the only through services but additional trains were gradually provided to enable servicemen and others to spend the day in Lynn and Norwich and return late. One ran from Norwich City to Lynn, and another on Saturdays only from Norwich Thorpe to Cromer Beach via Mundesley. From 1940 onwards two or three Melton trains ran to and from Cromer GE for London connections, and in the summer of 1943 a through train from Melton, Holt and Sheringham to Liverpool Street was restored, leaving early in the morning and returning in the evening. A passenger could spend five hours in London, and the service was also very useful for leave travel. From early in 1944 there was also an up through train in the afternoon.

A further reduction of service occurred at the time of the Normandy landing in June 1944 but it mainly affected the few additional trains which had been put on. The Melton—Liverpool Street service continued to run, and the trains taken off in the summer were restored at the end of the year, when an improved North Walsham—Yarmouth service was also run on some days.

SUNDAY TRAINS AGAIN

A through train on Sundays between Norwich Thorpe and Holt via Cromer GE appeared in April 1945, the first Sunday train in the timetable since 1939. The down train had an Overstrand connection from Whitsun onwards. In the summer there were two trains from Norwich Thorpe via Mundesley on Sundays, one to Sheringham and one to Holt, and the weekday Norwich Thorpe—Sheringham—Melton service was improved. A Holt Sunday train continued in the winter, the first advertised passenger train Holt had seen on a winter Sunday since E & M days.

RESTORATION OF EXPRESS SERVICES

The morning westbound and afternoon eastbound Leicesters were restored in the summer of 1946 but on a slower schedule than before the war. They again made the traditional Bourne—South Lynn non-stop runs, and had Norwich, Cromer, and Yarmouth and Lowestoft, portions, but no Gloucester, Birmingham or West Riding through carriages. There were also advertised Saturdays only trains between Derby and Leicester and Yarmouth, and between Bourne, Spalding and Hunstanton. Two down and three up Liverpool Street—Melton trains were provided daily (one from Holt only), besides Sheringham through carriages on other trains, and one Holt and Sheringham to Liverpool Street train on Sundays. Heavy snowfalls early in 1947 were followed by floods, which affected the line near the Welland, east of Spalding. At the same time there was a coal shortage, and services were reduced.

Further improvements were made in the summer of 1947. Through coaches to Birmingham re-appeared on the Leicesters, although Leeds and Manchester were now served by LNE routes instead of M & GN. More through trains were provided on Saturdays only, and by a daily Cromer and Holt train it was again possible to visit Yarmouth for a day as in 1914. On the Liverpool Street line two of the best trains were accelerated, named 'The Norfolkman' and 'The Broadsman', and given through coaches for Sheringham via Mundesley. The Sunday Holt—Liverpool Street through train continued to run in the winter.

CHAPTER EIGHT

The Eastern Region's Administration

NATIONALISATION

Under the Transport Act, 1947, which brought about nationalisation, the systems of both the M & GN and N & S joint committees were transferred along with their parent companies and other railways to the British Transport Commission on 1 January 1948. The controlling body of the railways was called the Railway Executive, though that organisation and title did not last long. The M & GN and N & S lines, along with the King's Lynn Dock & Railway, were assigned to the Eastern Region, which at that period corresponded very closely to the former Southern Area of the LNE—the old GN, GE and GC. So they were still directed from Liverpool Street, as they had been since 1936. It is an interesting fact that the M & GN changed much more after that year, 1936, than it did after either 1922 or 1947. In 1936 there was a vital change of administration, accompanied by considerable changes in the locomotive and carriage stock, in the signalling, and in other matters (Chapters 7 and 10). In 1923 there had been no change of administration, rolling stock or signalling, and in 1948 the change of administration from an area of the LNE to a region of nationalised British Railways was a change more in name than in fact. The system was administered from the same place, mainly by the same officials, and there were no material changes in rolling stock or signalling, at least initially.

CHANGE OF STATION NAMES

On 27 September 1948 a plan for rationalising station names was put into effect. Murrow M & GN became Murrow West,

Murrow on the March—Spalding line—Murrow East, Fakenham Town—Fakenham West, Fakenham (old GE)—Fakenham East, Aylsham Town—Aylsham North, Aylsham (old GE)—Aylsham South, Wisbech M & GN—Wisbech North, Wisbech (old GE)—Wisbech East, North Walsham (old GE)—North Walsham Main, and Cromer (old GE)—Cromer High. A further change occurred in 1950 when the harbour goods stations at Wisbech became North and East respectively. As another piece of rationalisation, in April 1950 the portion of the old Midland westwards from Little Bytham Junction as far as Edmondthorpe was transferred from the London Midland Region to the Eastern Region.

THE PASSENGER SERVICES

The post-war rise in the popularity of holiday camps caused additional facilities to be provided. In 1948 a through train ran again on summer Saturdays from Liverpool Street to Caister station, via Cambridge, Norwich Wensum curve, and Antingham Road Junction, where it reversed, and stopped at Hemsby and Caister camp halt, which was re-opened along with the other halts between Yarmouth and Potter Heigham. Except on Saturdays the halts were served by additional trains which were one class only. In the summers of 1949-50 there were three in each direction between North Walsham and Yarmouth on Sundays, the first Sunday trains in the timetable for this section since 1914. At the same time more summer Saturday Hunstanton trains from Leicester, Bourne and Peterboro' were operated. From the summer of 1950, there were summer Sunday Hunstanton trains from and to Eye Green, Bourne and Spalding, serving the intermediate stations. They were the only Sunday trains serving the local stations on the old western section ever to be shown in the timetables. From 1949 new starting and returning points appeared for some of the summer Saturday trains; one of the Nottingham trains ran to and from Mansfield, and another Beeston, and a Birmingham train ran to and from King's Norton. In October 1951 the daily all-year-round Leicester was again given a restaurant car, attached between Leicester and South Lynn. From the 1952 season it operated twice a week to and from Yarmouth, and from the

1955 season daily in the summer. Rather elderly ex-GN and GE cars were generally used. The 'quality' holiday traffic to Cromer and 'Poppyland' however, declined further and some of the best hotels closed. Many holiday visitors now came in caravans, and did not use rail at all.

CLOSURES AND ECONOMIES

Several closures, economies and alterations took place from 1951. On 18 June the Essendine and Bourne line, the route of the old GN trains to Lynn, was closed. Hellesdon station was closed to passengers on 15 September 1952. On the same day the passenger service on the old GE Wroxham—Aylsham—County School branch was taken off but the line remained open for goods. Early in 1953 it was decided that the Mundesley—Overstrand—Roughton Road Junction section should be closed; this, of course, was the last N & S section to be opened, and doubts had been expressed in the first place as to whether it would ever pay. Efforts had been made to develop it by providing through services and conductor-guard locals and halts which were cheap to operate and maintain, but the district remained quiet, and the trains were subjected to bus and private car competition. The last trains ran on Easter Monday, 6 April. Liverpool Street to Sheringham and Melton through carriages which had been running via Mundesley were again detached at Cromer Junction or ran in and out of Cromer High.

BREYDON VIADUCT CLOSED

In the same year it was decided to close Breydon viaduct as it was expensive to maintain and in need of partial reconstruction, and divert traffic to other routes. Closure took place on 20 September. The Lowestoft through coaches on the Leicesters, the ordinary passenger service between Yarmouth Beach and Lowestoft, and the M & GN route freight trains were withdrawn. But a good service was provided to and from South Town, as well as a through train between Birmingham and Lowestoft on Saturdays. The following summer a daily service was provided from Derby and Leicester to Lowestoft and

Gorleston via the old GE routes. Two goods trains each way continued to run daily between Beach and Caister Road Junction for the Quay line.

CONCENTRATION AT CROMER BEACH

Early in 1954 it was announced that the long-considered concentration at Cromer Beach would be effected, and Cromer High closed. Beach comprised a main platform with an overall roof and a short bay previously used by the Mundesley trains. To accommodate the principal Liverpool Street trains, which were generally of nine coaches, the main platform was considerably lengthened. The booking and parcels offices were modernised, a new bicycle store provided and the signalling layout altered. The short single-line section from the gasworks siding to the station was doubled. The alterations were successfully undertaken during the summer and completed on 19 September. Cromer High was closed to passengers the following day.

The best Liverpool Street—Cromer schedule, which had recovered to 3 hours 10 minutes by the acceleration of 'The Norfolkman' and 'The Broadsman' in the summer of 1951, was now still only 3 hours 14 minutes in the case of 'The Broadsman', despite the greater distance, but other trains were slower. The whole train often reversed at Beach and worked to and from Sheringham or Melton. Thus two adjacent sections of the N & S on either side of Roughton Road Junction had a different fate within eighteen months. One was closed, and the other became almost a main line. An occasional excursion from Kings Cross appeared at Beach, but came via Hitchin, Cambridge and Norwich Thorpe.

SPALDING

At the start of the 1955 winter services, on 18 September, the daily Leicesters, which had run non-stop between Bourne and South Lynn for so many years, began to stop at Spalding and reversed there. This was not an easy operation, as the train had to move forward off the platform and back on to the fresh engine waiting on another line, so that at first there were delays. In the summer of 1956 the Spalding stop was made 'except Saturdays' and the trains again used the avoiding line along with the other summer Saturday through trains. It was also used on Sunday by a Hunstanton train.

DIESEL TRAINS

The first appearance of open two-coach diesel sets which could be made up into four-coach or even longer trains, also occurred on 18 September 1955, when they began to operate on some of the Norwich Thorpe—Cromer Beach—Sheringham —Holt services. On the Mundesley line from April 1953 to the summer of 1956, services were operated by a steam push-and-pull train working in and out of North Walsham Main. But in the summer of 1956 the steam push-and-pull was replaced by diesel sets with conductor-guards, who issued Mundesley tickets on the train, so that the booking office could be closed. Further economies were effected by running the diesel as 'one engine in steam', no tablet being required. Probably the last passenger trains between North Walsham Town and Mundesley were the special trains provided from Chesterfield to Mundesley for the Derbyshire schools camping association, which reversed at North Walsham Town.

The Eastern Region considered making increased use of diesel sets, which were then being introduced in many districts all over the country. They were more economical than a three-coach steam train and, on the M & GN, had the additional advantage of reducing the difficulties at reversing stations. On 18 September 1957 they took over the operation, except for the long distance through trains, of the rest of the Melton—Cromer service and of the Melton—Norwich City service. Some ran through between Norwich City and Cromer, and one started at Norwich City and returned to Norwich Thorpe after reversal at Cromer. But, although there were increases in patronage and revenue, these were still not sufficient to indicate that with complete dieselisation the passenger service would show a profit.

GOODS TRAFFIC: ROAD COMPETITION

The so-called 'denationalisation' of road transport by the Transport Act of 1953 had a very serious effect on the goods traffic. From 1948 much freight, which in many cases would have been better kept on rail, especially for long journeys, was conveyed on British Road Services vehicles owned by the BTC, on the natural arguments that the receipts would go into the same BTC 'national' pocket anyway, and that the customers had often said they preferred road transport. But the 1953 Act removed a very large number of vehicles from BRS, which were purchased by private hauliers (often the same hauliers that had owned them before nationalisation) who were entitled as of right to 'Special A' licences for the vehicles for five years. Thereafter these hauliers frequently carried the traffic which the vehicles had been conveying for BRS—much of which might have been better sent by rail. Furthermore, the rule was abolished whereby private hauliers were restricted to a 25-mile radius (except for specified traffics) without BRS permission. So the private haulier again competed generally for traffic, with the same advantages, especially direct conveyance from farm to market as before. There was also much irregular running of lorries carrying fruit and vegetables from the district, which was not punished as it ought to have been, in the interests both of the railways and of the many honest road hauliers who complied with the law. The consequences of all this began to be felt seriously in 1955-6. More favourable rates for fruit were offered, but they did not attract traffic back to rail in any large quantities. What was left of the fish traffic also suffered from road competition accentuated by irregular running of lorries.

From September 1956 a regular traffic of stone was sent from Holt to Bawtry near Doncaster, for which more than thirty former iron ore hopper wagons were used. Unfortunately another loss of valuable traffic in the same district occurred in 1957, when the army began to run down its Stiffkey and Weybourne camps. Holt and Weybourne had been two of the busiest stations for military traffic on a system which had carried so much before, during and after two great wars; both camps were closed in 1959.

FLOODS AGAIN

In consequence of the Welland floods, the catchment board

diverted the river three-quarters of a mile to the east of Clay Lake box (formerly Cunningham's Drove). The line was temporarily diverted to the south and special sidings provided in August 1951. The level crossing now had to be manually operated instead of mechanically from the signal box. A new single-line girder bridge over the new course of the river was opened on 7 June 1953.

On 31 January 1953 a combination of gales and spring tides again caused severe flooding. The station and goods yard at South Lynn were inundated. At Yarmouth both South Town and Vauxhall were flooded, leaving only Beach in use. Lowestoft Central was 3 ft under water. Owing to the condition of the GE line near Lynn the Royal train used the M & GN route.

CHAPTER NINE

Closure

SPECIAL INVESTIGATION

Because of the many difficulties and continued losses in working, and the serious financial position of the railways as a whole, the Eastern Region appointed a special committee to consider the closure of most of the M & GN. It made a full investigation, and upon its report the region recommended substantial closure to the British Transport Commission on 19 May 1958. The Minister of Transport, the Transport Users Consultative Committees, and the unions were informed.

A statement to the press issued on 13 June referred to attempts made to improve services and operate them more economically, and stated that losses had been reduced. But it added there were 'big losses on other services, and the extent to which they could be financed out of proceeds of profitable services had been limited by recent trends. A new point of balance must be found between obligations of public service, and requirements of the railway budget'. It referred to the duplication of former GE and M & GN routes, often close together, and indicated how compensating services could be provided; it reiterated the difficulty of retaining passenger services in rural areas where buses were more convenient and quoted the 'beneficial results' of the diesel services, but stated there was now sufficient experience to show that to make them profitable all over the system there would have to be an increase in traffic which was 'simply not available' in the area. Furthermore the volume of freight traffic was not sufficient to justify continuance of the line as a separate route. It was estimated that a saving of £500,000 would be effected, besides avoidance of heavy engineering expenditure, particularly for rebuilding the West Lynn (referred to as the Clenchwarton) bridge.

Under the proposals Peterboro'—Yarmouth, Saxby—Sutton Bridge and Melton—Norwich would disappear as passenger routes. Compensating holiday services to Cromer and Yarmouth by GE routes were promised, with improvements. Arrangements with the Lincolnshire Road Car and Eastern Counties bus companies for substitution of local and, in some cases, long distance buses would be made; these were agreed on 28 August. Peterboro'—Yarmouth, and Little Bytham Junction—Sutton Bridge would also disappear as through freight routes, but Peterboro'—Wisbech, Spalding—Sutton Bridge, Lynn—Gayton Road and Melton—Norwich would remain in use for goods.

The matter was formally submitted to the local TUCC, the East Anglian, on 13 September. For the benefit of members who desired to inspect the line a special train was run on 26 September. On 30 September there was a joint meeting of the East Anglian and East Midland TUCCs at Peterboro'.

The attitude of so many of the general public to railway closure proposals has often been unreasonable and illogical. They used the bus to reach the next village or the large town, they went to the seaside by coach, they owned private cars in rapidly increasing numbers, and they sent goods, often for long distances, by lorry. Yet, when there had been a railway in their district for many years, they professed they could not understand why it should be closed. If the coach or lorry did not come, or the car broke down, they expected the railway to be there, without considering whether it was now suitable to the general needs of the district, or whether it paid.

THE TUCC INQUIRY

The formal inquiry before the East Anglian TUCC was held at the Shirehall, Norwich, on 14-15 October. Mr Johnson, General Manager, Eastern Region (later Sir Henry Johnson, Chairman of British Railways), presented the case for closure. He referred to the BTC's deficit which was already £27 million and mentioned recent statements by ministers 'that railways should shed non-paying services'. Obligations dating from days of near monopoly could no longer be maintained and the spending of large sums of money under the 1955 modernisation plan could only be justified if non-paying lines were discarded. The holiday traffic was limited to a short season and was largely 'Saturdays only', and the Norwich—Melton diesels had only increased traffic by 10 per cent. The total saving from closure would be nearly £1 million, while coal merchants and other traders would be assisted by the granting of facilities at GE stations and by negotiation of suitable terms.

OBJECTIONS

It was noticeable, in a long list of objectors, how few represented substantial traffics. The only objections concerning fish traffic related to Cromer crabs and to the conveyance of fish from the north of Scotland to Yarmouth—a clear confirmation of the decline of the traffic. Several public bodies in the fruit-growing areas complained, but only three consignors did, a sad and eloquent comment on the reduction of the fruit traffic. The Stalham representative, speaking for Broadland, stressed the importance of the line for people going on the Broads, but admitted that only 25 per cent arrived by rail; at one time, it would have been nearly 100 per cent. It was also admitted that the cattle market there was now entirely served by road. Naturally the holiday camps objected, as campers arriving by rail would have to come via Yarmouth Vauxhall, with (so it was alleged) inconvenient buses and roads between there and the camps, instead of coming in their special train to Caister, Hemsby, or the halts. But even here it was admitted that only 25 per cent of the campers arrived by rail.

The Yarmouth representative admitted the general decline of the fishing industry and said it was important in the town's interest that there should be more holidaymakers by way of compensation. The inadequate size of Yarmouth Vauxhall station and carriage sidings to cope with more holiday trains was a serious ground of complaint, as Mr Johnson admitted. He explained the problem of keeping so many carriages for a short holiday season and promised enlargement of the station and sidings.

People living between Melton and Norwich said the diesels

were useful and well patronised, and that the buses were inconvenient and insufficient. Murrow also complained of the bus services, and Whaplode, which had no diesel service, asked for one. It was the well-known problem of the rural area where neither the train nor the bus was likely to pay. Some of the districts, in a more favourable atmosphere, might have qualified for subsidised assistance to the railway—or the bus operator—and several objectors suggested this. There were many references to congestion on narrow roads, actual and prospective (by, for example, the representative of Hunstanton, which did not want to lose its trains by the M & GN route). But if so much of the traffic had gone to the roads, then the roads should have been improved.

There were, of course, faithful rail users who objected: Anglian Building Products at Lenwade, East Anglian Grain at Rudham, Cooper Roller Bearings at Lynn, a turkey consignor at Drayton, a mushroom farmer near Martham, several coal merchants, and some holiday passengers from Leicester. The Norfolk Farmers Union referred to fertilisers and feeding stuffs, and there was also the sugar beet traffic. But such traffics, though important to the consignors, when set against the traffics no longer carried only emphasised the difficulties of railway officers who recommended closure, and of the TUCCs and the minister in making decisions. It was significant how little was said about flowers and vegetables, once so valuable.

The National Union of Railwaymen referred to the possible extension of diesel operation, suggested the new fruit rates should have had a longer trial and mentioned the value of the line in national emergencies and the good condition of the track. It also spoke of the value of the Spalding—Saxby line as a through route, and as a means of access to the Bourne—Sleaford line, still in use for goods to Billingboro'. There was a danger that passengers might have to travel via London at increased fares.

Mr Johnson's reply included references to the alternative facilities offered, particularly to Cromer, Sheringham and Hunstanton, negotiations with East Anglian Grain, concentration facilities for coal, continuance of Melton—Norwich services for goods, and better buses for Murrow.

CLOSURE

THE DECISION

Despite Norfolk County Council's suggestion of a two year postponement and a further review of the situation then, the committee substantially approved the closure proposals, finding that the saving would be £640,000. It said the NCC's suggestion of postponement could cost £2 million and found that the alternative facilities offered were reasonable. It did not agree that the Norwich—Melton diesel passenger service should be retained, and did not accept all the extra costs alleged by the coal merchants, but said the railway should give them favourable consideration. It recommended special treatment of East Anglian Grain, modernisation of Yarmouth Vauxhall, and improved bus services for Murrow.

On 11 November the East Midland committee, sitting at Bourne, also heard objections. It approved the proposals, subject to retention of the Spalding—Bourne line and the section thence to Billingboro' for freight.

After Mr Chambers, the secretary, had inspected the lines affected and made a report, the Central Transport Consultative Committee approved the closure proposals on 26 November. The Bourne—Little Bytham section would be entirely closed, as would the old Midland line thence to South Witham, but the portion from there to Saxby would remain open for goods.

SERVICES IN THE LAST TWO YEARS

Attempts were still being made to attract more holiday passengers by altering places served by the Saturday trains. In 1957-8 one train came from Chesterfield and the Erewash valley stations, and the Mansfield trains ran to and from Shirebrook. There were still at least eleven Saturdays only trains from the Midlands advertised in those summers, including the Hunstanton trains but not the trains for the camps. In 1958 one Saturdays only train ran through from Norwich Thorpe to Peterboro' via Cromer Beach and Melton.

The names Great Northern and Great Eastern were officially revived by the Eastern Region for areas on 1 January 1958, so that the M & GN for the last year of full operation was part of what was formally described as the GE. There was another serious blizzard on 25 February 1958. Several trains were held up by snow drifts, and the eastbound Leicester was diverted via March and the GE route.

Eye Green, Thorney and Wryde stations were closed to passengers on 2 December 1957, and North Drove followed on 15 September 1958. The North Walsham Town—Antingham Road Junction section, which had for some years been very little used, was closed on 8 April 1958, as a bridge on it had become unsafe. A single-line trailing connection was laid between the GE line and the M & GN line south of the stations, and was brought into use on 4 May. The Liverpool Street—Caister holiday camp trains used it in the summer, reversing there instead of at Antingham Road Junction. The Spalding avoiding line subsided dangerously at the end of the year, and for the last few weeks of operation was used only by light engines.

28 FEBRUARY 1959

The minister duly confirmed the findings of the TUCCs, and the sad last day of so much of the line was Saturday 28 February 1959. With the above exceptions the full service was maintained to the end. A journey on the westbound Leicester from South Lynn on Saturday 14 February, when it was reasonably well patronised, gave no indication that the end was so near. On the last day large crowds turned out both to travel on the trains and to watch. The last westbound Leicester reached Spalding (after nine Norwich Thorpe—Sheffield football specials had arrived via the GE route) bearing a placard 'That's Yer Lot', the work of a shunter. Other trains had decorations too, among them a laurel wreath with 'Farewell M & GN', and 'Farewell Crab and Winkle'—supposed to be associated with Yarmouth's coat of arms. The last passenger train of all was the 10.48 pm from Yarmouth Beach to Stalham.

One might wish that the public could have been informed more fully of the decline of traffic, either at the inquiries before the TUCCs, or through the press. The TUCCs and the minister could only deal with the situation as it was and did not enquire how, for example, the loss of fruit or fish traffic came about. The public could have more readily appreciated the reasons for such a substantial closure if it had been more generally known how traffics had been lost. Many traffics, even at their best, were seasonal, and when such traffic had declined to negligible amounts the problem of keeping the line open became even greater.

SURVIVING FREIGHT SERVICES

It was found that the Gayton Road—East Rudham section could be operated cheaply so, as the East Anglian TUCC had recommended special consideration for East Anglian Grain, it was kept open for goods with one train daily each way. The attraction of Gayton Road itself was the conveyance of sand for industrial purposes.

There was still considerable freight traffic on the Melton—Norwich City line. Through trains had to go a long way round to get there, and went over the Newstead Lane Junction—Runton West Junction spur, which had been little used since the closing of Cromer High and the transfer of all traffic to Cromer Beach. It was decided to build a connecting line at Themelthorpe, north of Whitwell, with the Aylsham South—County School line. The junction faced north, to allow direct running between Aylsham South and Norwich City. A junction at this point had been considered as far back as 1880 but laid the other way, for through running between Aylsham South and Melton (see Chapter 3). The new junction was brought into use on 12 September 1960 and the section from Themelthorpe to Aylsham South, which had been closed to goods as well as passengers, was reopened; the Themelthorpe—Melton section was closed. For economy the route from Wroxham through Aylsham to Themelthorpe was operated as a light railway. One of the principal users of the line was Anglian Building Products of Lenwade, which had been an objector at the closure inquiry. Other traffics included roadstone, glass bottles and coal to Norwich City.

Most of the old Union line at Yarmouth, which had remained in use after the closure of Breydon viaduct, was closed in February 1959. But the M & GN's own coal yard at

White Swan, north of the junction with the GE tramway, was still served by trains coming through the Vauxhall goods line; so 200 yd of the M & GN remained in use until closure in 1976.

In order to retain access to the Dogsthorpe and Eye Green brickfields, and to Wisbech North and the harbour line there, and avoid the expense of retaining for limited traffic the bridge over the Midland and GN lines north of Westwood Junction, Peterboro', it was decided to make a junction at Murrow between the M & GN and the March—Spalding line. The connecting line left the latter just south of the level crossing of the two lines, and turned west to join the M & GN so that trains could run direct between March and the brickfields, and reach Wisbech North after reversal at the new West Junction. The connection was laid in on 17 December 1960, and first used on 2 January 1961. The section from Wisbech Junction, north of Westwood, over the bridge to Dogsthorpe was formally closed on 26 March 1961, but the last train had run on 31 December 1960.

The 1958 North Walsham connecting line and the M & GN Town Goods Yard remained in use for some time, and part still is, as the GE yard was not large enough for all traffic.

COMPENSATING SERVICES

The compensating holiday services in the summer of 1959 by GE routes had some unusual features. A Derby Saturdays only train used Friargate station there, and ran via the GN, Sleaford and March, the first Yarmouth train from Friargate shown in the timetables since 1914. There was a Shirebrook train, and Ollerton and Sheffield trains used former Lancashire, Derbyshire & East Coast routes. As some compensation for loss of the Birmingham carriages on the Leicesters, a daily service ran all-year-round between Birmingham and Norwich Thorpe by the LNW route and Peterboro' East with a restaurant car. But there were no daily through Leicester trains, which survived only on summer Saturdays, when there was also a Leicester—Sheringham. The up 'Broadsman', 7.54 am from Cromer Beach with through carriages from Melton, reached Liverpool Street in 2 hours 51 minutes, a schedule reminiscent of the best days of the Liverpool Street—North Walsham non-stop runs. Other trains had a 2 hour 55 minute schedule with a Norwich change. The Melton—Cromer Beach line had a good service, and there were Sunday trains to and from Holt, but not Melton.

The GE East Suffolk line from Beccles to Yarmouth South Town was closed to passenger traffic on 2 November 1959. The Liverpool Street—Ipswich—Beccles—South Town service was diverted via Lowestoft Central and the N & S line through Gorleston, which presented a scene of great activity, especially in the following summer when so many trains from Liverpool Street and the Midlands were run over it. The track was improved and the bridges strengthened.

Weybourne station was by now little used and the up loop and signal box went out of use on 6 June 1961. However, the Duke of Edinburgh visited Weybourne on 30 May 1963 in the royal train, the last appearance of a steam-hauled train on the line.

It was soon found uneconomical to work so many trains through, all year round, between Liverpool Street and Cromer Beach, Sheringham and Melton, as the patronage did not justify it. Accordingly from the summer of 1962 through Liverpool Street—Cromer and Sheringham trains were confined to summer Saturdays, some using the Wensum curve, as in the days of the North Walsham non-stops. But Cromer Beach could still be reached in 3 hours all year round, with a change at Norwich.

MORE CLOSURES

On 21 April 1963 the Newstead Lane—Runton West Junction line was closed, the Runton West, and Newstead Lane to Runton East Junction sections singled, and the Runton East—Cromer Beach section adapted as two single lines instead of a double line. At Cromer Beach the old type of apparatus for tablet delivery (see Chapter 5 and Fig 4) can still be seen in use.

The Beeching report, published in April 1963, recommended withdrawal of the passenger services between Melton and Sheringham, and between North Walsham and Mundesley. Action was postponed for a time, but the minister approved the proposals and passenger services ceased between Melton and Sheringham on 6 April 1964, and between North Walsham and Mundesley on 5 October.

Limited freight traffic included that of the sheet factory at Melton, and some sugar beet and fertiliser, but it was decided to close both sections at the end of the year. The Bawtry stone traffic from Holt had not survived the 1959 closures, but there was some beet from Paston right up to the end.

To accommodate the holiday traffic, Yarmouth Vauxhall and its sidings, were improved and enlarged as promised. But from 1962 the policy was adopted of bringing the best, and later all, the through Liverpool Street trains there (running in and out of Thorpe, or using the Wensum curve), instead of via Lowestoft and Gorleston to South Town, so that the N & S line there did not become the main London—Yarmouth route, as had seemed likely in 1960. The original scheme for the Eastern Counties, of course, was for a line from London to Yarmouth via Ipswich and Norwich.

MORE ECONOMIES

The Leicester and Derby to Cromer and Sheringham Saturday trains did not run after the summer of 1966. In that year there were still Liverpool Street—Cromer and Sheringham summer Saturday trains, while there was a limited Sunday service to Sheringham from 31 July to 11 September only.

Further economies were effected on 2 January 1967 by making all stations between Norwich Thorpe and Cromer and Sheringham unstaffed halts. Sheringham station was closed to ordinary traffic, and a new halt provided on the east side of the level crossing. The latter is quite unstaffed, but Cromer Beach is unstaffed only from the passengers' point of view, as it has signalmen, and also offers goods facilities. The diesel sets have conductor-guards, as the North Walsham—Mundesley— Cromer Beach and some of the Yarmouth—Potter Heigham locals used to have.

No through trains from Liverpool Street to Cromer and Sheringham, and no Sunday Sheringham and West Runton services were shown in the published timetables for the summer of 1967, but advertised only by special notice there was a through Liverpool Street—Cromer and Sheringham train on Saturdays only from early June to early September, composed of diesel sets. The three trains each way on Sundays between Norwich and Cromer all worked to and from the new halt at Sheringham (stopping at West Runton) also only advertised by special notice for the same period. In the summer of 1968 these Sunday trains for Sheringham and West Runton were shown in the public timetables, but the through Saturday train between Liverpool Street and Sheringham was not; it ran again from early June to early September by special notice.

Similar arrangements were adopted on the N & S Yarmouth South Town—Lowestoft Central line from 12 September 1966; all the diesel sets had a conductor-guard, and Gorleston-on-Sea, Hopton, Corton and Lowestoft North became unstaffed, like Gorleston Links. But here there were still twelve passenger trains each way all year round.

After the disappearance of through goods trains to and from the M & GN on this line owing to the closure of Breydon viaduct in 1953, there was a daily pick-up between Lowestoft Central and South Town. But this ceased on 4 November 1967 and the same weekend the line was singled. As Gorleston, Hopton and Corton boxes had already been closed, Lowestoft North box, closed on 5 November, was the last N & S box in use. The passenger service was withdrawn in May 1970, so this N & S section is closed too.

There is a regular Birmingham—Leicester—Peterborough—March—Norwich Thorpe service, including Sundays. The summer Saturday Liverpool Street—Sheringham was in the timetable, 1970-5, but not since. However, the Norwich—Cromer—Sheringham local service has been increased, including Sheringham Sunday trains all the year round.

GOODS SERVICES WITHDRAWN

The Dogsthorpe—Wisbech, Spalding—Bourne—Billingborough and Spalding—Sutton Bridge sections were operated as economically as possible by singling double sections and abolishing crossing places and signal boxes. On the Thorney—Murrow section the old 'staff and ticket' method was reintroduced. But owing to freight concentration at larger stations these sections too were eventually closed. A portion of the old GN Billingborough—Bourne line from Billingborough to Hacconby sidings was the first to go, on 15 June 1964. Spalding—Bourne—Hacconby followed on 5 April 1965; it was used for storing trucks for some time but was later taken up. Spalding—Sutton Bridge was closed on 1 May 1965, the Wisbech harbour (M & GN) branch on 4 January 1965, and the Wisbech—Murrow section on 31 October. Murrow—Dogsthorpe was operated for a time on the 'one engine in steam' principle but was closed on 18 April 1966.

Freight on the South Lynn—Gayton Road—East Rudham section ended on 6 May 1968. King's Lynn Harbour Junction to South Lynn is in use. The old South Lynn goods yard is closed; activity is now concentrated at the site of the old engine shed on the opposite side of the line. The British Sugar Corporation factory (see Chapter 6) at South Lynn still provides valuable traffic. The King's Lynn Harbour branch (see Chapters 2 and 6) is still in use as far as the first swing bridge, and the King's Lynn Dock lines are in full operation.

Early in 1969 goods traffic ceased to be dealt with at Norwich City, so the section from there to Drayton was closed on 3 February of that year, and goods trains via Themelthorpe only ran as far as Drayton.

Thus, the M & GN has almost disappeared. Born in the days of expansion and competition between railway companies, it long gave good service to the public. But in changed conditions, when railways, especially in country districts, are faced with competition from other forms of transport and are beset with difficulties, it is not surprising that it did not survive. Statistics of the main closure 28 February 1959, effective officially as from 2 March 1959.

Mileage closed entirely	79 m 24 ch*
„ „ for passenger trains	161 m 40 ch
Stations closed entirely	30†
„ „ to passengers only	24

* does not include Little Bytham Junction to South Witham (LMS line) 5 m 5 ch
† includes Langor Bridge and Bluestone goods depots

CHAPTER TEN

The Rolling Stock

EARLY DAYS. MIDLAND ENGINES

Midland engines on the Peterboro'—Sutton Bridge—Lynn passenger services were at first 2-2-2s. But from 1874 they were generally 2-4-0s of Kirtley's last design, the 1070 series. These had 6 ft 2½ in drivers and 18 by 24 in cylinders, and were built at Derby. As they also worked on the Leicester line, they were stationed at Peterboro', with two, generally Nos 1071 and 1073, outshedded at Lynn. They were rebuilt by Johnson in 1887 and continued on the line until the joint engines took over. They were renumbered 127-146 in 1907, and had long careers. Midland goods engines, including those on the few Midland trains on the Sutton Bridge—Bourne section, were usually Kirtley 0-6-0s, including Nos 524-5 and 530, with one generally shedded at Lynn. They had 5 ft 2 in drivers and 17 by 24 in cylinders.

GN ENGINES

GN engines for branch service in the 1860s included old Sharp 2-2-2s, 2-2-2 tanks (rebuilt from tender engines), Sturrock 0-4-2 tanks, and from 1872, Stirling 0-4-4 tanks. But after 1871 the GN generally used standard Stirling mixed traffic 0-4-2s on the Bourne—Spalding—Lynn service. They had 5 ft 7 in drivers and 17 by 24 in inside cylinders. No 13 was at Lynn GE shed for a time, and No 85 was at Spalding (both built at Doncaster in 1871-2). Nos 557-9 (Sharp Stewart, 1876) were also used. It is surprising that the tanks were not employed more, as some trips were short, and several trains reversed at Spalding. But the 0-4-2s were regarded as good maids-of-all-work. One nearly fell into the river after passing signals at danger when the old Sutton Bridge was open; the leading wheels overhung the water before the engine was pulled back.

GY & S ENGINES

The GY & S's first engines in 1877 were two small 0–6–0 saddle tanks, *Ormesby* and *Stalham* (later Nos 15 and 16). They were built by Fox Walker of Bristol. Black Hawthorn then supplied a similar engine, but early in 1878 it was transferred to the L & F and named *Ida* after the chairman's daughter; it later became No 7. To replace it, in 1881 Black Hawthorn sent the Y & NN (as it had become) another, *Aylsham* (later No 17).

Dimensions of engines of the E & M and M & GN, in original condition, are given in Appendix 5.

L & F ENGINES

Two of the earliest engines on the L & F were even smaller, *Alpha* and *Vici*, 0–4–0 tanks from Hudswell Clarke. At first they belonged to Wilkinson & Jarvis. *Alpha* appeared in October 1878, worked on construction of the line, and with *Ida* ran trains from the opening day. *Vici* arrived in December 1880. They were taken officially into the company's stock in 1881 and numbered 4 and 5. *Holt*, similar to *Ida*, arrived the same year and later became No 6. This engine was later renamed *Chairman*.

4–4–0 TANKS

The two locomotive departments were closely associated at an early date, and the 4–4–0 tanks appeared almost simultaneously on both lines. They were pretty little engines, but were nevertheless quite powerful and proved successful on passenger trains. They were designed by Massey Bromley, just before his appointment as locomotive superintendent of the GE, and were built by Hudswell Clarke. The first, *North Walsham* (later No 32), was delivered to the Y & NN in September 1878, and the second, *Hillington* (later No 8), came to the L & F in November. *North Walsham* had its slide bars and crosshead enclosed by iron casing to keep out sand on the Yarmouth—Ormesby section. The next pair, *Martham* (later No 31), and *Fakenham* (later No 9) had slightly more heating surface and 1 in larger cylinders, and were delivered to the Y & NN and L & F respectively in March and June 1879. The latter was the only one of the class to have the Westinghouse brake. The next, *Norwich* (later No 10), which came to the L & F in October 1880, was similar but had increased water and fuel capacity. Two more, identical to *Norwich*, came in October 1881, *Great Yarmouth* (later No 19) to the Y & NN, and *King's Lynn* (later No 20) to the L & F.

0–6–0 TANKS

In December 1880 the L & F obtained three 0–6–0 tanks from Sharp Stewarts. They belonged originally to a class of eighteen supplied in 1873-4 to the Cornwall Minerals Railway; when the Great Western took over that line it kept nine and returned nine to the makers. On the L & F they had their bunkers enlarged, and cabs fitted, and were named *Melton Constable*, *Reepham* and *Blakeney* (later Nos 1-3).

In anticipation of the opening of extensions, the L & F ordered some 4–4–0 tender engines, but as they were not delivered in time five more of the ex-Cornwall Minerals engines were obtained from Sharp Stewart. To increase their coal and water capacity for main-line work, Sharp Stewart supplied four-wheel tenders with them, and also sent similar tenders for the original three, so that the whole class was used as tender engines from 1883. These five received numbers 11-14 and 18.

With their small driving wheels they were still not really suitable for long journeys and in 1890-2 four of them were rebuilt at Melton as 2–4–0s, to the design of Mr Marriott, Nos 18, 13, 3 and 14 in that order. The whole engine was raised 2½ in and new 4 ft 7 in driving wheels were fitted; the leading wheels remained 3 ft 6in. The side tanks were removed and splashers substituted, and new cabs were provided.

BEYER 4-4-0S

The first four 4-4-0s ordered by the L & F were built by Beyer Peacock in 1881 and delivered in March 1882. They were somewhat similar to Adams' design for the London & South Western (recently executed by Beyers) but smaller. With copper-capped chimneys and Ramsbottom safety valves they had a handsome appearance. They had the Westinghouse brake, and their numbers were 21-24.

LIVERIES

The L & F livery was green with black and white panel bands, red frames, and vermilion buffer beams and cab insides, but the first set of Cornwall Minerals tanks were painted chocolate. The carriages were four-wheeled, varnished teak, with clerestory roofs. Y & NN engines were a darker green. The carriages were rather similar to those on the L & F but were also of darker colour.

E & M ENGINES

Four more 4-4-0s ordered by the L & F just before the amalgamation and built early in 1883 were delivered in November. They differed slightly in appearance, as the domes were higher, and were painted chocolate, with red, white and blue lining; this was adopted as the E & M livery. Their numbers were 25-8. There were some derailments of these heavier engines on the light permanent way, so the whole class was provided with jacks.

Three more 4-4-0s, Nos 29-31, arrived in November 1886 and had GN Stirling-pattern chimneys. Four more came in May 1888, Nos 32-5. They were fitted with vacuum as well as Westinghouse brakes for working the through trains to Kings Cross. To make way for them, 4-4-0 tanks, Nos 31-2, were renumbered 40-1.

The L & F numbered its engines shortly before amalgamation and they retained their numbers afterwards, when the Y & NN engines, which had previously had only names, were numbered too. Soon the names began to disappear from most of the engines.

In November 1883 the E & M bought two 2-4-0s from the London & North Western, originally Lancaster & Carlisle engines built in 1857 to Allan's 'Crewe' design. On the LNW they had been Nos 377 *Rickerby* and 384 *Luck of Edenhall*, later 1101 and 1112, and had been rebuilt by Webb. On the E & M they were at first Nos 29-30 and later 42-3.

HEADCODES

When the old route to Lynn from Bawsey was in use the headcode was a green disc with a white rim at the point of the chimney, and a green light at night. A white disc with a black cross was also used as a headcode by the E & M; but the M & GN committee did not use such indications, and adopted the standard headlamp code in the 1900s.

CARRIAGE STOCK

In 1893 the committee took over in all, 39 engines and, according to the records, 104 coaches. The latter consisted of 30 old four-wheelers, 28 six-wheelers which were regarded as E & M standard, 28 obtained second-hand from the North London, and 18 six-wheelers transferred from the Midland. Mr Johnson, reporting to the committee in 1894, said that there were 121 coaches; but the discrepancy can probably be accounted for by some old carriages which had been converted to vans, being reckoned as coaches, and by the return to the Midland and to the GN of some old carriages of theirs which had been transferred and were now nearly worn out.

The committee broke up many of the older vehicles, and hired some from the parent companies, so that early in 1901 it owned only about 70; there were over 80 on hire from the GN and Midland, and over 40 more were required. Disputes arose over the hiring terms, and Mr Marriott considered it better for the committee to own its carriages, as the Somerset & Dorset did. Accordingly, the GN and Midland transferred the vehicles, so that by 1906 the committee owned 220. Many carriages were lit by gas instead of the old oil lamps, and a gas works was established at Melton. Some of the E & M standards which had roofs arched high at the sides, were painted dull red-brown, grained to represent mahogany, with blue door edges and frames, and others were painted and grained varnished teak. They long retained these liveries under the committee's regime.

E & M ENGINES WITHDRAWN

After the committee took charge, the 4-4-0 tender and tank engines remained in use for a long while, but most of the other E & M engines disappeared in a few years. Several went at once on to a duplicate list. This happened to 6 and 7 which became 6A and 7A, were sold in 1894 to T. W. Ward (later Ibstock Brick Co.) and survived for many years. No 15, after working as a shunter at Yarmouth, painted black, was sold to a colliery in 1900; No 17, as 17A, was works shunter at Melton until 1901 when it was scrapped. The four Cornwall Minerals, rebuilt as 2-4-0s, and the former LNW 2-4-0s, all went on the 'A' list and were scrapped within about three years. The other Cornwall Minerals, still 0-6-0s, remained in use for longer. The last in service was No 12A, broken up in 1902; its last duty was on the construction of the Yarmouth—Gorleston section over Breydon water. The wheels and some other parts of these engines, and of those rebuilt as 2-4-0s, were used in the construction of new 0-6-0 tank engines to be described later, while their four-wheeled tenders remained in use as water tanks for many years. The little 0-4-0 tank engines, and No 16A, an 0-6-0 tank, were to have long careers under the committee. All former E & M engines working for the committee retained their E & M numbers except as noted.

ASSISTANCE BY GN AND MIDLAND ENGINES

When the through trains from the Midlands via Saxby and Bourne were put on, they were worked for some years by the Midland west of the latter point. Old No 198A, a Kirtley 2-4-0 built by Beyers in 1867 and rebuilt by Johnson in 1882, was stationed at Saltley, Birmingham, for this purpose. Other engines used included some 6 ft 8½ in 2-4-0s of Kirtley's

THE ROLLING STOCK 177

famous '800' class of the batch built at Derby and numbered from 60, and some of the '1492' class (renumbered from 272 in 1907). These latter were the Johnson 7 ft 2-4-0s of 1881, and were the last Midland 2-4-0s built. Before the committee had sufficient engines to operate the whole joint system, some GN and Midland engines were hired to assist. The Midland engines included No 185A (similar to No 198A), which was stationed at Yarmouth, some of the '1740' class of 7 ft Johnson 4-4-0s of 1885-7, and others of the '1808' class of 6 ft 6 in Johnson 4-4-0s of 1888-91, which were very similar to the M & GN 4-4-0s that were arriving at that time. The GN engines were standard Stirling 6 ft 7 in 2-4-0s, including the then new Nos 996-7, built at Doncaster early in 1894. Some of the engines left later in 1894, as soon as the first of the M & GN 4-4-0s arrived, and others remained until 1899. Midland goods engines stationed at Spalding at this period included Nos 1711, 2018-9 and 2630. Some of the older class were later at Bourne. There were also Midland 0-4-4 tank engines on some locals west of Spalding.

THE JOHNSON 4-4-0S TAKE OVER

The first batch of ten Johnson 4-4-0s for the M & GN, ordered in 1893, arrived in June-July 1894. They were Nos 36-9 and 42-7. The second batch of sixteen came later the same year, Nos 48-50, 1-7, 11-14 and 17-18. They were built by Sharp Stewart. They were very similar to the Midland '2203' class of 1893, save that the M & GN engines did not have the flush-lagged smokebox, but the more usual pattern. The third batch also from Sharps, Nos 51-7, came in 1896, and the fourth, from Beyers, Nos 74-80, in 1899. They were similar to the contemporary Midland '2581' class, except that they had slightly less water and coal capacity. In the committee's livery which was described as yellow, golden ochre (not such a bright yellow as that of the London, Brighton & South Coast), these 4-4-0s were handsome engines indeed. From 1894 to 1925 they were known as the 'C' class. Some for a time had 'Jt M & GN' on the tender, instead of the usual 'M & GN'.

The whole class remained in use as the principal passenger engines until 1936, and frequently hauled goods trains too.

Except for those later rebuilt with large boilers, they were altered little. It is interesting to note that nearly all the Midland engines of similar design were 'renewed' (in fact replaced) by standard class '2' 4–4–0s after comparatively short lives, while the M & GN engines remained in service for a much longer period. Early in 1905 three of them were first provided with steam heating apparatus for working on the through Kings Cross trains. From 1899 when they were all in service the appearance on an M & GN passenger train of one of the parent companies' engines was rare, except on specials and at busy holiday times. One of them, stationed at Norwich, took over the operation of the through express to and from Leicester in October 1902; previously this service had been worked by a Midland engine west of Bourne. The committee used the automatic vacuum brake, which in 1893 was the standard of the parent companies.

THE JOHNSON 0–6–0S

The standard Midland Johnson 0–6–0 goods design was introduced on the M & GN in 1896, when eight of the type arrived, Nos 58-65. They were similar to the '2284' series then appearing on the Midland, and were from the same makers, Neilson. In 1899 eight more appeared, Nos 66-73, built by Kitson; they were very similar to the Midland '2391' series from the same makers. The 0–6–0s were used for goods traffic all over the system, and often ran passenger excursions and relief trains at busy times. They were the 'D' class.

THE IVATT 0–6–0S

Next year, 1900, Mr Johnson reported to the committee that owing to increased traffic there was a shortage of engines, especially for goods. This was characteristic of other lines at the time, when both the GN and Midland obtained American 2–6–0s. For the M & GN, however, the committee chose a standard GN type. Twelve of a batch of thirty-five Ivatt 0–6–0s being built by Dübs & Co for the GN were obtained, and became Nos 81-92. They were generally used for goods on the old Western section. In fact, the author cannot remember ever

THE ROLLING STOCK

seeing one at Cromer or Yarmouth. Perhaps they preferred to stay near other GN engines! They were the 'Da' class.

CLASSES OF ENGINES

Designation of classes of engine by letter was done officially by the locomotive department. But the 4–4–0, 0–6–0 and 0–4–0 tanks were never given a class letter.

REBUILDING OF BEYER 4–4–0S

From 1896 all the Beyer Peacock outside-cylinder 4–4–0s were rebuilt in order of their ages; the first to be so treated was No 21 in 1896 and the last, No 35 in 1909. They received 140-lb boilers similar to the Johnson 4–4–0s but slightly shorter, and the Ramsbottom safety valves in consequence disappeared. There were other changes in their appearance too, as some were fitted with what were called 'Melton' chimneys rather Midland in style, and one had an Ivatt chimney. Several received extended smokeboxes. Nos 33-5 had larger cabs and tender weather boards for working tender first. Some had train heating apparatus of Midland type, and others the Laycock heating apparatus for use with GN stock. In the 1900s they were frequently on the Cromer line but by 1919-21 they could be seen on North Walsham—Yarmouth slow trains, and on the Lowestoft line. There were generally one or two at Spalding. They often hauled light goods trains. Between 1914 and 1927 Nos 21-8 received 160-lb boilers and extended smokeboxes, while Nos 29-30 received extended smokeboxes only. The whole class was given larger tenders and throughout their careers on the M & GN were known as the 'A's.

NEW TANK CLASSES

Between 1897 and 1905 nine smart little 0–6–0 tank engines were built at Melton for shunting duties, and some parts from the old Cornwall Minerals engines were incorporated in them. Their original numbers, in order of appearance, were 14A, 1A, 3A, 11A, 15, 12A, 17A, 2A and 16. They had connecting rods on the second pair of wheels, and were equipped with the vacuum brake. In January 1907 those with the 'A' numbers were renumbered 93-9.

When the Lowestoft line was opened, Mr Marriott designed a handsome 4–4–2 tank engine. The first of the class, No 41, appeared from Melton in 1904. The chimney was 'Melton' design, but the closed dome and the 1904 Derby-pattern Ramsbottom safety valve were characteristic of contemporary Midland practice. The outside cylinders produced a similar appearance to that of the Beyer 4–4–0s. Two more, Nos 20 and 9, came in 1909, and the whole class had tablet exchangers and Midland train heating apparatus. They ran, as intended, on the Lowestoft line, but they also worked between North Walsham and Yarmouth, on the Cromer and Mundesley lines, and between Lynn and Spalding. It is surprising that Mr Marriott provided no more, in view of the reversing stations, and the popularity of the 4–4–2 tank type on other lines at the period. They were the last engines to be built new for the committee, and were the 'A tank' class.

TRAVELS OF 4–4–0 TANKS

The 4–4–0 tanks were rebuilt with larger boilers, beginning with No 41 in 1894, and ending with No 19 in 1903. The new boilers had mountings in accordance with Derby practice, Melton chimneys and brass dome casings. As altered, they had 821 sq ft of heating surface and 140-lb pressure. No 41 was withdrawn in 1904 and used as a stationary engine in Melton works, but the others had long and varied careers. In 1906 four of the class, Nos 8, 10, 19 and 40, were lent to the Midland, and used on rail motor services, one of them between Harpenden and Hemel Hempstead. The carriage portion was an old Midland Pullman car, with a driving compartment and connections fitted so that the combination could be driven from either end. At first the engines kept their M & GN yellow livery and their old numbers, but they were later painted Midland red, fitted with Midland chimneys, and given the numbers of the cars to which they were attached. They returned to the M & GN in 1912.

While they were away, the Midland lent the M & GN three standard Johnson 0–4–4 tanks, Nos 141-3. They retained these

THE ROLLING STOCK

numbers and Midland colours, but had M & GN in transfers on the tank sides. They were frequently used on the same services as the 4–4–2 tanks, described above.

The same four 4–4–0 tanks, Nos 8, 10, 19 and 40, departed again in May 1917, this time requisitioned by, and sold to, the government as the M & GN's contribution of engines for war service. At different times they were on camp lines at Pirbright, near Farnborough, Fovant in Wilts, and Rhyl, at a factory line near Paisley, and shunting on the GN at Holloway. Meanwhile No 20 (20A since 1909) remained at Melton, and drew an inspection saloon for the directors and Mr Marriott, while No 9 (9A since 1909) was generally running between Spalding, Bourne and Saxby.

JOHNSON 4–4–0S WITH LARGE BOILERS

The first serious modification of the Johnson 4–4–0s was in 1906, when three received extended smokeboxes. Then in 1908 two, Nos 39 and 55, were rebuilt at Melton with larger boilers. As altered, they had round-topped fireboxes and standard Midland 'H' type boilers, but flush circular extended smokeboxes, instead of the contemporary Midland pattern. No 39 had 1,428 sq ft of heating surface (1,303 tubes, 125 firebox), whereas No 55 had 1,347 sq ft (1,222 tubes, 125 firebox). No 55 had a Derby 1904 taper chimney but No 39 and the others rebuilt later had the 1907 parallel pattern with deflector. Nos 45 and 53 received large boilers in 1909, of the non-superheated Belpaire type similar to those of the contemporary Midland class 2s, but the smokeboxes were Melton's own design, and the coupling rods were plain. Nos 56, 57, 52, 54, 46 and 51, in that order, were similarly rebuilt in 1912-15; they had 1,410 sq ft of heating surface. All these rebuilds had 175-lb pressure and Ramsbottom safety valves. They took over the through Leicester—Norwich operation of the express, two being stationed at Norwich for the purpose for many years. Later on M & GN engines were frequently seen at Leicester and Nottingham on through holiday trains, and in 1923 they took over the operation throughout of the slow trains between Spalding and Nottingham.

Nos 39 and 55 also received Belpaire boilers to correspond

in 1925. The other eight were again reboilered in 1925-30. Ross 'pop' safety valves were fitted to some for a time, but these were found to be too noisy in a district where there were still many horses, and were replaced by the Ramsbottom type in 1933. Later, some blastpipe and chimney experiments were made, Nos 45 and 55-6 in 1933 receiving stovepipe chimneys of unpleasing appearance. It is surprising that none of these fine powerful engines were ever superheated. From rebuilding until 1925 they were known as 'C rebuilds' but thereafter as class 'C'.

Nos 6, 36, 44, 50, 77, 2 and 49 were rebuilt in 1930-1 with small type Belpaire boilers having 1,089 sq ft of heating surface and 160-lb pressure; they also received larger cabs. The twenty-three other standard 4–4–0s remained substantially in their original state, having similar mountings when reboilered, though from 1935 onwards some had shorter chimneys. The whole thirty, without large boilers, were termed class 'B' in 1925.

THE COMMITTEE'S CARRIAGE STOCK

Of the carriages supplied to the M & GN by the parent companies those provided by the GN were generally its standard non-corridor six-wheelers, varnished teak and lettered M & GN. They could be distinguished from the E & M standards by their different shape. Some were corridor six-wheelers, including a few early East Coast Joint Stock dating from 1890. A number of the latter, including some brake-vans, could be seen at Yarmouth in 1920 still lettered ECJS. The corridors were also used on the North Walsham—Mundesley—Cromer conductor-guard train, and on the Mundesley—Peterboro' through service as late as 1932. The Midland provided some non-corridor six-wheelers with low roofs, which were lettered M & GN but retained their lake livery for some time. From 1914 a few bogie carriages were specially built, and some GN bogie brakes appeared; but generally the E & M, GN and Midland six-wheelers remained usual on the ordinary trains, with modern GN and Midland bogies on the through expresses. In 1934 150 six-wheelers were still in use. From 1920 steam heating was provided on all carriages which had previously been without it.

GOODS VEHICLES

At the time of handing over, the E & M had 718 goods vehicles. The committee had 586 in 1914 and 352 in 1927. Larger numbers were not needed, as so many of the parent

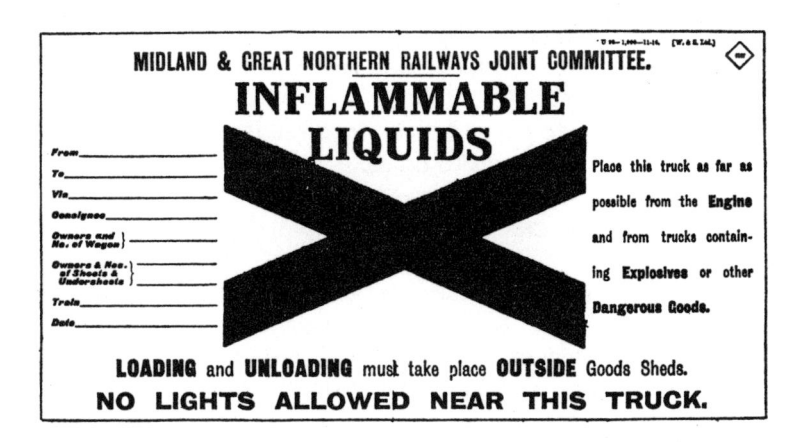

```
┌─────────────────────────────────────────────────────────┐
│   MIDLAND & GREAT NORTHERN RAILWAYS JOINT COMMITTEE.    │
│                  INFLAMMABLE                            │
│                    LIQUIDS                              │
│  From____                                               │
│  To_____                          Place this truck as far as │
│  Via_____                          possible from the Engine │
│  Consignee_                                             │
│  Owners and }                      and from trucks contain- │
│  No. of Wagon }                                         │
│  Owners & Nos. }                   ing Explosives or other │
│  of Sheets &   }                                        │
│  Undersheets   }                                        │
│  Train___                          Dangerous Goods.     │
│  Date___                                                │
│                                                         │
│   LOADING and UNLOADING must take place OUTSIDE Goods Sheds. │
│       NO LIGHTS ALLOWED NEAR THIS TRUCK.                │
└─────────────────────────────────────────────────────────┘
```

companies' trucks worked through, though the M & GN had its own fish- and fruit-vans. Some trucks were built at Melton. From 1928 most of the goods vehicles were transferred to the parent companies' ownership.

0–6–0S REBOILERED

In 1906 Johnson 0–6–0 No 62 received a large Midland boiler, complete with Derby-style fittings, similar to that fitted to 4–4–0 No 39, and in 1909 No 69 was similarly treated. Nos 68 and 71 of the same class received large Belpaire boilers in 1921, and in 1924-5 Nos 62 and 69 followed suit. The heating surface was 1,410 sq ft and the pressure 175 lb. The Ivatt engines had extended smokeboxes from 1907, and between 1920 and 1927 received larger GN pattern boilers, with 1,235 sq ft heating surface and 160-lb pressure. Some of both classes were given stovepipe chimneys.

LONG-LIVED SMALL TANKS

In 1901 No 16, the old Y & NN 0–6–0 tank, became the Melton works shunter; she was renumbered 16A in 1905 and remained in service until 1937. *Alpha*, the 0–4–0 tank which had been No 4A since 1894, was used by the engineering department, and was sold to Colmans in July 1917. The sister engine, *Vici*, which became No 5A in 1894, also worked for the engineering department; it later lost its number and was treated as a service vehicle. It still existed in Melton yard in 1929 but disappeared in 1930. Both were painted black, and retained their names to the end, the only engines to do so.

CHANGES IN THE LIVERY

The yellow livery appeared to get darker in the course of years, and by 1921 was officially described as light brown instead of golden ochre. In 1923 a dark brown chocolate livery with yellow lines was adopted for the goods engines, and in 1929 the passenger engines followed suit. A few engines were painted a dark green in the late 1920s.

LAST YEARS OF THE BEYER 4–4–0S AND 4–4–0 TANKS

All the old Beyer 'A' 4–4–0s remained in service until 1933, but in that year and in 1934 Nos 29, 30, 31, 33 and 34 were broken up, in that order. Nos 21-2 and 35 followed early in 1936. Nos 23, 26-8 and 32 were all running when the LNE took over but were scrapped in 1937. Like the other M & GN engines when the LNE management took charge they received 'O' in front of their numbers, but were withdrawn too soon to be listed as LNE stock. No 25 had broken frames, and No 24 a bad boiler, so 25's boiler was put on 24's frames, the combination was renumbered 025 and taken into LNE stock. It was working in 1938, and was regarded in one sense as the oldest LNE 4–4–0, and in another sense as the newest! It was withdrawn in 1941 after sixty years' service.

The 4–4–2 tanks were still on the Mundesley trains in the early 1930s, including the through summer Yarmouth trains and the runs into North Walsham GE station. No 20A, the inspection 4–4–0 tank, lasted until 1931, and No 9A survived on the Mundesley conductor-guard train until 1933. Of the four taken over by the government two went to colliery lines in Scotland; old No 8 lasted at Fleet's colliery, Tranent, East Lothian, until 1935. Old No 40 went to the Llandarcy oil-refinery sidings, South Wales, and remained in use until 1934. Old No 10, renamed *Kingsley*, went to the Longmoor Military Railway, where it lasted for many years, being finally used for re-railing practice. It was the last survivor of the class when scrapped in 1953.

OPERATION OF THE LEICESTERS

In the 1920s the 'C' rebuilt engines used to work the Leicesters throughout between Leicester and Yarmouth instead of between Leicester and Norwich. Early in 1928, however, No 543 a Midland class 2 once worked the Leicester through to Norwich, in an emergency when the usual M & GN engine was not available. But the practice in the early 1930s was for one 'C' to be changed for another at South Lynn, one engine working between South Lynn and Leicester, and the other between South Lynn and Yarmouth. By then the 'C's were finding it difficult to keep time on the heavier trains, which weighed up to 450 tons, despite good maintenance and blastpipe alterations to improve steaming. Thanks to good driving they and the small-boilered engines often did well, but they were ageing. Derby was approached for assistance and lent a compound 4–4–0 and a Horwich 2–6–0, but when these were found to be unable to clear some bridges and loops safely, two superheated class '3P' 4–4–0s with Belpaire fireboxes, Nos 758-9, were sent in their place. They were stabled at South Lynn and Yarmouth, worked the Leicesters and other heavy trains, and were regarded by the M & GN drivers as the finest engines they had ever had. In the summer of 1936 they were both at Yarmouth and worked the Leicesters on alternate days. But when the LNE took over they were returned to the LMS, along with two LMS class '4F' 0–6–0s, Nos 3913 and 4265, which had also been borrowed, and had been stationed at South Lynn since 1934.

THE LNE REGIME

Responsibility for the locomotive department was formally transferred to the LNE on 1 October 1936, and within a few months many M & GN engines had been withdrawn and replaced by various LNE types.

For a short time afterwards the 'C' class 4-4-0s again hauled the Leicesters but the LNE then provided 'D9's, ex-GC Robinson 4-4-0s, rebuilt with large boilers. One of these locomotives, No 6021 *Queen Mary*, was the only named engine ever to work the Leicesters.

WITHDRAWAL OF M & GN ENGINES

The first 'B' class 4-4-0 and Johnson 0-6-0 to go were Nos 045 and 068 respectively, late in 1936. By February 1937 eight more 'B's had gone, and another Johnson 0-6-0. Some of the engines with 'O' prefix retained M & GN on their tenders for some time, but others were lettered LNER. Altogether, by the end of the year, fourteen 'B's had gone, three 'C's and three more Johnson 0-6-0s. More followed, and by the end of 1938 only fourteen 'B's remained, all lettered LNER.

The LNE reclassified the survivors in 1942. The remaining 'B's, Nos 011-12, 038, 043 and 076 became class 'D52'. The Belpaires, Nos 02, 06, 050 and 077, became 'D53'. The surviving 'C's, Nos 046, 051-2 and 055-6, became 'D54', but they did not last long after this. The last 'C's in service, Nos 055-6, were withdrawn early in 1944, and the last M & GN 4-4-0s of all, Belpaires Nos 050 and 077, went in 1945. Breaking up took place generally at Stratford. The remaining unrebuilt Johnson 0-6-0s, Nos 059, 061, 064-5 and 070 became class 'J40', and the surviving rebuilt engine, No 071, 'J41'. The latter was withdrawn in 1943, and the last of the unrebuilt engines, No 059, in 1944.

One of the 4-4-2 tanks, No 020, was withdrawn shortly before the reclassification but Nos 09 and 041 became C17. No 041 was still on the Mundesley trains in 1940 but was withdrawn in 1943, and No 09 followed in 1944.

LNE ENGINES

Among the first LNE engines to arrive were ex-GN rebuilt Ivatt 4–4–0s and by 1937 there were as many as twenty. Their duties included the Nottingham—Spalding trains, so that GN engines were again on the old Midland & Eastern, which the GN had worked for many years but not since the mid-1890s. No 3400, old No 400, the original Ivatt 4–4–0 of 1896, was on this service. The appearance of these ex-GN engines at Nottingham Midland and of the ex-GC engines at Leicester London Road caused considerable interest. But in 1942 a Midland engine sometimes worked the Spalding train to Bourne, and the ex-GN 4–4–0 took over there. In 1941-6 the Ivatt 4–4–0s were doing most of the Melton—Norwich work and could be seen on the Cromer line. The only appearance of an ex-GN Ivatt Atlantic was when one of the smaller class worked to Lynn in 1938.

Goods engines that arrived included ex-GN Ivatt 0–6–0s, ex-GE Holden 0–6–0s, and a few ex-GC 0–6–0s. A few ex-GN Ivatt 4–4–2 tanks and ex-GC Parker 2–4–2 tanks also appeared. Ex-GE 2–4–2 tanks, long familiar on the N & S line and at Sheringham, appeared on the M & GN proper, especially when the Melton—Cromer service was more closely associated with ex-GE Cromer trains; and a few ex-GE 0–6–0 tanks also came. Some of the 0–6–0s had continuous brakes for passenger working.

MORE POWERFUL TYPES IN USE

When they took over the best trains, the 'D9' 4–4–0s were already over thirty years old, and they were heavy on fuel and water. They were on the Leicesters and the through Kings Cross express for only about two years, and were then transferred to the ordinary trains. Later on they left the M & GN, and the last two, including *Queen Mary*, were scrapped in 1950. It was stated that North Eastern Rs and North British 'Glens', might be tried on the Leicester, and there were hopes of a more successful Robinson GC design, the 'Directors'. Actually, some ex-GN 'K2' two-cylinder 2–6–0s and ex-GE rebuilt 'Claud Hamilton' 4–4–0s arrived. The former were rough riders, but the 'Clauds' were used all over the system, especially during the 1939 war. They were rather sluggish on very heavy trains, such as wartime specials, and on the Leicester, which they could be seen working after its restoration in 1946. For a time it seemed strange to see such characteristic GE types as these and the 2–4–2 tanks on the M & GN. Eventually, it was decided that a six-coupled type was needed on the Leicesters, so some ex-GE Hill 4–6–0s, reclassified as 'B12/3', arrived in 1948 and worked the service satisfactorily. Their well-kept appearance and good cabs were appreciated, and their visits to Leicester London Road caused interest. The big 4–6–0, equipped with a tablet exchanger lettered M & GN, could be seen waiting in the siding where the M & GN 'C' 4–4–0 used to be.

THE LAST M & GNS

The Ivatt M & GN 0–6–0s, which had become class 'J30' when taken over, lasted a relatively long time under the LNE regime, as they were similar to other ex-GN LNE engines and so were easier to fit with spare parts. Nos 082, 084-5, 087, 089, 090 and 092 were again rebuilt with smaller ex-GN type boilers, becoming class 'J4'. In the LNE 1946 renumbering scheme the class was allotted numbers 4156-67 but Nos 090-1 were withdrawn before they could receive their new numbers and the rest were all withdrawn in five years. No 085, renumbered 64160, was the last M & GN engine to survive on the line and went to Doncaster for scrapping on 24 November 1951.

The 0–6–0 tanks also lasted well. No 097 was scrapped in 1943 but in 1946 the others were allotted 8482-9 for Nos 098, 093, 096, 095, 015, 099, 094 and 016 respectively. Nos 015, 093 and 099 were withdrawn without receiving their new numbers. The last of the class to go was No 016—seen by the author at Melton in August 1946 still so numbered—in August 1949.

CARRIAGE STOCK CHANGES

A change in the carriage stock took place in the early 1930s, when both the LMS and LNE sent a number of bogie vehicles

THE ROLLING STOCK 189

of pre-grouping vintage, both corridor and non-corridor. They included examples of old LNW, Midland, North Eastern and GC stock. The majority were in varnished teak, but some of the LMS ones remained red, as had the early acquisitions from the Midland in the 1890s. When the LNE took over, the carriages, unlike the engines, all remained lettered M & GN, but had 80,000 added to their numbers.

VISITS BY NAMED ENGINES

The ex-GN 4–4–0s, also an elderly class, were removed from the M & GN in late 1947, but a Gresley 'K4' three-cylinder 2–6–0 No 1997 *MacCailin Mor* (from the West Highland line) appeared at Melton at that time. Besides this engine and *Queen Mary* it is believed that the only other appearances of named engines in later years were on a wartime troop special hauled by the rebuilt ex-GE 4–4–0 *Claud Hamilton* and when the LNE 'B2' 4–6–0 *Royal Sovereign* was used on royal journeys from Wolferton over the M & GN west of Lynn. There were, of course, visits to Sheringham by named 'Sandringham' class 4–6–0s on Liverpool Street trains. The 'K4' 2–6–0's visit seems to have been an isolated incident rather than a trial for future use of the type on the M & GN.

THE BR ERA

In 1950-1 the Eastern Region of British Railways allocated to the M & GN section a number of its Ivatt class '4' 2–6–0s, which performed much of the passenger and goods work in the last years, including the Leicesters. They had 17½ by 26 in outside cylinders, 5 ft 3 in drivers, taper boilers of 225-lb pressure and Walschaerts valve gear; they were fitted with tablet exchangers which in many cases were still lettered M & GN. Nos 43080-3, built at Darlington, were among the first to arrive and were stationed at Peterboro'. More of the Darlington series followed, and Nos 43058-69 came from Doncaster. These Peterboro'-based engines worked the Essendine—Bourne line before its closure in June 1951. Next came Nos 43104-6 to South Lynn early that summer, and Nos 43107-10 a little later, Nos 43147-51 to Melton at the end of the year, and Nos 43157-

61 to Yarmouth in 1952. Also on the line were Nos 43142-6.

Despite the heavy influx of new engines there was still quite a variety of motive power. Several of the rebuilt 'Clauds' and 'Super Clauds' were still working on the M & GN, besides a few ex-GN 4-4-2 tanks. Ex-WD 2-8-0s sometimes came on freight trains in 1948, and in 1955 there were several 'J17' 0-6-0s and two 'J39's. Large ex-LMS class '4F' 0-6-0s often worked through with Saturday holiday trains in the later years. In the summer an ex-LNE 'N7' 0-6-2 tank sometimes visited Melton. It was reported that this engine was intended to bank heavy trains, but this does not seem to have been the case.

The big 'B12/3' 4-6-0s were regarded as rather large for any but the heaviest trains. In 1955 they sometimes worked through between Leicester and Yarmouth but on other occasions engines were changed at South Lynn. Sometimes the 4-6-0 would operate west of Lynn and a class '4' 2-6-0 east of there, or *vice versa*. After the Spalding stop was inserted in September, an engine change always took place there. On the first day of the altered arrangements one 2-6-0 was changed for another.

THE N & S JOINT

The N & S committee never owned any rolling stock. M & GN engines hauled M & GN trains on the section, and GE (LNE from 1923) engines hauled GE trains, until October 1936. Thereafter the ex-GE, GN and GC engines which had come to the M & GN worked former M & GN services on the N & S. Class '4' 2-6-0s were very rare on former N & S lines, as the Yarmouth Beach—Lowestoft and Mundesley—Cromer services disappeared in 1953 (see chapter 8) and diesels were being brought into use; the only operation on the N & S for which they were suitable would be Norwich Thorpe, Sheringham and Melton trains via Roughton Road Junction.

THE ENGINE SHEDS

During the committee's administration the M & GN had its own sheds at South Lynn, Melton, Norwich City, Cromer Beach and Yarmouth Beach. At the committee's expense the GN built

THE ROLLING STOCK 191

a new shed at Bourne, which became M & GN property but was also used by GN and Midland engines. The M & GN also had a small separate shed at Spalding. At Peterboro' from 1894 to 1936 M & GN engines were stabled at the Midland Spital shed, near the Midland tracks north-west of North station. On 1 October 1936, when the LNE took over, they were moved to the old GE shed at Peterboro' East and on 1 May 1939 to the former GN New England shed. The M & GN also had a small shed at Mundesley on the N & S.

THE LAST YEARS

In the last few years fewer locomotives were required owing to the introduction of diesel units (Chapter 8), but occasionally there were interesting workings by large engines. In January 1959 'B17' 4–6–0 No 61654 *Sunderland* worked a Weybourne—Norwich City train strengthened for football traffic (in replacement of a diesel set); and on 22 August 1959 'Britannia' Pacific No 70041 *Sir John Moore* worked a Liverpool Street—Sheringham express and drew the stock on empty to Melton for stabling.

There were also some unusual appearances in the last few weeks of the Leicesters, including a 'B1' 4–6–0 No 61159, at Christmas 1958, a Gresley 'K2' 2–6–0 No 61771 and a Midland class '2' 4–4–0 in January 1959; but for the last days the Ivatt 2–6–0s were again in use. Class 'B1' 4–6–0 No 61399 could be seen on the surviving through freight trains to Norwich City in 1959 and No 61119 of the same class took the Duke of Edinburgh's train to Weybourne in May 1963. Ex-WD 2–8–0s also appeared on the Norwich City freight trains (see Chapter 9).

EPILOGUE

A Midland & Great Northern Joint Railways Preservation Society was formed in April 1959. At first, hopes were entertained that the North Walsham Town—Yarmouth Beach section would be re-opened by the society and later the Themelthorpe—Melton section; but it was not found possible to carry out either of these schemes and after the closure of the Melton—Sheringham line the society concentrated its efforts on the Sheringham—Weybourne section. In 1965 the name the 'Poppy Line' was put forward as a suitable title but in 1967 the society became North Norfolk Railways Limited. Relaying was carried out at Weybourne station and the track between there and Sheringham kept in good condition. At first the society's showrooms and offices were at Weybourne but were moved to Sheringham station after the ordinary services there were transferred to the new halt in January 1967. Application for an Order to reopen the section as a light railway was (despite minor local opposition) granted to British Railways in 1973. There were private trips for society members. Sir John Betjeman was a patron. The order was transferred to North Norfolk Railways on 7 May 1976, and public services began in July, generally steam operated. The NNR has a supply of rolling stock. An ex GE J. Holden 0-6-0 (564, LNE 7564, rebuilt 1912) and two 0-6-0Ts, *John D. Hamer*, a Peckett, built 1939, and *Colwyn*, a Kitson, built 1933 (the former painted in old yellow M & GN colours) generally haul the trains. There are ex LNE (including an ex GN articulated suburban set) and ex LMS coaches. There are also an ex LNE B12/3 4-6-0, 8512 built 1928 to GE S. D. Holden – J. J. Hill designs, four diesel locomotives, two diesel buses, two ex SR Brighton Belle Pullmans, and some wagons. There is also a museum, including some directors' saloons. There are plans for extending to Kelling, and perhaps Holt. The M & GN Circle is another interested society.

Appendixes

APPENDIX 1

DATES OF OPENINGS

1858	15 November	Spalding—Holbeach (Norwich & Spalding)
1862	3 July	Holbeach—Sutton Bridge (Norwich & Spalding)
1866	1 March	Lynn—Sutton Bridge (Lynn & Sutton)
,,	1 August	Spalding—Bourne (Spalding & Bourne)
,,	,, ,,	Peterboro'—Sutton Bridge (Peterboro' Wisbech & Sutton Bridge)
*,,	,, ,,	Wisbech Harbour branch (Peterboro' Wisbech & Sutton Bridge)
1877	7 August	Yarmouth—Ormesby (Great Yarmouth & Stalham)
1878	16 May	Ormesby—Hemsby (Great Yarmouth & Stalham)
,,	15 July	Hemsby—Martham (Great Yarmouth & Stalham)
1879	16 August	Lynn—Massingham (Lynn & Fakenham)
1880	17 January	Martham—Catfield (Yarmouth & North Norfolk)
,,	3 July	Catfield—Stalham (Yarmouth & North Norfolk)
,,	6 August	Massingham—Fakenham (Lynn & Fakenham)
*1881	8 June	Sutton Bridge Dock branch (Midland & Eastern)
,,	13 June	Stalham—North Walsham (Yarmouth & North Norfolk)
1882	19 January	Fakenham—Guestwick (Lynn & Fakenham)
*,,	15 May	Yarmouth Beach—White Swan Junction (Yarmouth Union)
,,	1 July	Guestwick—Lenwade (Lynn & Fakenham)
,,	2 December	Lenwade—Norwich (Lynn & Fakenham)
1883	5 April	Melton Constable—North Walsham (Eastern & Midlands)
1884	1 October	Melton Constable—Holt (Eastern & Midlands)
1886	1 January	South Lynn—Bawsey (Eastern & Midlands)
1887	16 June	Holt—Cromer Beach (Eastern & Midlands)
1894	1 May	Little Bytham Junction—Bourne (M & GN)
,,	,, ,,	Little Bytham Junction—Saxby (Midland)
,,	,, ,,	Spalding avoiding line (M & GN)
1898	1 July	North Walsham Town—Antingham Road Junction (M & GN)
,,	,, ,,	Mundesley—Antingham Road Junction (Norfolk & Suffolk)
,,	,, ,,	North Walsham GE—Antingham Road Junction (GE)
1903	13 July	Caister Road Junction—Gorleston North Junction (M & GN)
,,	,, ,,	Coke Ovens Junction, Lowestoft—Gorleston North Junction (N & S)
,,	,, ,,	Yarmouth South Town—Gorleston North Junction (GE)

1906	23 July		Runton east Junction—Newstead Lane Junction (M & GN)
	,, ,,		Roughton Road Junction—Runton west Junction (N & S)
,,	,, ,,		Roughton Road Junction—Cromer Junction (GE)
,,	2 August		Roughton Road Junction—Mundesley (N & S)

* Goods only.

† These, except as noted, are openings for passenger traffic. Separate openings for goods traffic are given in the text.

APPENDIX 2
MILEAGE TABLES
Midland & Great Northern and Norfolk & Suffolk Joint Committee Railways

		miles	chains	miles	chains
Saxby station	⎫	0	04		
Saxby Station Junction		0	00		
Edmonthorpe & Wymondham		2	34		
Pain's Siding box	Midland Rly	4	54		
Buckminster Sidings box		5	68		
South Witham		6	74		
Castle Bytham	⎭	11	16		
GN bridge No 43		12	73		
Little Bytham Junction		13	07		
Bourne Tunnel, West end		16	55		
,, ,, East end		16	70		
Bourne West Junction	⎫	18	01		
,, Station	GNR	18	09		
,, East Junction	⎭	18	24		
Twenty		21	74		
Counter Drain		23	38		
North Drove		25	25		
Cuckoo Junction		26	30	26	30
Spalding, junction with GN				27	55*
,, station, GN				27	74
,, junction with GN				28	08
Welland Bank Junction		27	53	28	61
Clay Lake		27	74		
Cunningham's Drove		28	37		
Weston		30	07		
Moulton		31	47		
Whaplode		32	53		
Holbeach		34	73		
Fleet		36	78		
Gedney		38	23		
Long Sutton		39	35		

* Spalding M & GN Goods branch 16 chains.

APPENDIXES

	miles	chains	miles	chains
Sutton Bridge Dock Junction	42	36		
Peterborough GN station			0	00
Westwood Junction			0	51
Wisbech Junction			0	59
Dogsthorpe Siding			3	33
Eye Green			5	12
Northam Brick Co's Siding			5	27
Thorney			8	44
Wryde			10	64
Turf Fen box			12	77
Murrow			14	40
Wisbech St Mary			17	59
Barton Lane Crossing			19	28
Wisbech			20	11
Horse Shoe Lane box			20	52*
Ferry			22	51
Tydd			25	16
Sutton Bridge Junction	42	62	27	26
,, ,, station	42	76	27	40
,, ,, East box	43	10	27	54
Walpole	45	56	30	20
Terrington	47	56	32	20
Clenchwarton	48	79	33	43
West Lynn station	51	34	35	78
Single Line Junction box	51	56	36	20
South Lynn station	51	79	36	43
,, ,, Junction	52	10	36	54
King's Lynn Harbour Junction ⎫	52	38	37	02
,, ,, Exton Road box ⎬ GER	53	35	37	79
,, ,, station ⎭	54	05	38	49
Gaywood Road Junction (site)	55	15		
Bawsey Junction (site) see below	58	37		
South Lynn station	0	00		
,, ,, Junction	0	11		
Hardwick Road (Goods)	1	15		
Gayton Road	3	52		
Bawsey Junction (site) see above	4	56		
Grimston Road	6	39		
Hillington	8	40		
Wilson's Ballast Siding	11	64		
Massingham	13	19		
East Rudham	16	32		
Raynham Park	18	29		
Fakenham Town	22	10		
Langor Bridge (Goods)	25	17		
Thursford	28	50		
Melton Constable West Junction	31	49		
,, ,, station	31	55		
,, ,, East Junction	31	64	31	64
Hindolvestone			33	62

* Wisbech Harbour Goods branch 68 chains.

MIDLAND & GREAT NORTHERN JOINT RAILWAY

	miles	chains	miles	chains
Guestwick			36	19
Whitwell & Reepham			40	20
Lenwade			42	45
Attlebridge			44	14
Drayton			48	36
Hellesdon			50	72
Norwich City			52	77

Thurning Ballast Siding	35	32
Corpusty & Saxthorpe	36	48
Bluestone	39	35
Aylsham Town	43	19
Felmingham	46	44
North Walsham Junction	48	62
,, ,, Town station	48	68
Honing	51	63
Stalham	55	50
Sutton Staithe halt	56	65
Catfield	57	56
Potter Heigham	60	41
Potter Heigham Bridge Halt	60	78
Martham	63	21
Hemsby	66	06
Great Ormesby	67	63
Scratby Halt	68	24
California Halt	68	56
Caister Camp Halt	69	56
Caister-on-Sea	70	43
Salisbury Road box ⎫ Newtown Halt ⎭	72	40
Yarmouth Beach	73	14

Yarmouth Yard box	0	00		
Caister Road Junction	0	42	0	42

North Quay Junction (with GE) near White Swan			1	18

Breydon Water Bridge North end	1	12
,, ,, ,, South end	1	34
North Gorleston Junction (with N & S Jt)	2	53
Gorleston North	3	25
Gorleston-on-Sea	4	49
Gorleston Links Halt ⎫	5	49
Hopton-on-Sea N & S Jt	6	50
Corton ⎭	8	57
Lowestoft North	10	11
Coke Ovens Junction ⎫ GE	11	64
Lowestoft Central ⎭	12	25

Melton Constable station	0	00
,, ,, West Junction	0	06
Briningham Junction	1	09
Holt	5	11
Kelling Sidings	6	69
Weybourne	8	55

APPENDIXES

	miles	chains	miles	chains
Sheringham (original station)	11	30		
„ Halt	11	42		
West Runton	13	07		
Runton West Junction	13	65	13	65
Runton East Junction	14	32		
Cromer Beach	15	16		
„ „	0	00		
Runton East Junction	0	64		
Newstead Lane Junction	1	20	14	36
Roughton Road Junction (with GE)	2	58		
Cromer Links Halt ⎫	3	36		
Overstrand ⎬ ⅋ ⥊	4	24		
Sidestrand Halt ⎭ z	5	39		
Trimingham	6	56		
Mundesley-on-Sea	9	22		
Paston & Knapton	11	00		
Antingham Road Junction	13	79		
North Walsham (GE)	14	39		
North Walsham Junction	14	31		
„ „ Town station	14	37		

Numbering of mileposts

Section	from zero at
Little Bytham Junction—Bourne West Junction	Saxby Station Junction
Bourne East Junction—Sutton Bridge Junction	Bourne East Junction
Cuckoo Junction—Spalding, junction with GN	„
Spalding, junction with GN—Welland Bank Jcn	Spalding, jcn with GN
Peterboro'—Sutton Bridge Junction	Peterboro', Wisbech Jcn
Sutton Bridge Junction—South Lynn Junction	„
South Lynn Junction—Harbour Junction (GE)	„
South Lynn Junction—Yarmouth Beach	South Lynn Junction
Yarmouth Beach—North Gorleston Junction	„ •
North Gorleston Junction—Coke Ovens Junction	Lowestoft, Coke Ovens Junction
Melton Constable West Junction—Cromer Beach	South Lynn Junction †
Runton West Junction—North Walsham Junction	North Walsham Junction
Melton Constable East Junction—Norwich City	South Lynn Junction

• reversing at Yarmouth Yard box

† reversing at Melton Constable West Junction

APPENDIX 3

Single Line Sections in 1914

	Crossing Stations
Thorney—Murrow	
Horse Shoe Lane Junction, Wisbech—Sutton Bridge Junction	Wryde
Twenty—Cuckoo Junction, Spalding	Tydd
Cunningham's Drove Box, Spalding—Sutton Bridge Dock Junction	Moulton, Holbeach, Gedney
Over Cross Keys Sutton Bridge	
Over West Lynn Bridge	
Grimston Road—Raynham Park	Hillington, Massingham, East Rudham
Corpusty—Yarmouth Beach north box	Aylsham, North Walsham Town, Honing, Stalham, Potter Heigham, Martham, Great Ormesby
Melton Constable—Norwich City north box	Whitwell, Drayton
Briningham Junction, Melton Constable—Runton West Junction	Holt, Weybourne, Sheringham
Cromer, Gas Works siding—Cromer Beach station box	
Over Breydon viaduct	
Caister Road Junction—White Swan Junction	
Wisbech Harbour branch	
Sutton Bridge docks branch	

Norfolk & Suffolk joint

Single line section in 1914

	Crossing Stations
Antingham Road Junction, North Walsham—Newstead Lane Junction	Mundesley, Trimingham, Overstrand, Roughton Road Junction

Midland line from Saxby

Single line in 1914

	Crossing Stations
Saxby—Little Bytham Junction box	Edmondthorpe, South Witham

APPENDIX 4

THE BOARD OF DIRECTORS
OF THE M & GN JOINT COMMITTEE, 1889-1936

1889-1904	Lord Colville of Culross, KT, GN (chairman of GN 1880-95)
1889-92	Lord de Ramsey, GN
1895-1904	
1889-91	A. B. Foster Esq, GN
1889-90	Sir M. W. Thompson Bt, Midland (then chairman of Midland)
1889-1900	Sir Frederick Mappin, Bt, Midland
1889-1911	G. E. Paget Esq, Midland (chairman of Midland 1891-1911; became, 1897, Sir Ernest Paget, Bt)
1890-5	L. C. Probyn, Esq, GN, sat occasionally, not formally appointed
1891-4	F. W. Fison, Esq, GN
1891-8	H. T. Hodgson Esq, Midland (deputy chairman of Midland 1904-18)
1914-18	
1893	J. Noble Esq, Midland, sat occasionally, not formally appointed
1893-1901	L. R. Starkey Esq, Midland
1895-1917	The Rt Hon W. L. Jackson MP, GN (chairman of GN for same period; became Lord Allerton, 1903)
1898-9	Sir Henry Oakley, GN (former general manager, GN)
1906-12	
1901-12	Lord Farrer, Midland
1901-31	Gustav Behrens Esq, Midland (LMS from 1923)
1904-6	Sir Frederick Banbury Bt, MP, GN (chairman of GN 1917-22)
1919-22	
1905-18	Sir Francis Mowatt, GN
1911-19	G. Murray Smith, Esq, Midland (chairman of Midland for same period)
1914-36	Oliver Bury, Esq, GN (LNE from 1923) (former general manager GN)
1918-31	F. L. Steel Esq, GN (LNE from 1923) (deputy chairman of GN 1918-22)
1919-34	Charles Booth Esq, Midland (LMS from 1923) (chairman of Midland 1919-21)
1920-2	Sir John Beale, KBE, Midland
1922-35	Frank Tatlow, Esq, Midland (LMS from 1923) (former general manager of Midland)
1923-31	W. Burgh Gair Esq, LNE
1931-6	H. T. Bailey Esq, LNE
1931-2	Sir Charles Trotter, CB, LNE
1931-6	Sir Alan Anderson, KBE, LMS
1931-6	Sir Thomas Williams, LMS
1932-6	Lt-Col The Hon A. C. Murray, CMG, DSO, LNE
1932-5	William Whitelaw Esq, LNE (chairman of LNE)
1934-6	D. Vickers, Esq, LMS
1935-6	A. E. Pullar Esq, LMS
1936	The Rt Hon Lord Burghley, MP, LNE
1936	Sir Gerald Talbot, KCVO, CMG, LNE

The senior member from the GN generally took the chair at one meeting, and the senior member from the Midland would take the chair at the next, and so on. There was no official 'chairman' of the M & GN.

MIDLAND & GREAT NORTHERN JOINT RAILWAY

APPEN

Dimensions of
EASTERN & MID

Building Date	No	Previous Name or No		Builder	Previous Owner
1873 (arrived 1880)	1	Melton Constable	1	Sharp Stewart	L & F (previously CMR)
1873 (arrived 1880)	2	Reepham	2	Sharp Stewart	L & F (previously CMR)
1873 (arrived 1880)	3	Blakeney	3	Sharp Stewart	L & F (previously CMR)
1878	4	Alpha	4	Hudswell Clarke	L & F (from contractors)
1880	5	Vici	5	Hudswell Clarke	L & F (from contractors)
1879 (arrived 1881)	6	Holt (renamed Chairman)	6	Black, Hawthorn	L & F
1877	7	Ida	7	Black, Hawthorn	GY & S then L & F
1878	8	Hillington	8	Hudswell Clarke	L & F
1879	9	Fakenham	9	Hudswell Clarke	L & F
1880	10	Norwich	10	Hudswell Clarke	L & F
1873 (arrived 1881)	11-14		11-14	Sharp Stewart	L & F (previously CMR)
1877	15	Ormesby		Fox, Walker	GY & S
1877	16	Stalham		Fox, Walker	GY & S
1881	17	Aylsham		Black, Hawthorn	Y & NN
1874 (arrived 1881)	18		18	Sharp Stewart	L & F (previously CMR)
1881	19	Great Yarmouth		Hudswell Clarke	Y & NN
1881	20	King's Lynn	20	Hudswell Clarke	L & F
1881 (arrived 1882)	21-4		21-4	Beyer Peacock	L & F
1883	25-8			Beyer Peacock	(ordered by L & F)
1857 (arrived 1883)	29*	Rickerby	377 1101	Rothwell	L & C, then LNW
1857 (arrived 1883)	30*	Luck of Edenhall	384 1112	Rothwell	L & C, then LNW
1879	31*	Martham		Hudswell Clarke	Y & NN
1878	32*	North Walsham		Hudswell Clarke	Y & NN
1886	29-31			Beyer Peacock	
1888	32-5			Beyer Peacock	

* Old 29-30 were renumbered 42-3 in 1886

APPENDIX 5

Locomotives
LAND ENGINES

Type	Driving Wheels ft in	Heating Surface sq ft	Cylinders				Pressure psi
0–6–0T	3 6	823	16½	×	20	(outside)	140
0–6–0T	3 6	823	16½	×	20	(outside)	140
0–6–0T	3 6	823	16½	×	20	(outside)	140
0–4–0T	2 6	172	8	×	15	(outside)	120
0–4–0T	2 6	172	8	×	15	(outside)	120
0–6–0T	3 6	556	13	×	20	(outside)	140 (later 120)
0–6–0T	3 6	556	13	×	20	(outside)	140 (later 120)
4–4–0T	4 6	565	14	×	20	(outside)	140 (later 130)
4–4–0T	4 6	622	15	×	20	(outside)	140 (later 130)
4–4–0T	4 6	622	15	×	20	(outside)	140 (later 130)
0–6–0T	3 6	823	16½	×	20	(outside)	140
0–6–0T	3 6	458	13	×	20	(outside)	140 (later 120)
0–6–0T	3 6	458	13	×	20	(outside)	140 (later 120)
0–6–0T	3 6	556	13	×	20	(outside)	140 (later 120)
0–6–0T	3 6	823	16½	×	20	(outside)	140
4–4–0T	4 6	622	15	×	20	(outside)	140 (later 130)
4–4–0T	4 6	622	15	×	20	(outside)	140 (later 130)
4–4–0	6	1,033	17	×	24	(outside)	140
4–4–0	6	1,033	17	×	24	(outside)	140
2–4–0	5 2	1,083	17	×	20	(outside)	120
2–4–0	5 2	1,083	17	×	20	(outside)	120
4–4–0T	4 6	622	15	×	20	(outside)	140 (later 130)
4–4–0T	4 6	565	14	×	20	(outside)	140 (later 130)
4–4–0	6	1,083	17	×	24	(outside)	140
4–4–0	6	1,083	17	×	24	(outside)	140

Old 31-2 were renumbered 40-1 in 1886

ENGINES SUPPLIED TO OR BUILT BY THE MIDLAND & GREAT NORTHERN JOINT COMMITTEE

Building Date	Nos	Builder	Type	Driving Wheels ft in	Heating Surface sq ft	Cylinders	Pressure psi
1894	36-9, 42-7	Sharp Stewart	4–4–0	6 6	1,240 (1,130 tubes, 110 firebox)	18 × 26 (inside)	160
1894	48-50, 1-7, 11-14, 17-18	Sharp Stewart	4–4–0	6 6	1,240 (1,130 tubes, 110 firebox)	18 × 26 (inside)	160
1896	51-7	Sharp Stewart	4–4–0	6 6	1,240 (1,130 tubes, 110 firebox)	18 × 26 (inside)	160
1896	58-65	Neilson	0–6–0	5 2½	1,240	18 × 26 (inside)	150
1899	66-73	Kitson	0–6–0	5 2½	1,240	18 × 26 (inside)	150
1899	74-80	Beyer Peacock	4–4–0	6 6	1,240 (1,130 tubes, 110 firebox)	18 × 26 (inside)	160
1900	81-92	Dübs (intended for GN)	0–6–0	5 1½	1,126	17½ × 26 (inside)	170 (later 160)
1897*	14A	Melton Works	0–6–0T	3 6½	737	16 × 20 (outside)	140
1898*	1A	Melton Works	0–6–0T	3 6½	737	16 × 20 (outside)	140
1899*	3A, 11A	Melton Works	0–6–0T	3 6½	737	16 × 20 (outside)	140
1900	15	Melton Works	0–6–0T	3 6½	737	16 × 20 (outside)	140
1902*	12A, 17A	Melton Works	0–6–0T	3 6½	737	16 × 20 (outside)	140
1903*	2A	Melton Works	0–6–0T	3 6½	737	16 × 20 (outside)	140
1905	16	Melton Works	0–6–0T	3 6½	737	16 × 20 (outside)	140
1904	41	Melton Works	4–4–2T	6	1,099	17 × 24 (outside)	160
1909	20, 9	Melton Works	4–4–2T	6	1,099	17 × 24 (outside)	160

* These engines were renumbered 93-9 in 1907

Author's Note

My mother's family, named Clowes, has lived in Norfolk for a very long time. My·grandfather, the late Dr Francis Clowes, JP, for many years lived at Sutton Hall near Stalham, which the Yarmouth & North Norfolk Railway (afterwards part of the M & GN) reached in 1880. My grandfather was then the doctor in the village, and his daughter, my mother, was only a little girl. But she could vividly remember the opening of the line. Recollections of conversations with her, with my grandfather, and with his old coachman (the late W. Kerrison of Stalham—a great enthusiast for the line) have been very useful in compiling this work. I spent many happy holidays at the hall, and on the Broads, and later came to know the whole of the country served by the M & GN well. I have been informed that I travelled for the first time on the Kings Cross—Cromer express in 1908, and my memories of journeys on the through trains from the Midlands to Norfolk date back to 1913. I knew many of the staff of the line, and have spoken with some, and their relatives, who had very early recollections of it. In 1933 I was shown round the old head offices at King's Lynn, where there were useful records.

The Midland & Great Northern Joint, a railway casualty of the late 1950s, was a very interesting system. Its handsome yellow engines (mainly of Midland types), varnished teak six-wheeled coaches (largely of Great Northern origin), somersault GN signals, automatic tablet exchangers for single-line operation, and (later) concrete buildings and fittings, became almost as much part of the north Norfolk scene as a square church tower, a windmill, or a wherry's sail.

Acknowledgements

Warm thanks are due to many who have provided valuable information. There are so many friends and colleagues on British Railways who have helped, but I should particularly mention Mr Claud Hankin, lately divisional manager, Norwich, and his officers, especially the late E. Tuddenham, whose lamented death occurred while I was completing this work, and whose articles in the *Railway World* on the lines in the Cromer area were of special value. There are the staffs of British Railways Record Office and British Railways Legal Library, who were unfailingly courteous in finding old records and statutes; and my former senior colleague, Mr G. H. P. Beames, to whom I am indebted for 1891 Airy maps. There is the M & GN Circle, especially Mr D. Thomas of Spalding and Mr Michael Back of Long Sutton, who supplied station plans. There is the M & GN Preservation Society, now North Norfolk Railways Limited, where I should particularly thank Mr B. L. Ridgway and Mr Bill, both of Sheringham.

Mr T. G. Hepburn of Nottingham has supplied many of the illustrations; Mr H. C. Casserley has provided illustrations and information about the carriage stock, and Mr A. C. Erroll special information about the promotion of the Lynn & Fakenham Railway. To Colonel Rixon Bucknall I am indebted for illustrations, some of a very early date taken by Dr Tice Budden, and for references in his books. Mr C. R. Clinker's wide knowledge of dates has been of great value and he has prepared the table of distances. I must also thank other friends at the Railway Club and the library there; Mr R. S. McNaught, who has supplied a photograph taken in 1862, and Mr D. H. Ballantyne and Mr P. H. Groom who have provided illustrations of the line in the 1950s. The editor of the *Isle of Ely and*

ACKNOWLEDGEMENTS

Wisbech Advertiser and Pictorial has given information about Wisbech.

Others no longer with us that I should mention include the late Kenneth Brown (sometime president of the Railway Club) from whose researches I obtained valuable material about the Eastern & Midlands, and with whom I walked over the old disused Lynn—Bawsey line in 1933; and the late H. P. Le Mesurier (sometime engineer of the Bengal—Nagpur Railway) for information about the Spalding avoiding line of which he was resident engineer.

Sir Robert Marriott and other members of the family have kindly written to me, as has Mr R. Gamble of Cromer, who was long on the staff of the M & GN like his family before him.

The maps and sketches are based on original drawings prepared by my son, Michael, who also reproduced station plans kindly supplied by Mr Back.

Bibliography

General Works
Acworth, Sir William. *The Railways of England.* (1889)
Grinling, C. H. *History of the Great Northern Railway.* 1st edn (1889); 3rd edn, Borley, H. V. and Ellis, C. Hamilton (1967)
Lewin, H. G. *The Railway Mania and its Aftermath.* (1937)
Tatford, B. *Story of British Railways.* (1946)

Periodicals
Bradshaw's Railway Guide
Bradshaw's Railway Manual
Directory of Railway Officials
Locomotive Carriage and Wagon Review
Modern Railways
Railway (later Transport) and Travel Monthly
Railway Gazette
Railway Magazine
Railway News
Railway Pictorial
Railway Times
Railway World
Railway Year Book
Railways
Trains Illustrated

Reports
The Law Reports, High Court, Chancery Division

Law Times Reports
Reports of the Light Railway Commissioners
Reports of Railway and Canal Commission

Articles of particular interest
The Locomotive Carriage and Wagon Review
  Vols 27-8, 1921-2. Dewhurst, P. C. 'The Midland & Great Northern Joint Railway and its locomotives'
The Railway Magazine
  Vol 3, 1898, July. Hanson, A. 'Poppyland and One Way to it'
  Vol 15, 1904, September. Sekon, G. A. 'Railways in Poppyland'
  Vol 23, 1908, August and September. Hopwood, H. L. 'The Midland & Great Northern Joint Railway'
  Vol 51, 1922. Gairns, J. F. 'Fruit Traffic on the Midland & Great Northern Joint'
  Vol 53, 1923, August and September. Ahrons, E. L. 'Locomotive and Train Working in the latter part of the nineteenth century; the Midland & Great Northern Joint Railway'
  Vol 79, 1936, August and September. 'The Midland & Great Northern Joint Railway, (1) Its Traffic', by A. Maxwell, (2) 'Its Locomotives 1900-35', by F. T. Gillford
Railway Pictorial
  Vol 3, 1950, continued in:
Railways
  Vol 12, 1951. Wells, Alan. 'The Locomotives of the Midland & Great Northern Joint Railway'
Railway World
  Vol 25, 1964, June, Tuddenham, E. 'The M & GN Route to Cromer'
  Vol 26, 1966, July. Tuddenham, E. 'The Norfolk & Suffolk Joint'
Trains Illustrated
  Vol 8, 1955, February, April. Newman, Marcus. 'The Midland & Great Northern Joint Railway'
  Vol 8, 1955, May. Boyles, W. W. 'The Midland & Great Northern Joint Railway'
  Annual, 1960. Freeman Allen, G., and McNaught, R. S. 'A Souvenir of the Midland & Great Northern Joint Railway'

Index

Index

Illustrations are indicated by figures in bold type

Abandoned lines, 59, 95
 (*see* Closed lines)
Abandoned schemes for lines, 12, 14, 20-3, 32, 43, 48, 51, 55-6, 60-1, 63, 84-5, 88, 92-4, 104
Accidents, 94, 104, 139, 146-7
Acts of Parliament, 12, 13, 14, 15-16, 19, 21, 22, 23, 24, 30, 32, 34, 37-8, 39, 43, 44, 45, 46, 56, 58, 64-5, 74-5, 83-4, 86, 91, 99, 105, 109, 121, 137, 152, 156
Agricultural traffic, 11, 27, 37, 55, 59, 102-3, 120-1, 128, 136-7, 148, 157, 162, 163, 170
Air raids, 122, 147, 148-9
Aldred, Mr, 34, 39, 51, 57
Allerton, Lord (*see* Jackson)
Amalgamations, 13, 14, 20, 22, 25, 28, 34, 40, 48-9, 51, 73-4, 104, 129
Ant, River, 27, 41, 44-5, 91
Antingham Road Junction, 84, 85, 91, 130, 135, 153, 164, 193, 197-8
Army (*see* Military Traffic; War)
Aslett, Mr, 52, 59, 68
Attlebridge, 27, 49, 196
Aylsham, 13, 27, 32, 40, 41, 43, 44, 45, 52, 111, 140, 145, 153, 154, 165, 196, 198, **107**

Ballast, 104, 111, 196
Banbury, Sir F., 106, 199
Bankers, of railway, 34, 39, 51
Banks (*see* Gradients)
Barton Lane Crossing, 70, 95, 195
Bawsey Siding, 21, 59, 175, 193, 195
Beccles, 97, 167
Beeching, Dr (now Lord), 167
Beyer Peacock & Co, 62, 174, 176, 177, 179, 184, 200
Billingboro', 162-3, 169
Birmingham, 13, 19, 78-9, 95, 131, 150, 154, 166, 176
Black, Hawthorn & Co, 172, 200
Blakeney, 12, 14, 27, 32, 43-4, 47-8, 60-1, 63, 88, 104
Bloxham, Mr, 98
Bluestone, 52, 121, 196
Board of Trade, 34, 46, 114, 120
Boston, Stamford & Birmingham Ry, 13, 14, 19
Bourne, 19, 20, 22-4, 25-7, 29, 31, 49, 55-6, 61, 63-4, 65, 68, 70, 78-9, 80, 91, 110, 117, 130, 138, 145, 150, 153-4, 155, 163, 169-70, 187, 189, 191, 193-4, **107**
Bourne & Essendine Ry, 19
Bourne & Lynn Joint Ry, 24-5, 49, 61, 65

Bradford, 100, 117, 127, 131
Bradshaw's Guide, 70, 145
Brakes, 62, 174, 176, 180, 187
Brake Vans, 175, 182
Brereton, the Rev I., 32
Breydon Viaduct, 33, 86, 96-7, 139, 154, 169, 176, 196, 198
Brick Traffic, 103, 166
Bridges, 22, 33, 38-9, 47, 49, 59, 70, 88, 91, 96, 111, 140, 160, 194, 196
Briningham Junction, 95, 196, 198
British Railways, 152, 160, 189
British Road Services, 157
British Transport Commission, 152, 157, 159
Broads, the, 27, 37, 41, 63, 84, 86-7, 109, 117, 131, 148
Bromley, Mr M., 172
Buckminster, 80, 194
Bunn, Mr J., 34
Bure, River, 27, 33, 38-9, 52, 96
Buses: horse, 14, 63;
motor, 118, 133, 136, 137, 149, 158, 163
Bytham: Castle, 78, 194;
Little, junction; 65, 70, 78, 153, 160, 193, 197, 198, 71;
Station, 56, 64, 65

Caister, 27, 33, 37, 43, 80, 84, 93, 111, 134-5, 140, 153, 161, 164, 196;
Camp halt, 134-5, 153, 161, 164, 196
Caister Road Junction, 25, 33, 96, 138, 155, 193, 196, 198
California: Cliffs, 80, 135;
Halt, 135, 196
Cambridge, 12, 153, 155
Camps, holiday, 134-5, 153, 156, 161, 164

Carriage stock, 62, 65, 66, 69, 75, 87, 104, 110, 127, 128, 132, 142, 156, 175-6, 182, 188-9, 192, **54**
Catfield, 27, 38-9, 41, 94, 116, 193, 196
Cattle traffic, 11, 25, 27, 52, 55, 57, 59, 80, 103, 161
Central Norfolk Ry, 32, 45, 52
Chambers, Mr, 163
Cheshire Lines, 25, 61, 73, 77
Churchill, Sir Winston, 106
Clay Lake, 79, 83, 139, 158, 194
Clenchwarton, 21, 22, 160, 195 (see also Lynn, West)
Cley, 43, 61
Closed lines, 59, 154-5, 164, 166-8, 169-70
Closed stations, 59, 121, 149, 154-5, 164, 168
Closure procedure, 160-5, 167-8
Clowes, Mr, 34
Coaches (see Carriage stock)
Coal traffic, 11, 27, 30, 103, 121, 132, 161-3, 165
Cobbold, Mr, 15
Coke Ovens Junction, 85, 97, 193, 196
Colmans, Messrs, 103, 184
Commissioners: Light Railway, 34, 94;
Railway and Canal, 56-7, 61-2, 105
Committees: Bourne & Lynn, 24, 65;
M & GN, 1889-1893, 65, 69-70, 74;
1893-1947, 65, 74-5, 77-151, 152, 175-89;
Railway Executive, 120-1, 147;
Transport Users Consultative, 159-65

INDEX

Concrete, use of, 123
Conductor-Guard trains, 128, 130, 154, 156, 168, 169
Contractors: Finnegan, 99; Handyside, 88; Mousley, 84; Waring & Eckersley, 22, 28; Wilkinson & Jarvis, 32, 40, 43, 49, 124
Cornwall Minerals Ry, engines from, 173, 176, 179, 200, **17, 54**
Corpusty, 27, 52, 95, 196, 198
Corridor stock, 87, 98, 128, 132, 182, 189
Corton, 27, 97, 169, 196
Counter Drain, 23, 26, 194
County School, 27, 32, 41, 43, 154
Cromer, 12-13, 32, 45-6, 58-9, 60-1, 62-4, 68, 73-4, 79, 82, 84-6, 87, 92-5, 99, 100-2, 109, 110, 112, 117-18, 121-2, 127-8, 130-4, 145-6, 150, 153, 155, 156, 160, 163, 165, 166-7, 168-9, 179, 180, 182, 187, 190, 193, 197, 198;
    Beach, 46, 59, 60, 87, 101-2, 126, 128, 131, 133-4, 139, 155, 156, 165, 166-7, 190, 193, 197, 198, **18, 35, 126**; GE, 59, 87, 92, 99, 119, 149-50, 153, 155, 165;
    Junction, 100, 101, 128, 133, 146, 154, 194;
    Links Halt, 130, 197
Cross keys (see Sutton Bridge)
Crowland, 22, 26, 88, 128
Cuckoo Junction, 70, 79, 194, 198
Cunning, Mr, 80, 94
Cunningham's Drove, 79, 83, 139, 158, 194, 198 (see also Clay Lake)

Curson, Mr, 44, 52, 80, 95
De Ramsey, Lord, 92, 199
Derby, 42, 95, 109, 123, 129, 156, 166, 171, 177, 181, 185
Dereham, 12, 27, 32, 39, 41, 48-9, 55, 94
Diesel trains, 156, 159, 161-3, 168-9, 191
Dimensions, of locomotives, 171, 173, 176-7, 189, 200-2
Directors, 15, 24-5, 28, 32, 34, 50-2, 57, 85, 92, 94, 141, 199
Distances (see Mileage)
Dividends, 25, 37, 41-3, 46, 66, 74-5
Dogsthorpe, 103, 166, 169, 195
Doncaster, 21, 29, 99, 123, 171, 177, 189
Doubling of lines, 59, 70, 83, 91, 95, 101, 117, 155
Drayton, 27, 43, 49, 130, 162, 170, 196, 198
Dübs & Co, 178, 202
Dyke, Mr, 24

East Anglian Light Ry, 94
East Anglian Ry, 14-15, 19, 22
East Norfolk Ry, 32, 41, 45
East Rudham, 44, 162, 165, 170, 195, 198
Eastern & Midlands Ry, 29, 31, 39, 48-9, 50-75, 77-8, 100, 150, 173-6, 193, 200-1
Eastern Counties Ry, 12-15, 19, 168
Eastern Region, British Railways, 152-70, 189-191
Eastern Union Ry, 15
Eccles, 92
Eckersley, Mr, 22, 28
Edenham & Little Bytham Ry, **56, 78**

Edmondthorpe, 78, 153, 194, 198
Engineers, 30, 37, 39, 46-7, 52, 59, 70, 77, 88, 95, 97, 124, 131
Engines (*see* Locomotives)
English, Messrs, 29, 30
Erosion, coast, 80, 92, 111
Essendine, 19, 23-5, 26, 154, 189
Excursion traffic, 117-18, 120, 127, 132-4, 146
Expresses, 55, 62, 68, 78-9, 86-7, 93, 95-6, 117, 127-35, 146, 150, 153-6, 164, 166 (*see also* Kings Cross; Leicesters)
Eye Green, 22, 24, 26, 95, 153-4, 166, 195

Fakenham, 12, 14, 27, 28, 34, 39, 40-41, 43-4, 47, 62, 67, 87, 153, 193, 195
Fares, 25, 37, 40, 70, 109
Felmingham, 27, 52, 196
Ferry, 24, 26, 195
Fish Traffic, 11, 46, 52, 59, 98, 120, 128, 138, 142, 145, 157, 161, 183
Fishing, in rivers, 38-9, 63
Fleet, 16, 26, 194
Floods, 29, 92, 110-12, 150, 157-8
Flower traffic, 13, 137, 162
Folkes, Sir W. B., 32, 39, 51
Fox, Walker & Co, 172, 200
Freight traffic (*see* separate headings)
Fruit traffic, 13, 102-3, 121, 128, 136-7, 157, 161, 183

'Garden of Sleep' Poem, 86
Gardens, station, 140
Gasworks, 42, 102, 142, 155, 176, 198
Gayton Road, 21, 26, 58, 140, 160, 165, 195

Gaywood Road Junction, 21, 39-40, 44, 48, 59
Gedney, 16, 26, 194, 198
Gloucester, through train, 131, 146, 150
Golf, 84, 92, 97 (*see also* Cromer Links, Gorleston Links halts)
Goods traffic (*see* separate headings)
Goods vehicles, 75, 123, 183, **35**
Gorleston, 84-5, 97, 122, 149, 154-5, 168, 197;
  Links halt, 97, 122, 127, 169, 196;
  North Junction, 97, 196;
  North Station, 97, 149, 196;
  -on-Sea Station, 97, 145, 169, 196
Government control, 120, 129, 147
Gradients, 24, 37, 40, 45, 49, 52, 60, 77-8, 101
Great Central Ry, 77, 96, 104-6, 109, 123 (*see also* Manchester Sheffield & Lincolnshire Ry)
Great Eastern Ry, 19, 20-1, 27-9, 39, 40-1, 43-5, 48, 52, 56, 59, 62-3, 73, 83-7, 103, 105-6, 109, 118, 136, 138, 193-4, 196-7
Great Northern Ry, 13-14, 16-19, 23-5, 28-9, 30-1, 46, 49, 61-5, 73-5, 77, 83, 87, 104-6, 109, 110, 122-3, 127-8, 129, 131-2, 171-2, 175-7, 178-9, 194, 199, 202, **17**
Great Northern & Great Eastern Joint Ry, 29, 77, 139
Great Ormesby (*see* Ormesby)
Great Western, 120, 136, 173
Great Yarmouth (*see* Yarmouth)
Great Yarmouth & Stalham Light Ry, 32, 34-8, 172, 193

INDEX

Grimston Road, 21, 26, 40, 195, 198
Grouping, of railways, 106, 152
Guestwick, 47, 196

Haddiscoe, 37, 84, 118, 127, 149
Halts, 97, 122, 127, 130, 134-5, 140, 148, 153, 169, 196-7
Happisburgh, 27, 84-5, 92
Hardwick Road, goods station, 21, 58, 85, 195
Hastings, Lord, 32, 51, 60
Headcodes, 175, **125**
Hellesdon, 27, 49, 92, 111, 154, 196
Hemsby, 27, 37, 41, 134, 153, 161, 193, 196
Hereward the Wake, 31
Hillington, 40, 62, 195, **89**
Hindolvestone, 27, 47, 140, 146, 196, **90**
Holbeach, 13, 15, 16, 26, 70, 79, 102-3, 137, 193, 194, 198
Holt, 13, 27, 32, 43-4, 47, 60, 88, 93, 123, 147, 149, 150-1, 156-7, 193, 196, 198
Honing, 11, 27, 45, 95, 196, 198
Hopton, 37, 97, 169, 196
Horse Shoe Lane Junction, 24, 70, 195, 198
Horsey, 27, 84, 92
Hudson, George, 13
Hudswell Clarke & Co, 172, 200
Hunstanton, 26, 28, 134, 145, 150, 153, 156, 162;
& West Norfolk Ry, 34, 39

Ipswich, 15, 86, 112, 168
Ivatt, Mr H. A., engines designed by, 178, 187-8, **144**;
Mr H. G., engines designed by, 189, **107**

Jackson, Mr (Lord Allerton), 92, 199
Jarvis, Mr 34, 39-40, 43, 46, 124
Johnson, Mr H. (now Sir Henry), 160, 161, 162;
Mr S. W. (Midland Locomotive Superintendent) 78, 176-8

Kelling siding, 43, 45, 61, 104, 129, 139, 196
Kings Cross, 50, 60, 68, 78, 101, 105, 110, 112, 117-18, 121, 133, 140, 146-7, 155
King's Lynn (*see* Lynn)
Kingsley, Charles, 31;
engine named, 185
Kirtley engines, 171, 176-7
Kitson & Co, 178, 202

Lacons, bank and brewery, 34; siding for, 78
Lacon, Sir E., 34, 39, 51, 78, 172;
Miss Ida, 172
Lancashire & Yorkshire Ry, 21, 99-100
Langley, Mr, 131
Langor Bridge siding, 27, 47, 91, 95, 195
Le Mesurier, Mr, 70, 205
Leeds, 99, 109, 127, 130-1, 134, 150
Legal Proceedings, 14, 38, 56-7, 61-2, 66-8, 69, 74, 105
Leicester, 13, 23, 63, 78, 95, 112, 123, 136, 145, 162, 166
'Leicesters' expresses, 78, 95, 121, 134, 141, 146, 154, 164, 166, 185, 187, 188, 190, 191, **36, 72, 107-8**
Lenwade, 27, 47, 140, 162, 165, 196, **90**
Level Crossings, 41, 94, 116-17

Light Railways, 32, 34, 38, 46, 88, 94, 128, 165 (see also Commissioners)
Liverpool, 12, 96, 109, 130, 132, 135, 145
Liverpool Street, 62, 87, 93, 109, 129, 131, 134, 141, 149, 151-2, 154-5
Liveries, 129, 174, 177, 184
Locomotives, 37, 40, 45, 46, 52, 62, 75, 77-8, 87, 95, 110, 115, 122, 136, 140, 142, 146, 171-91, 200-2, **125**, **126**, **143**, **144**
London traffic, 12; (see also Kings Cross; Liverpool Street)
London, Mr 129
London & North Eastern Ry, 106, 129, 132-3, 135-7, 140, 141-51, 152, 186-9
London & North Western Ry, 57, 122, 175, 200
London, Midland & Scottish Ry, 129, 130, 133-4, 136, 141-2, 146, 184, 185-6
London Midland Region, British Railways, 153
Long Sutton (see Sutton)
Lowestoft, 12, 27, 84-5, 96, 98-9, 102, 109, 121, 127-8, 138, 142, 145, 154, 168-9, 193, 196;
    Central, 97, 102, 158, 169, 196;
    North, 97, 102, 169, 196
Lynn & Dereham Ry, 12, 14
Lynn & Ely Ry, 13
Lynn & Fakenham Ry, 12, 28, 32, 34, 39-41, 43-50, 51, 172-4, 193, 200
Lynn & Hunstanton Ry, 28, 34
Lynn & Sutton Bridge Ry, 19, 22-3, 193

Lynn, King's, 12-13, 21-3, 25-6, 27-30, 39, 44, 47, 52, 57-9, 60, 66-7, 68, 80, 85, 93, 106, 121-2, 127, 133-4, 138, 142, 145, 149, 154, 162;
    Austin St, 21, 44, 48, 52, 59, 85;
    GE Station, 21, 22, 39, 44, 59, 93, 195 (called Lynn Town by E & M, 59);
    Harbour, 22, 138, 170;
    South, 22, 26, 48, 58-9, 62, 68, 70, 79, 87, 117, 145, 153, 158, 164, 170, 186, 193, 195;
    West, bridge, 21, 22, 91, 160, 195, **108**;
    station, 21, 22, 59;
    Dock & Ry, 21, 27, 39, 66, 147, 152, 170

Macdonald, Mr, 88
Madden, Mr, 80
Manchester, 62, 77, 96, 99-100, 109, 128, 130, 132, 134-5, 150
Manchester Sheffield & Lincolnshire Ry, 77, 105 (see also Great Central Ry)
Mania, Railway, 12-14, 15, 19, 34
Mann, Mr 47, 52, 59
Maps, 20, 21, 26-7, 33, 38, 42, 59, 79
March, 13, 20, 28, 164
Marriott, Mr William, 44, 52, 59, 77, 94-5, 97, 111, 123, 124, 129, 130, 131, 173, 175, 180, 181
Marriott, Sir R., 205
Marriott, 2nd Lt Stanley, 123
Martham, 27, 37, 55-6, 93, 140, 162, 196, 198, **17**

INDEX

Massingham, 12, 27, 39, 40, 62, 114, 193, 195, 198
Mellett, Mr, 52
Melton Constable, 43, 47, 52, 55, 68, 87, 92, 110-11, 117, 122-3, 129, 130, 142, 145-6, 149, 160-1, 163, 165, 176, 179, 181, 186, 187, 189, 190, 191, 195, 197, 198, 202; **18, 42; 125**
Midland Ry, 13, 19, 22-3, 24, 29, 56-7, 61-6, 70, 73-5, 78, 83, 92, 95, 105-6, 109, 127, 171, 175, 176-7, 178-9, 180-2, 183, 194, 198-9
Midland & Eastern Ry, 22-3, 28, 31, 47-8, 50-1, 61, 193
M & GN Circle 204;
Preservation Society (see North Norfolk Rys Ltd)
Mileage, 16, 22, 23-4, 34, 37, 39, 40-1, 43-4, 45, 58, 91, 97, 194-7
Military Traffic, 120, 122, 124, 147-9, 157, 162
Ministry of Transport, 127, 159, 166, 167
Moulton, 16, 194, 198
Mundesley, 63, 68, 75, 83-6, 91-3, 99, 100-2, 109, 110, 112, 115, 118, 121, 127-8, 130-1, 133-4, 135, 138, 146, 148, 149, 150-1, 154-6, 167-8, 180, 182, 184-5, 186, 191, 193, 197, 198, **143**
Murrow, 20, 26, 28, 95, 139, 162-3, 166, 169, 195, 198

Naval Bombardment, 122
Nene, river, 16, 22, 29, 88 (see also Sutton Bridge)
Newman, Mr, 131

Newstead Lane Junction, 59, 93, 99, 100-1, 165, 167, 194, 197, 198
Newtown Halt, 33, 134, 196
Nicolson, Mr, 37, 39
Non-stop runs, 79, 87, 93, 99, 114, 117, 130
Norfolk & Suffolk Joint Ry, 85-6, 91-3, 96-7, 99, 100-2, 122-3, 128, 133, 138, 149, 152, 190, 193, 196-7, 198
Norfolk Ry, 13-14
North Drove, 23, 26, 164, 194
North Norfolk Rys Ltd, 192, 201
North of Norfolk Ry, 13
North Walsham, 32, 38, 44-6, 52, 55, 91, 101-2, 111, 127, 131-2, 138, 149-50, 153, 156, 164, 167, 168, 185, 193, 197, 198
Northern & Eastern Ry, 12
Norwich, 11-13, 15, 27, 34, 43, 49, 50, 55-7, 62-3, 79, 80, 95, 103-4, 110-11, 117-18, 136, 146, 160, 162-3, 164, 167, 185, 187, 193, 196, 198;
Central station, proposed, 48, 55-6;
City station, 49, 110, 134, 146, 148-9, 156, 165, 191, 196, 198, **72;**
GE Stations, Thorpe, 48-9, 55, 135, 148-9, 156, 163-4;
Victoria, 49
Norwich & Brandon Ry, 13
Norwich & Spalding Ry, 15-16, 19, 22, 25, 28, 34, 49, 193
Nottingham, 95-6, 100, 130, 132, 134, 145-6, 149, 153, 181, 187

Oakley, Sir Henry, 94-5, 199
Offices, 52, 59, 75, 86, 129, 152

218 MIDLAND & GREAT NORTHERN JOINT RAILWAY

Openings, 16, 22-3, 30, 37, 40-1, 44-6, 49, 52, 58, 60, 70, 78, 91, 96, 100-1, 165-6; List of, 193
Ormesby, Great, 27, 37, 80, 92, 135, 193, 196, 198
Otway, Mr, 51, 57
Ouse, river, 22; **108**
Overstrand, 27, 59, 84, 92, 101-2, 110, 127-8, 130, 140, 154, 197, 198

Paget, Mr, 92, 199
Pains siding, 78, 194
Palling, 27, 84, 92
Passing Loops, 70, 95, 112-16, 128, 198
Paston, 27, 91, 168, 197
Pepper, Mr, 40
Permanent Way, 16, 41, 68, 80-1, 162, 174
Peterboro', 12-14, 16, 23-5, 26, 30-1, 55-7, 61-2, 86-7, 91, 98, 100, 103, 117, 128, 133-4, 160, 163, 166, 191, 195;
  GE East station, 24, 26, 98-9;
  GN North station, 14, 24
Peterboro' Wisbech & Sutton Bridge Ry, 16, 19, 21, 23, 30, 47-8, 49, 51, 193
Petrie, Mr, 94, 123, 124
Piggs Grove Summit, 47
'Poppyland', 66, 86, 109, 131, 154
Potter Heigham, 38-9, 63, 87, 111-12, 117, 132, 135, 153, 196, 198;
  bridge, 38;
  halt, 135, 153, **71**
Pudding Norton, 40, 43

Rails (*see* Permanent Way)

Rates, 106, 124-5, 136, 157
Raynham Park, 27, 44, 95, 195, 198
Read, Mr, 28, 51, 56-7, 64, 66-7, 69
Receivership, 66-7, 74
Reedham, 12, 56
Restaurant cars, 100-1, 109, 128, 130-1, 133-4, 135, 145, 153-4, 166
Revenue, 25, 37, 43, 55, 73, 104, 109, 156-7
Reversals, 25, 44, 48, 59, 62, 70, 87, 91-2, 97, 99, 112, 155-6
Road Traffic, 11-12, 136, 145, 154, 156-7, 160;
  competition with, 124, 127, 131-3, 136-7, 142, 156-7, 159-62
Rolling stock, hire of, 67-9, 74, 175 (*see also* Carriages, Goods Vehicles, Locomotives)
Roughton Road Junction, 59, 91, 99, 100-1, 119, 154, 197-8
Royal Journeys 40, 60, 86, 158, 167
Running Powers, 14, 19, 20-1, 23, 39, 58, 63, 85
Runton: east junction, 59, 81, 92, 100-1, 167, 197;
  west junction, 59, 100, 138, 165, 167, 147-8, 197-8;
  West station, 45, 49, 60, 92-3, 140, 169, 197

Salthouse, 27, 61
Saxby, 22, 63-5, 68, 70, 78, 80, 118, 135, 138, 145, 160, 162-3, 176, 181, **108**
Scott, Mr Clement, 86
Scottish traffic, 98, 102, 112, 135, 145
Scratby halt, 135, 196

INDEX

Sea transport, 121, 148
Sheds, engine, 41, 133, 190-1
Sharp Stewarts, 173, 177, 200, 202
Sheffield, 96, 100, 109, 164, 166
Sheringham, 11, 27, 45, 60, 62, 84, 87, 92-3, 99, 100-1, 110, 112, 133-5, 140, 146, 150-1, 156, 162, 167-9, 190-1, 192, 197-8
Shops, locomotive, 41, 44 (see also Melton Constable)
Sidestrand, 140, 197
Sidings, 70, 78, 83, 98-9, 121, 129, 138 (see also separate headings)
Signals and signalling, 80, 82-3, 91, 97, 112-17, 123, 128-9, 139, 142, 152;
  somersault signals, 81, 91, 142
Single line operation, 62, 68, 70, 82, 87-8, 91, 96, 101, 104, 112-17, 128-9, 138-9, 155, 167, 169, 188;
  Sections, list of, 198
Skegness, 135
Slade, Mr, 51, 57
Sleaford, 29, 99, 100, 109, 127, 138, 166;
  & Bourne line, 29, 138-9, 162-3
Somerset & Dorset Joint Ry, 52, 64, 77, 114, 175
South Town (see Yarmouth)
South Witham, 65, 78, 80, 163, 194, 198
Spalding, 12-14, 15-16, 19, 20-1, 23, 25-6, 28-9, 31, 34, 49, 70, 78-9, 80, 83, 99, 103, 118, 128, 134-5, 137, 138-9, 150, 153, 155-6, 160, 162, 164, 166, 169, 171, 177, 193, 194, 198

Spalding & Bourne Ry, 19, 22-3, 193
Speeds, 16, 62, 68, 78, 86-7, 93, 99, 110, 117, 121, 127-8, 130, 140, 150, 155, 166-7
Staff, 44, 52, 59, 68, 75, 80, 92, 94-5, 117-18, 124, 129, 139, 140, 142, 147-8
Stalham, 27, 32, 34, 37, 41, 44-5, 87, 119, 132, 135, 140, 161, 164, 195, 196, 198
Stamford, 13, 19, 24, 25, 26, 61;
  & Essendine Ry, 23
Starkey, Mr, 92, 199
Steam Heating, 178-9, 182
Stiffkey, 27, 48, 60-1, 147
Stirling, Mr P, engines designed by, 110, 171, 174, 177
Stratford, 142, 186
Strikes, 110, 124, 127, 132
Sugar beet traffic, 137, 162, 168, 170
Sunday services, 37, 41, 47, 55, 100, 118, 121, 132, 134-5, 138, 150, 151, 153
Sutton (near Stalham) 41;
  Staithe Halt, 135, 196
Sutton Bridge, 13, 14, 15, 16, 19, 21, 22, 26, 30, 54, 57, 61, 62, 70, 88, 94, 102, 118, 128, 137-8, 160, 169, 171, 193, 195, 198;
  Cross Keys Bridge at, 22, 26, 54, 70, 88, 91, 172, **54**;
  Stations at, 16, 22, 24-5, 88, **89**;
  Docks, 29, 30, 49, 70, 88, 105, 193
Sutton, Long, 16, 17, 102-4, **17**;
  Sutton St Mary, 13
Symes, Mr, 52

Tablets, 62, 68, 82; (Tyers') 112-16, 128-9, 139, 180, 188;
  Mechanical exchange, 114-17, 180, 188
Tait, Mr, 52
Tenders, 171, 173-4, **54**
Terrington, 22, 26, 70, 91, 102, 195
Themelthorpe, 43-4, 165, 170
Thorney, 13, 21, 26, 95, 101, 164, 195, 198
Thurne, river, 27, 38-9, 41, 56, 63
Thursford, 47, 62, 95, 195
Tickets, 106, 109, 118-19, 120-1, 140, 148
Timetables, 70, 145
Toft Tunnel, 70, 104, also called Bourne Tunnel, 194
Town Holiday trains, 117, 131, 132
Townshend, Lord, 32, 39
Tramways, 41 (see also Yarmouth Union)
Trimingham, 27, 101, 128, 140, 197-8
Twenty, 23, 26, 70, 110, 138, 194, 198
Tydd, 24, 26, 195, 198

Vegetable traffic, 13, 103, 121, 137, 157, 162

Walker, Mr, director of L & F, 32, 39;
  traffic manager of M & GN, 131, 141
Walpole, 22, 26, 102, 195
War, 16, 120-4, 147-50, 181, 188
Waring, Mr, 28, 47, 51-2
Water traffic, 12, 103
Welland Bank Junction, 70, 194

Welland, river, 16, 70, 150, 157-8
Wells, 11, 27, 28, 88, 104
Wensum: curve, 86, 153, 167, 168;
  river, 47, 49;
  Valley Ry, 32
West Norfolk Ry, 28, 34
Weston, 16, 26, 194
Westwood Junction, 20, 23, 139, 166, 195
Weybourne, 60, 93, 157, 167, 191-2, 196, 198
Whaplode, 16, 26, 128, 162, 194
Whitaker, Mr, 114
'White Swan', The, Yarmouth, 43, 138, 166, 196, 198
Whitwell, 43, 140, 165, 196, 198
Wilkinson, Mr, 15, 37, 43, 51, 56, 77, 124
Wilson, Major, 146
Wisbech, 12-16, 19, 21, 27, 53, 57, 95, 102, 109, 118, 121, 130, 133, 136, 138, 140, 160, 166, 169;
  EA, 14-15;
  GE East, 14, 153;
  Harbour, 14, 138, 153;
  Junction, Peterboro', 20, 95, 139, 195;
  M & GN (North) 24, 102, 145, 153, 166, **53**;
  M & GN Harbour, 21, 24, 27, 138, 153, 166, 169, 193; 195;
  St Mary, 24, 102, 195
Wiveton, 43
Worstead, 11, 27, 45
Wroxham, 27, 32, 154
Wryde, 24, 26, 101, 164, 195, 198

INDEX

Yare, river, 26, 33, 39, 43
Yarmouth, Great, 11-13, 35, 41, 43, 52, 55, 56, 58, 62-3, 80, 84-5, 97-9, 117, 121-2, 127, 130, 132-5, 138, 146, 150, 153, 160, 166-7, 173, 176, 180, 185, 193, 196, **37**
Yarmouth Great/Beach, 34, 41, 43, 97-8, 131, 134, 142, 145, 154, 158, 164, 168, 196, 198, **38**;
Harbour, 43, 84, 138;

South Town, 43, 97, 138, 142, 149, 154, 158, 167;
Vauxhall, 37, 43, 142, 158, 161, 163, 168
Yarmouth & Norwich Ry, 12-13
Yarmouth & North Norfolk Light Ry, 28, 37-9, 40-1, 43, 51, 173, 174, 193
Yarmouth Union Ry, 43, 46, 48, 193
Youell, Mr, 34